AGBONKHIANMEGHE E. OROBATOR, S.J. (EDITOR)

THEOLOGICAL REIMAGINATION

CONVERSATIONS ON CHURCH, RELIGION, AND SOCIETY IN AFRICA

For David:

In grateful appreciation of your commitment and passion for the issues that matter in church and society. Many thanks!

Paulines

PAULINES PUBLICATIONS AFRICA

THEOLOGICAL REIMAGINATION: CONVERSATIONS ON CHURCH,
RELIGION, AND SOCIETY IN AFRICA
© St Paul Communications/Daughters of St Paul
ISBN 9966-08-862-8
Year of publication 2014

Cover Painting by Bullen Alier Ajak

aulines

PAULINES PUBLICATIONS AFRICA
Daughters of St Paul
P.O. Box 49026
00100 Nairobi GPO (Kenya)
Email: publications@paulinesafrica.org
Website: www.paulinesafrica.org

Cover Design, Layout and Typesetting by Antony M. Wamwaki
Printed by: Don Bosco Printing Press, P.O. Box 158, 01020 Makuyu (Kenya)

Paulines Publications Africa is an activity of the Daughters of St Paul, an international religious congregation, using the press, radio, TV and films to spread the gospel message and to promote the dignity of all people.

Contents

PART ONE
African Theology and Religious Identity:
Source and Critiques

PART TWO
African Theology: Methods and Models

PART THREE

Theological Reimagination of the Nature and Mission of Christianity and Church in Africa

Acknowledgments

The idea for the Theological Colloquium on Church, Religion, and Society in Africa (TCCRSA) took a few years to come to fruition. Key moments of confirmation include the 2010 Expert Seminar on the second African Synod and the 2012 Bilingual Expert Seminar *Catholic Theological Ethics in the World Church (CTEWC) in Africa After Trento: Engaging the African Synod.*

Both events, held in Nairobi, Kenya, confirmed my insight that a change in direction in conducting theological study and research in Africa was due and imperative. The new direction would shift from individual, isolated theologians ruminating on faith and life issues, to a community of theologians and representatives of allied disciplines conversing, collaborating, and conducting research on Church, religion, and society. Although revolutions in information communication technology have made meetings a virtual reality, the African proverb "Mountains don't meet, people do" still carries an important lesson. And for this project to succeed, people had to meet.

I am profoundly grateful to a European family foundation and the Society of Jesus (Jesuits) that helped fund the meetings and joint research projects of African theologians in TCCRSA. I am grateful to past and present members of the CTEWC Planning Committee for the Future, led by Jim Keenan and Linda Hogan, for the opportunity to appreciate the significance of cross-cultural theological research and scholarship.

The response to the inaugural call for participation exceeded all expectation. The original plan envisaged not more than thirty-five participants; the enthusiastic interest expressed in the project necessitated increasing the number, albeit limited funding meant capping it at fifty-five participants each year. I am grateful to the participants for their active involvement and commitment to TCCRSA.

Special thanks go to the translators from Hekima College for their patient and selfless service, Martin McHugh for his editorial assistance, and Paulines Publications Africa for its commitment to publish the outcomes of TCCRSA.

My companions, collaborators, and colleagues in the Eastern Africa Province of the Society of Jesus have continued to grant me the opportunity to undertake theological research and writing while tasked simultaneously with the responsibility of leading the province. *Asanteni sana!*

All along, *Kijana wa Zamani* Joe Healey, MM, has generously supported and encouraged my theological initiatives. *Asante sana,* Joe!

As always, the love and belief of Chuks Afiawari, SJ, and Oghomwen n'Oghomwen Anne Arabome, SSS, render this endeavour profoundly meaningful and fulfilling. Thank you!

Agbonkhianmeghe E. Orobator, SJ
Nairobi, May 2014

PREFACE
About Theological Colloquium on Church, Religion, and Society in Africa (TCCRSA)

The Theological Colloquium on Church, Religion, and Society in Africa (TCCRSA) is a three-year theological research project in the currents of the fiftieth anniversary of Vatican II. The colloquium aims to develop, model, and sustain a new and innovative methodology and process of theological reflection, research, and study at the service of the African Church and the World Church. From 2013 to 2016, the colloquium will convene a community of African Catholic scholars doing theology or using Roman Catholic theological/ethical (re)sources in their academic disciplines to identify, analyse, and study a wide variety of issues in the African Church and society. TCCRSA focuses yearly on general themes:

- **Year 1 (2013/14):** African Theology in the Twenty-First Century: Identity and Profile, Contexts, and Models;
- **Year 2 (2014/15):** The Church We Want: Theological Voices from Within and Outside the Church at the Service of *Ecclesia in Africa;*
- **Year 3 (2015/16):** An Agenda for Vatican III: Ideas, Issues, and Resources from Africa or the World Church. (This third and final colloquium is scheduled to coincide with the fiftieth anniversary of the conclusion of Vatican II, 1962–1965).

Each colloquium will create a forum for conversation, listening, presentation of commissioned papers and responses, and joint working/research sessions among participants. Participants will come from:

1. The theological academy and allied disciplines;
2. The ecclesial hierarchy;
3. Civil society/practitioners.

The colloquium aims for a pan-African participation and representation of linguistic (French, Portuguese, and English speaking), gender (women and men), geographical (North Africa and sub-Saharan Africa: east, west, central, and south), generational (established theologians and young/new scholars), and ecclesial (laity, religious, clergy, and bishops) composition. It also includes African theologians in the Diaspora.

Each colloquium comprises plenary, panel, and palaver sessions. In a plenary session, one speaker delivers a commissioned paper on a topic of major significance in African Christianity/theology that may not have previously received serious theological consideration. A panel discussion includes three or four panelists discussing a point of relevance in African Christianity/theology. During a palaver session, two speakers present position papers on an issue of concern/contention in African Christianity/theology. During each session, all participants engage in open conversations to contribute to and clarify understanding of the topic under consideration.

Select materials presented at the colloquium will be edited and published. Thus, by 2015–2016, three volumes will have been published on Church, religion, and society in Africa, reflecting participants' research and scholarship and the dynamics of the colloquium's progress. A fourth volume will contain the most innovative essays from the first three volumes.

Altogether, TCCRSA will achieve the following goals and objectives over the three years:

1. Create and consolidate a new community of African scholars at the service of Church and society.

2. Critically identify, explore, and study emerging ideas and issues in theology in Africa.

3. Generate a new set of materials and resources for theological education and learning in Africa through the published volumes.

4. Initiate and experiment with a new way of doing conversational, cross-disciplinary, collaborative, and multigenerational theology.

5. Create a platform for constructive theological conversation, engagement, and interaction between theologians and the hierarchy/leadership of the Roman Catholic Church in Africa and beyond.

6. Build the capacity, reinforce the confidence, and enhance the methodological competence of a new/young generation of African theologians.

TCCRSA is envisioned as a pioneering multiyear, multilevel theological research project in African theology with a wide-ranging, positive impact on the study of theology, religion, Church, and society in Africa and beyond.

Agbonkhianmeghe E. Orobator, SJ,
Convener and Series Editor

Introduction:
Doing Theology as a Collaborative Effort

Agbonkhianmeghe E. Orobator

O f all the models of conversational and communicative styles in African cultures, *palaver* seems the most theologically fertile. Some derisive portrayals of this style exist, including its depiction as pointless banter presided over by an African chief. The essays in this volume result from an experience of African palaver that doubles as a joint theological research project with a clear theme, purpose, and objective.

Focusing on Church, religion, and society in Africa, this project gathers African theologians in conversation about issues that shape all three institutions. As the title indicates, their conversations pivot on "reimagination," and the choice is not arbitrary. Imagination relates to the power of the mind to undo the confines of the status quo and scale seemingly insurmountable boundaries with boundless creativity and audacity. Applied to theology, reimagination creates alternative worlds of meaning and purpose that embody God's self-revelation in innovative and creative ways. Theological reimagination depicts the central task of this research project and the commitment of each participant and author.

The African theological enterprise has since shed its self-imposed innocence and *naïveté* that once reduced it to merely aping theological models and answers fabricated for overseas context and consumption. If one needs proof of Africa's theological maturity, one need not look beyond this volume. As the outcome of a collaborative theological project, this volume demonstrates the creativity of theological imagination in Africa with theologians asking their own questions and discovering their own answers.

While imagination is the gift of the individual mind, in the context of Africa, individual prowess has a social premium; its exercise takes place in a communal framework. No matter how dexterous a single finger is, says an African proverb, it cannot catch a louse in the hair. Whether as palaver or Ubuntu, the theological enterprise operates as a collaborative effort regulated by the communicative ethics of mutual listening and respectful dialogue. The inaugural gathering of the Theological Colloquium on Church, Religion, and Society in Africa (TCCRSA) yielded conversations that produced these essays, living proof of collaboration as a fruitful methodology of theological research and scholarship.

As with other recently published works in African theology, the mode of research and scholarship adopted in this volume takes the form of conversation.[1] In the context of TCCRSA, conversation in theology creates a space in which new scholars engage with established scholars and lay women and men, religious, clergy, and ecclesiastics sit at the same table to expand the boundaries of inquiry and clear new paths for theological scholarship in Africa and the world church. The emerging model of theologising facilitates intergenerational conversation that transcends gender, status, language, and geography in the community called church.

This conversation also operates at another level, namely, the encounter between Christianity and other religious traditions, in this case African religion. The essays in this volume draw on Christian traditions and sources: Scripture, Church fathers, and the scholastics, but these foundational sources do not exhaust the field of theological scholarship. When it comes to doing theology in Africa, there are alternative and complementary sources. In diverse ways, the authors of this volume appeal to African religious traditions, cultures, histories, and contexts as valuable and valid sources of theologising. Of critical importance is the conversation and dialogue that must exist between Christian and African sets of theological sources alike.

Speaking of theological sources, the authors look beyond documentary materials as well as inward to rich mines of personal experience. These essays demonstrate beyond doubt that the authors ask personal, pertinent questions not as ivory-tower academicians but as believing and practicing Christians who have experience to substantiate their claims. Theirs resembles a contemporary appropriation of the scholastic definition of theology as faith seeking understanding with the fundamental difference that while *fides quaerens intellectum* hinges on a Cartesian *Cogito ergo sum*, the quest of the authors of this volume pivots on the epistemological axiom of *umuntu ngumuntu ngabantu*.[2]

As will soon become evident in the contributions of several authors such as Arabome, Dowling, Dube, Kamaara, Mayemba, and Mejía, theology is indissociable from the theologian's personal faith narrative, quest, and journey as these unfold within and are fed by concerns of and from his or her Christian community. In fact, shared faith narrative, quest, and journey are grist for the theological mill.

Finally, the authors here represent less than half the number of participants in the first phase of the TCCRSA research project. In one sense, this volume serves as a sample of a wider theological conversation taking place in church, religion, and society in Africa. As the project moves to subsequent phases, the voices will increase in number and include more participants and contributors.

Though this volume's essays represent individual authors' participation in and contribution to the theological research project, all the authors are collaborators in a joint project. Their essays were presented and debated in live palaver sessions, following which they refined their arguments for wider dissemination.

This volume is divided into three parts, depending on the area where a group of contributors lays more emphasis. Part One focuses on conceptualising religious identity and understanding the role of theology in identifying the sources and resolving the debate. Part Two analyses issues of methods and models of theological research and scholarship. Part Three offers a theological reimagination of the community called church in light of questions relating to internal functioning and external mission.

These divisions need not set one part against the other; they are a convenience to aid comprehension. All three parts have a shared objective and reinforce a common theme, namely, reimagining church, religion, and society in twenty-first-century Africa.

Conversations

To start the conversation in Part One, **Laurenti Magesa** takes up the African continent's and its church's identity. In the maze and haze of globalisation as well as competing perceptions, visions, and interpretations of reality, Africa contemplates its identity at the crossroads of doubt, uncertainty, and confusion. The question of Christianity and African identity is by no means simple, certainly not as simple as Kamaara would have us believe in her essay that complements Magesa's. Its answer is not prefabricated; it is to be desconstructed and (re)constructed.

As Katongole, Iwuchukwu, and Kamaara note in various ways, this process unfolds in a radical departure from the old ways of being African and Christian. Thus, the unpredictable dynamics of this process carry a risk for Africa and Christianity: a dying unto self that permits the resurrection and creation of a novel reality. This nascent reality synthesises elements of the old and new and the local and the global, and it is truly African and fully Christian. Similarly, due attention must be paid to the language in which the African communicates and ritualises his or her story and identity and existential concerns and experiences.

Teresa Okure locates the source of African and other Christian theologies in the divine and creative Word of God that spoke creation into being. Theological investigation begins at the locus, the origin of God's Word about humanity and creation. Based on this understanding, Okure delineates the contours of a theology for the twenty-first-century African context. In the process, she surfaces thought-provoking questions for theologians: What is the necessity, purpose, and relevance of African theology? Does it serve life or does it merely seek knowledge? Are we servants of a theology fabricated for foreign consumption or craftspeople of our own theological works? In what ways does African theology satisfy the hunger of Africans for God and calm their fears of malevolent forces that oppose the Spirit of God? In raising these questions, her concerns echo those of Arabome, Ilo, Mayemba, Ngalula, and Uzukwu. Not surprisingly, as a biblical scholar like Béré and Nsongisa, she prioritises the Scripture as the source and soul of theology seeking to answer critical questions that confront Africans while drawing on largely untapped and under utilised local resources and materials.

She stresses that in the quest to serve life and respond to real needs, theology ought to relocate to the margins and neglected depths of African reality and cultures, including African women theologies, for inspiration and courage – itself a task of faith. Thus what Uzukwu recommends for ecclesiology, Okure advocates for theology in general – go to the margins! She predicts the result would be a theology grounded in African reality and anchored in the Word of God.

She tellingly proposes the idea of a "roundtable" theology that engages all the voices, especially women's, in a collaborative enterprise. Such a theology nourishes the people of God and answers their questions about God's presence and existence in Africa. Although she berates men theologians for being obsessed with method, her essay could well be a treatise on methodology. Nonetheless, her recipe for making theology good news in Africa is worth heeding: take seriously African women's theology, cultivate faith in local theological reflections, develop people-centered theology, create an empowering theology grounded in the life and ministry of Jesus Christ, and do theology in the open spaces of real-life situations that will close the gaps between Church, theologians, and the people.

Eloi Messi Metogo critically reviews the reality of change for theological research and scholarship in Africa. Far from being an ahistorical and static island, Africa is inextricably engaged in a dynamics of change and evolution within the dizzying vortex of globalisation; the drivers of change are not external to Africa. Besides the characteristic problems and difficulties of the continent are resources and solutions native to Africa. Like Mayemba, he advocates for a dynamic Africa that neither pines with nostalgia for things of old nor contents itself with "folkloric exhibitionism." The focus of theological analysis should be on fundamental issues that shape Africa's identity. Such issues include religious ignorance or what Katongole, quoting Scott Appleby, terms "weak religion," the fundamental constitution of the Church as people of God, autonomy of the local Church, and pastoral issues (magic, witchcraft, sacramentality, and so on). The concerns of African theology should also deal with the reality of suffering and death, economic dehumanisation and political violence, practical ecumenism, unbelief, and interreligious dialogue.

Paul Béré seeks to answer the question: "What role does biblical exegesis play in the theological research and scholarship of African theologians?" He focuses on the Old Testament in his review of African theology's historical trajectory. His discovery points to the absence of the Scripture as a key source of theological scholarship in African theology of Catholic extraction in contrast to the significant emphasis on the Scripture in Protestant theologies. The issue is not as simple as it might seem; deep fissures and tensions exist between practitioners of exegesis and proponents of biblical theology as well as between them and fundamental theologians. The situation raises the challenge of how to bridge the gap to create conditions for a sustained, penetrating study of the Scripture as an indispensable tool and component of theological discourse. A useful starting point is the recognition of the multiple and wide senses in which the Word of God functions as a medium of revelation and the ability to distinguish specific methodologies and foci of exegesis and biblical theology, deconstruct the cultural conditionings in the study of the Bible, and pay critical attention to context and broader interdisciplinary conversations.

Chantal Nsongisa agrees in substance with Béré on the centrality of the Scripture in theological discourse, research, and scholarship. The Christian experience of faith is grounded in the Scripture, an encounter with God, and makes sense in light of this foundational text. Knowledge of the Scripture is a fundamental condition and prerequisite for conducting an intelligent and intelligible discourse on God, also known as *theo-logy*. Devoid of Scripture, theology amounts to mere superficiality and curiosity without foundation. The data theology derives from the Scripture as its soul generates knowledge of God and personal faith and guides Christian life. However, granted that the Scripture is revelatory, one must question Nsongisa's assumption or claim that it alone grants a "better knowledge of God." As did Béré, she finds only superficial recourse to or use of the Scripture in African theology, but unlike Béré, she limits Scripture to the written text.

Béré's approach appears more nuanced, offering us various senses in which we can comprehend the Word of God. If the Word equates God's self-revelation in Jesus Christ, we ought to see beyond the written text and consider other media of God's ongoing self-revelation.

In light of Béré and Nsongisa's lament of the paucity of scriptural analysis in African theology, another question arises: if biblical scholars continue to insist on the specificity and distinctiveness of their discipline, are theologians to undertake in-depth study or exegesis of the Scripture? Ought not exegetes and biblical theologians combine efforts to put the resources of their scholarly research at the service of theological discourse in general? These queries underscore the pertinence and necessity of collaboration across disciplines that should characterise the work of theologians in Africa, be they exegetes, biblical theologians, theological ethicists, or fundamental theologians.

Eunice Kamaara responds to the same question that Magesa addresses; she explores the colonial roots of the development of African identity. In doing so, she grapples with some issues raised by Iwuchukwu about what constitutes authentic African belief, identity, and way of life. For her, African values are essentially Christian values and vice versa, and some readers might disagree with this. Her argument draws upon the principle of the fundamental dignity of the human person. Africans are no exception and should not be; they are endowed as all peoples are with rationality, free will, and spirituality. At the core of African identity are the values of dignity, community, ethics, and relationship. Christianity has given these values its own interpretation, but it is not to be taken as fixed, as her analysis of Vatican II's approach to culture demonstrates.

Nor does Christianity have a monopoly over these values. Rather than tread the familiar path of inculturation, she proposes the reconstruction and unification of Christian and African identities on the basis of the practice of love and justice. For her, to be truly African is to be truly Christian. This reasoning would seem a simplistic syllogism to the reader because it erodes if not eradicates the distinctiveness and differences that pertain between Christianity and African identities. Yet the essence of her argument can be retrieved and redeemed, albeit at the risk of encroaching on the borders of secular humanism: human values are more fundamental and universal than are external religious principles, manifestations, and features.

No doubt related to the dramatic growth of Christianity in Africa in the twentieth century, the tendency is to see Christianity as a relatively new religious tradition in Africa. Whether this tendency is the result of amnesia or excusable historical ignorance, the fact remains that Africa is home to some ancient Christian and theological traditions.

In that light, **Abba Daniel Assefa's** essay offers a fascinating sample of Mariology and Christology in the Ethiopic theological tradition. He analyses an ancient text of a devotee of Mary; interestingly, the exaltation never separates her from Christ. Assefa offers extensive insight into a symbolic, metaphoric, and poetic theology that thrives on a profusion of senses, images, and colours, and encompasses ecclesiology, pneumatology, eschatology, spirituality, and Scripture. His analysis contains several lessons and contributions to theological methodology. More important, it reminds us that theology is not mere discourse or speculation; it is a vehicle for encountering the divine and being embraced by the divine in worship, praise, ritual, and action.

Stan Chu Ilo begins and leads the conversation in Part Two by painting a comprehensive tableau of theology in Africa. His incisive presentation is much too complex to be squeesed into a few lines of summary; only the essential lines are presented here, leaving the reader to appreciate the complexity and depth of theological scholarship in Africa. A key lesson from Ilo's analysis that resonates with positions taken by other contributors (such as Aihiokhai, Arabome, Béré, Dowling, Dube, Okure, and Uzukwu) is the axiom that theology and its methodology are not divorced from faith and life of the Church, the community, and the cosmos. Whether viewed as method or model or both, theology entails a dynamic activity that takes seriously the Christian proposition of faith in a self-revealing God.

Considered historically and classified typologically, African theology represents a process that continues along intersecting axes of methodologies and models, such as inculturation, reconstructionist, feminist, liberationist, and ecological approaches. While we recognise the accomplishments of African theologies that draw on these methodologies and models, questions abound about the identity of the African theologian in Africa's disturbing socioeconomic and political context, ecclesial communities, and the methodological and epistemological *loci* of African theologians. Theology is not enough; the African theologian must pay attention to how history shapes faith and life in Africa. Theology cannot bypass the imperative to give an account of how God is revealed in the historical and contextual narratives of Africans.

Ilo identifies necessary shifts in African theology that evoke Dowling's contention that theology is not an exercise in doctrinal and magisterial parroting or simulation. Rather, theology consists of a critical exercise in listening to and discerning what and how God is revealed to the Church in the painful (Uzukwu would prefer the word *agonising*) realities and stories of the people of God. Ilo labels this approach as "African cultural hermeneutical methodology" whose practitioners are theologians deeply immersed in and knowledgeable about multiple, diverse events and data of faith and life in Africa without neglecting the requisite cross-disciplinary scientific tools essential for a correct interpretation of this data. They ultimately understand their project as ever-expanding accounts of the presence and growth of the Word of God in Africa. To validate this methodology, theologians and the people of God alike must find in it satisfaction for a quest for meaning, communication of God's Word, and deep resonance and relevance to what matters to Africans and their yearning for abundant life.

Josée Ngalula presents a critique of theological methodology in Africa. In her assessment, this theology is still too remote and isolated from the lived experience of African Christians and their communities. Echoing Arabome, Dowling, Ilo, Mayemba, Okure, and Uzukwu, she maintains that the task of the African theologian is to gather the fragments of the lives of people into a coherent narrative. The constitutive practices of this methodology include listening and dialogue. Rather than speculating on the possibilities and shortcomings of African theology, she offers an illustrative narrative of her methodological practice in the collection of essays "The Bible and Women in Africa." Her approach exemplifies a theology that makes a preferential option for women who often constitute the vast majority of church membership in Africa as well as the category of the impoverished. The locus of her theology is the local Christian community, where the experiences of local women become material for an in-depth theological reflection and analysis capable of generating new insights and effective and practical remedies.

Ngalula's essay notably answers Béré's concerns, concretises Mayemba's approach, and remedies Arabome's challenges. Furthermore, her approach validates the methodological principle that theology is essentially a collaborative effort. The theologian may take the lead as facilitator, but she or he does not monopolise the conversation, manipulate the agenda, or mute the Christian community's voices. This approach safeguards the agency of the people and respects their theological aptitude and creativity especially when it is a matter of redressing the wrongs of injustice. In sum, theology is a collaborative and ascetic discipline at the service of communities of the people of God. Quite clearly, Ngalula offers a concise and concrete agenda or program of African theology different from Mayemba's intellectual approach.

What is the role of a bishop as a theologian? How does a bishop do theology? In keeping with his down-to-earth and engaging style of ministry, **Bishop Kevin Dowling** thinks it is to enter into and be comfortable in the mess of ordinary people's lives and concerns. This requirement concerns theologians and the hierarchy of the Church in the context of Africa. Dowling offers a powerful narrative of his vocation as a bishop called to witness to the gospel through faithful service and compassionate accompaniment of the people of God broken by poverty and ravaged by disease. The concomitant lesson for the world church is unambiguous: pay attention to the signs of the times through which God speaks to and calls church leaders and theologians to task.

Dowling highlights two key principles in the exercise of theological and ecclesiastical leadership: subsidiarity and collegiality, the same aspects Uzukwu considers paramount in the theological conception of the church-family model. Both qualities of theological and ecclesiastical leadership yield a third element, namely, discernment. This third principle enables the Church to recognise God's revelations and actions through respectful listening to the people of God and paying attention to their material poverty and spiritual starvation. The model here accords with Uzukwu's idea of a listening church grounded in deep compassion and respect for people. Listening allows for an inclusive conversation that begins with the people and goes through the various levels of leadership, including theologians and bishops. For Dowling, whether a person is a theologian, a bishop, or both, the requisite virtues are the same: listening, discernment, and dialogue. The ability to incarnate these virtues in pastoral praxis makes a bishop a theologian.

Assuming teaching as the central function of the bishop, what role does theological research and scholarship play in the exercise of this function? This is the core question of **Bishop Rodrigo Mejía Saldarriaga's** essay. His response draws on personal experience and stresses the nonnegotiability of continuing theological formation and education of bishops. The present situation, in which the demands of ecclesiastical chores choke up-to-date theological learning, is lamentable and results in the "academic poverty" of bishops, especially in Africa. As an antidote to this condition, Mejía proposes collaboration between bishops and professional theologians without undermining or substituting the episcopal duty of teaching and reflecting theologically. Theologians and bishops need to function as allies committed to a common goal with mutual respect and trust.

From the perspective of a new scholar, **Bienvenu Mayemba** locates the context of theology in Africa in the interstices of postcolonial theory and postmodernism. He argues for an African theology that enters into dialogue with constitutive facets of postcolonial consciousness. One interesting implication of this methodological proposal is that it challenges African theologians to engage with a new generation of African youth in their own burgeoning terrains of information communication technology and social media. For this to happen, and recalling the position of Katongole, he identifies the necessary ingredients as creativity, imagination, and innovation in embracing past, present, and future African realities. This approach is not new. In Mayemba's understanding, there are African theological ancestors whose achievements challenge new scholars to fidelity and creativity or creative fidelity. He concretises his proposal with a sample outline of a course in African Christian theology. A cursory look at his proposal reveals further methodological characteristics of a new African theology. These include interdisciplinarity and attention to the contribution of indigenous

African theology and theologians. The outcome would be truly African and truly theological.

Marinus Iwuchukwu focuses his essay on the contribution of African theologians in the Diaspora to interreligious dialogue. The prospect and project of interreligious dialogue is mired in ideological and doctrinal extremism. Iwuchukwu proposes a new methodology to overcome this impasse; he christens this methodology "inclusive religious pluralism" based on the work of Jacques Dupuis. The challenge and urgency of this task affect African Christians and African Muslims in equal measure.

He points out that scholars engaged in this field are progenies of two worlds: African and European/Middle Eastern. Each scholar's ideological and intellectual emphasis is shaped by these worlds. There is no reason to fall into one of the other as though they were irreconcilable extremes. A middle way is possible for the African scholar that blends and balances the best of both worlds, taking into account the reality of postmodernism and the necessity of inclusive religious pluralism and dialogue. In navigating the claims and conflicts of religious affiliation in Africa and in the Diaspora, the key principle is inclusiveness. The African worldview accommodates religious plurality. In this sense, inculturation and incarnation, of which other contributors such as Aihiokhai speak, are dynamic rather than static activities that attend to the needs and demands of the present, past, and future.

Lilian Dube offers a personal narrative of theological teaching in the North American Diaspora. In the context of university teaching, academic requirements, technological tools, cultural pitfalls, and institutional controls must be dealt with. Crossing borders in theological teaching and scholarship may demand extra effort for the African theologian, but daunting as this may seem, for Dube, they are not insurmountable challenges. Her narrative offers encouragement to colleagues and potential African Diaspora theologians. Judging by her account, ongoing learning is a vital component of teaching African theology in the Diaspora.

The same can be said of theology in general in a rapidly evolving and globalising context. As does Arabome, Dube makes the point that theological learning and teaching benefit greatly when both find anchors in real-life situations and contexts. Essentially, as we see in the essays of Aihiokhai, Arabome, Ilo, Iwuchukwu, Katongole, and Uzukwu, African theology is not confined to the geographical space of the continent. The context of theological production and innovation transcends the boundaries of time and space, making the product – and the works of these Diaspora theologians – a universal theological good not only for the Church in Africa but also for the world church. The African theologian in the Diaspora serves as a bridge between two cultural worlds.

To begin the final set of conversations in Part Three, **Emmanuel Katongole** addresses the vexing irony of religious growth or expansion and socioeconomic and political distress in Africa. What difference if any does Christianity or Church make to Africa's predicament? As Uzukwu shows in his analysis, theology and ecclesiology cannot circumvent this question and its inherent ambivalence. Katongole assigns to theology the primary role of generating a lament that cannot be appeased by the external manifestations and trappings of Christianity's seemingly unstoppable progress in Africa. It is too easy to be mesmerised by numbers and overlook the Church's mission to be a catalyst of the transformation of the fundamental vision and imagination that underlie African society. Indications are that Christianity and the Church have not always embraced this mission; Christianity has become a religion trapped in the private, personal, and spiritual realms. Consequently, it is innocuous and offers little contribution to the advancement of society.

African Christianity needs a new direction that allows for the reimagination of Africa from its foundation. This task must begin with the Church itself; it must be able to rethink, reimagine, and reinvent its own social imagination and praxis. Katongole offers a vivid illustration of this task using the example of Bishop Paride Taban's Holy Spirit Peace Village in Kuron, South Sudan. Such examples and narratives offer fresh data for engaging, reimagining, and transforming theological discourse in Africa.

Having read **Elochukwu Uzukwu's** contribution, one is permitted to conclude that ecclesiology in Africa did not begin with the first African Synod (1994). Africa's contribution to ecclesiology dates to Patristic times in Christian North Africa under the theological influence and acumen of people such as Cyprian of Carthage and Augustine of Hippo. History shows that their brand of expansive, inclusive ecclesiology was gradually reduced to a monotheistic ideology of governance in which uniformity and paternalism overrode autonomy, collegiality, synodality, and communion.

What the first African Synod proposed as model of Church, that is, Church-family of God, drew its inspiration from Trinitarian theology and its attendant qualities of interdependence, reciprocity, and interrelationship. Uzukwu describes the concrete incarnation of Trinitarian ecclesiological metaphor of church-family in the sociopolitical context of Africa and the world church. This ecclesiological model offers a path to ecclesial reform and renewal. Uzukwu defines the resultant community as "a church of communion informed by a sibling relationship that imitates and displays communion as reciprocal interiority emerging from the life of the Triune God." He fleshes out the ecclesiological metaphor of the African Synod and expounds and interprets Vatican II's idea of the Trinitarian provenance of the Church in refreshing and innovative perspectives.

Of particular salience is the view that Trinitarian provenance does not mean that the church subsists in the elevated heights of power and privilege. On the contrary, a Trinitarian-inspired model of church-family originates in the marginal place of the skull, Calvary and Golgotha, where Jesus was crucified and whence flow water and blood as symbols of the release of the Spirit of the risen Christ for the edification (foundation) of the Church as a place of relationality and communion. The implication of his position – as is that of Dowling and Okure – is obvious: the need for a Church that relocates to the margins and embraces the lives of marginalised, oppressed, and impoverished poor, what Pope Francis calls "a Church which is poor and for the poor."[3] The indelible imprint of the Trinitarian communion becomes most visible in this marginal locus; it is here that the Church is mandated to heal and reconcile all women and men in the manner of a functional African family.

Uzukwu illustrates other aspects of church-family by exploring the indications of this model in the missiology of Spiritan founder Francis Libermann, who emphasised the autonomy and self-reliance of the local church regulated by principles of interrelationship and synodality. Fascinating as his analysis may appear, it needs to be said that (and Uzukwu alludes to this point) it would take the miracle of the Trinity and radical conversion to construct a church-family that fully embodies the qualities of interrelationship, collegiality, synodality, and reciprocity in the present sociopolitical context of Africa marred by ambiguity and disasters and regnant ecclesiological perspectives in the world church beholden to patriarchy and hierarchy. In essence, as Uzukwu puts it, the model of church-family remains a "dream ecclesiology."

Anne Arabome outlines the challenges to fitting African theology into a neat conceptual framework. Drawing on her personal history, she demonstrates that the sources, roots, and foundations of African theology are deeply embedded in African religion rather than in exclusively Christian sources. Like Aihiokhai's, her analysis underscores the pertinence of the hermeneutics of inculturation in proclaiming the gospel and in doing theology. When foisted on people without consideration for their context, Christianity and theology become instruments of alienation.

Her most critical point is one made also by Aihiokhai and Akossi – how and where women feature in this theological enterprise. Both Church and society still have much learning to do on how to recognise, honour, and embrace the unique and diverse gifts of women. Theological imagination remains truncated without a just and adequate engagement with this matter. So far, African theology delineates a man's world in need of dialogue, inclusiveness, wholeness, and conversation as its redeeming graces. Besides paying attention to the gender question, African theology that focuses on real-life issues rather than on mere rhetoric stands a better chance of claiming the label "authentic and Christian." She recommends Emmanuel Katongole's *The Sacrifice of Africa: A Political Theology for Africa* (Grand Rapids, Mich.: W. B. Eerdmans, 2011) as a concrete model of an appropriate theology for Africa that offers concrete examples and proposals of how African women create alternative theological discourse and life-giving narrative theology.

Drawing on her experience as a believing and practicing Catholic, **Marguerite Akossi-Mvongo** poses some uncomfortable questions and tells some inconvenient truths regarding instances of the exclusion of women from the ministerial life of the Church based on gender. As a Christian scholar, her interrogation lies in the axis of scientific inquiry and personal fidelity to the faith. It is not abstract or ephemeral but personal and fundamental. Like Aihiokhai, she underscores the necessity of discerning clearly and distinguishing correctly what is of God, that is, the core of the gospel, and what belongs to Caesar, that is, cultural, contextual, and historical accoutrements.

While the former is to be applied and promoted, the latter is to be critiqued and purified. She does not deny the progress made in gender inclusion since Vatican II. However, selective openings to women in material tasks and roles create the illusion of ministerial service; in practice, they amount to no more than forms of what Pope Francis has denounced as servitude. Her collection of real-life anecdotes buttresses her claim that a disconnect exists in the Church between rhetoric and practice.

Happily, she reminds us, women are here to stay; the sooner we get the message as Church and society, the sooner we can expect transformation to occur. To resist is to succumb to the vice of deliberate mutilation and impoverishment of the body of Christ.

Simon-Mary Aihiokhai tackles the recalcitrant problem of gender-based discrimination in the Church. Using the matrix of inculturation, he proposes ways of overcoming practices that undermine the role and contribution of women to mission and ministry. In particular, he draws on an inventory of ritual practices from African religious traditions and cultures to make a case for the inclusion of women in diaconal ministries. Looking closely at his analysis, we are confronted with the ubiquity of culture in the proclamation of the gospel; a culture-free proclamation sounds utopian and unrealistic. As he argues, humility emerges as an essential ingredient in speculating on such matters, even in identifying and proposing examples of ritual participation and inclusivity from African religion precisely because the cultures that underlie this religion have limitations and flaws. In Christian proclamation, the norm should be the person and teaching of Jesus Christ, but this norm does not preclude learning from cultures that Christian adherents routinely claim to evangelise, in order to admit women to ministries that enhance the evangelising mission of the Church.

Aloyse-Raymond Ndiaye analyses the role of religion *vis-à-vis* governance in Africa. He begins by underlining the fact that religious intolerance is not native to Africa, hospitality is. However, although African customs and religions contribute immensely to the development of human society, Africa cannot progress by resisting modern science and technology. This does not mean abandoning the wisdom of the elders; rather, it means critically appropriating it to change the prevailing context and condition of the continent.

While he notes examples of exploitation of religion for political ends, he affirms that religion properly construed and authentically practiced can guide political action in the interest of the common good. The Church in Africa has a vital role to play in the realm of politics, namely, promoting the rule of law, human rights, and democracy. An essential precondition for the realisation of this mission is collaboration between the Church and secular authorities. In so doing, the good news of Christianity will be proclaimed in the public sphere with justice, human rights, reconciliation, and forgiveness as constitutive elements.

Perhaps the most insightful point that Ndiaye makes concerns the role of the laity. Oftentimes, when the issue of the presence and role of the Church in managing social crises and political conflict surfaces, one tacitly assumes that this role is the exclusive preserve of prelates and clergy. Ndiaye challenges this assumption. Laypeople have a decisive and principal role to play; to deny or impede it would weaken their contribution and undermine the exercise of their Christian vocation in secular society. As Vatican II teaches, the competence and experience of the laity place them in a position to accomplish the mission of the Church in the public square.

Finally, for religion to become an asset in public and political governance, it must collaborate in the promotion of the culture of the rule of law, democracy, and human rights. As it concerns the Church, the laity ought to play the primary role in this collaboration.

Elias Omondi Opongo's incisive analysis of the complex and checkered historical interplay between religion and leadership or governance in Africa should be read in conjunction with Ndiaye's essay. The relationship is complex, but Opongo delivers a mixed verdict: good and bad, positive and negative. Religion and political governance may not be considered as one considering the divergence of their ends, but their compatibility of purposes means they are engaged and interacting with each other for good or ill.

Opongo traces the roots of Africa's ills to poor governance or lack of leadership. There are also conflicts in which religion has been a negative and a positive factor. Examples of the latter instance include situations of postconflict reconstruction, reconciliation, and peace-building. Engaging in the political sphere requires a delicate balance between proclaiming the gospel and falling into the snares of division and ethnicity. The Church in Africa is not a newcomer to the processes of democratic transitions either directly through facilitation and moderation or indirectly through pastoral letters on human rights, democracy, and freedom.

Notwithstanding its relative success in this area, myriad factors militate against effective and sustainable involvement in political issues, notably lack of finances. Reading between the lines and in light of Ndiaye's position, a perennial weakness in the church's engagement in sociopolitical issues is its tendency to limit this involvement to the top tier of ecclesiastical leadership. In fact, it is a problem of ecclesiology: the influence of church leaders does not filter into or derive from the recognition, participation, and initiative of grassroots Christian communities. The charism of prophetic and heroic leadership is not the sole preserve of church leaders; the laity is also endowed with this charism, as Ndiaye argues. Unless and until this lesson is heeded, the impact of the Church's initiative and commitment to the promotion of good governance will remain limited.

Another important point is the need to introduce a spiritual component as correlative to political processes. Reconciliation and healing are concrete examples of spiritual components of a political process that the Church ought to be adept at proposing and leading. Opongo mentions more factors that hamper the effectiveness of the church, such as the lack of a mechanism for participating effectively in policy formulation on key national issues and the dearth of model leadership in transparency and financial management in religious institutions.

Concerning the second factor, we are confronted here with the classic scenario of removing the splinter from one's eye as a condition for discerning and removing the splinter from a neighbour's eye! Although Opongo invites the Church to collaborate with research and educational institutions, he overlooks the crucial point made by Ndiaye that such collaboration implies *trusting* competent Christian lay women and men to lead the Church's mission of sociopolitical engagement and transformation guided by the principles, criteria, and norms of Catholic social tradition.

Having summarised the various positions and perspectives of the contributors and the focal conversation points, I leave the reader the task of assessing the relative strength of their argumentation and the depth of their imagination in relation to the renewal of church, religion, and society in Africa.

Endnotes

1   See Agbonkhianmeghe E. Orobator, ed., *Reconciliation, Justice, and Peace: The Second African Synod* (Maryknoll, N.Y.: Orbis Books, 2011); *Practising Reconciliation, Doing Justice, and Building Peace: Conversations in Catholic Theological Ethics in Africa* (Nairobi, Kenya: Paulines Publications Africa, 2013); Linda Hogan and A. E. Orobator, eds., *Feminist Catholic Theological Ethics: Conversations in the World Church* (Maryknoll, N.Y.: Orbis Books, 2014).

2   Nguni for "A person is a person because of/through other persons" (also *motho ke motho ka batho babang* in Sotho) or "I am because we are."

3   Pope Francis, *Evangelii Gaudium* (24 November 2013), no. 198.

PART ONE

AFRICAN THEOLOGY AND RELIGIOUS IDENTITY: SOURCE AND CRITIQUES

Truly African, Fully Christian?
In Search of a New African-Christian Spirituality

Laurenti Magesa

Introduction

D avid Tracy, a leading American theologian, describes the time we live in as "an age that cannot name itself." Traditionalists, modernists, and postmodernists, he says, all have different interpretations of the present moment in history as well as different expectations of and from it. According to him, "These three conflicting namings of the present situation are at the heart of the conflict of interpretations [of the current era]." They affect perceptions of both culture and Christian theology.[1] While Tracy notes he is describing the situation in the Western world, I contend that the condition of uncertainty is global and that its symptoms and impact on the African continent and Church are inescapable.

Indeed, one of, if not the most striking feature of, various dimensions of existence in Africa today is complexity brought about by a sense of overriding self-doubt induced by the experience of rapid change. Current developments belie former unequivocal perceptions of life aspirations. Multiplicity of visions and interpretations of reality manifestly characterise contemporary African life, often bringing about contradictory value-goals. These opposing expectations and goals are immediately present to many as real choices thanks to modern information and communication technology (ICT). ICT has made the phenomenon we call globalisation a fact of African life as well.

Emerging worldwide in a new way since the last several decades of the last century, the globalisation movement has bred a state of uncertainty that impacts very deeply the ways people view themselves and the world and everything in it. Empirically, globalisation involves an inevitable but generally destabilising, rapid, and relatively unrestrained social, economic, political, and cultural exchange. It facilitates easy mobility "of people, products, plants, animals, technologies and ideas,"[2] including negative environmental conditions across the globe. On account of this, on the social and theological levels, old claims to certain clearly defined identities are now radically challenged so that in Africa, the puzzle of whether we are "truly African" at the same time as we are "fully Christian" has increasingly taken on new urgency no longer as a theoretical conjecture but as a disturbing reality. And "in the process of trying to be both Christian and African, where do we put other religions," specifically Islam?[3]

Amidst the multiple social and religious identities that confront us and claim our allegiance in this politically and economically multipolar and polycentric but nonetheless intimately interconnected universe, who we "really" are is a question whose answer is by no means straightforward.

In Africa, there are a few if any who in one way or another do not feel overwhelmed by it. Globalisation has taken our "innocence" away, so to speak, and like everyone else, Africa stands naked to the world. Our old and neat but now clearly simplistic assertions of exclusivity in relation to our African or Christian identities are confounded. Concerning these, a new quest is under way.

Theological Issues at Stake

Pope Paul VI openly and directly encouraged the quest in the Catholic Church in Africa in the 1960s. On July 31, 1969, during a visit to Uganda, he declared to the bishops of Africa assembled in Kampala, "You [Africans] may, and you must, have an African Christianity." About ten years later, on May 3, 1980, Pope John Paul II affirmed the same to Africa through the bishops of the Democratic Republic of Congo, DRC (then Zaire): "You desire to be at the same time fully Christian and fully African,"[4] he insisted.

Since then, there have been numerous similar public calls by different actors in the Church, including African and Africanist theologians. Underlying the issue is the quest for identity. One might say that this quest perhaps encapsulates the deepest aspirations of the entire African Church (and the black subcontinent generally). The questions, however, are, What does "African Christianity" mean in practice? Is it merely a new version of African traditional religion (ATR)?[5]

Furthermore, after so many years of pastoral guidance and theological reflection, one wonders if the "road map" to Christian self-identity in

Africa is sufficiently clear and producing fruits. The story of Africa's encounter with Western Christianity, especially since the end of the nineteenth century, still makes this an extremely complex question, the noted attempts to address it notwithstanding. Thus, progress in the process often theologically referred to as inculturation or incarnation – the effort to transform the content and implications of the Christian faith to become comprehensively the "culture" of African Christians – is, in the opinion of some, agonisingly slow. For whatever historical, sociological, and psychological reasons, there may be a basic and general reluctance in the Church in Africa to become culturally both Christian and African. This process calls for some painful but necessary concrete steps to reach the goal of authentic self-identity in the Church.

Bluntly put, they consist in the demand to deconstruct or break down many historically established mental, social, theological, and attitudinal notions and structures that control life, including Christian life, in Africa to reconstruct them anew in what will be a different form but one intrinsically and radically faithful to the original. Although this may appear at first to be paradoxical or even self-contradictory as a proposal for a way forward, it is in essence the only way to realise the theological and pastoral aspiration of inculturation as a requirement for an authentically African Church.

Deconstruction and reconstruction constitute the current vocation of the Church in Africa: it is a process that leads to a new way of being truly African and fully Christian. In a real sense, the Church in Africa must be "no longer truly African, not fully Christian" in the old way to become "at the same time fully Christian and fully African." The process requires an act of the almost sacrilegious destruction of certain time-honored conceptions of both Africanness on the one hand and Christianity on the other to regain them anew in a more appropriate contextual manner.

The radical counsel of the Lord on true discipleship is pertinent here as a biblical metaphor for this process: "Whoever wants to save his life will lose it; but whoever loses his life for me will find it" (Matthew 16:25, John 12:24, 3:3 NIV). The loss and gain of life that Jesus is depicted as talking about here is exactly the kind symbolised and realised by his death and resurrection. The fundamental theological point these Christological events make is that Jesus' death was not a total destruction, an absolute break with, or complete disassociation from his earthly life. Nor did his bodily resurrection imply the reception of a totally different body than his historical one. Jesus rose from death with a new body in the sense that the same body had been transformed. This is to say that despite, or even because of, the apparent destruction of his earthly body, there remained an essential link and continuity between it and his glorified body in heaven.

As with Jesus, so will it be with us humans; the newness of our resurrected bodies will be, indeed, the fundamental mark of our new way of being with God in heaven. But this is a qualitative rather than a fictitious newness, one constructed as though from nothing. God never destroys but "saves" or transforms what God has created (see Romans 8:19–22).[6] The "new earth" we await at the end of time is this very earth transformed. In terms of inculturation and Christian self-identity, therefore, the new Christianity emerges from an intricate process of synthesis between the centuries-old Christian understandings (or traditions) of the liberating work of Jesus Christ and the African people's equally time-honoured, God-given cultural ways of being. The new Christianity refers to the life of faith of the self-same African-Christian transformed and renewed to become not merely a Christian *in* Africa but truly a Christian *of* Africa, an African-Christian.[7]

This is no easy task. It is one marked by uncertainty, but uncertainty is in this case not necessarily a liability but an act of hope, as American missiologist John C. Sivalon describes it. Potentially, it bears a chain of blessings: faith, contemplation, discernment, imagination, and creativity. According to Sivalon, "The gift of uncertainty generates the gift of change and growth. And, most important, the gift of uncertainty grounds our mission within the Mission of God."[8] Thus, the process of finding ourselves as truly African and fully Christian may be founded on the blessing of uncertainty, one that calls for imagination and creativity and grateful, graceful acceptance of growth-inducing change. Above all, uncertainty might help anchor the process of inculturation or authentic African-Christian identity in the mystery of the incarnation of Jesus Christ who, as God become human, is the image of true human identity.

The mystery of the Incarnation at its core involves death that leads to life, or seeming defeat that brings about solid triumph in the resurrection. The Incarnation as the prototype of true identity is a matter of "breaking boundaries."

Since human understandings and interpretations of the gospel are necessarily bounded by forms of situatedness that inform and limit human experience, a fuller appreciation of infinite divine revelation demands the exercise of a dynamic, spiral-like hermeneutics, one that continually tries to transcend local circumscriptions and circumspections. This requires openness, the sort that is the hallmark of true religion or true gospel Christianity. Current understandings of the gospel should never be considered absolute, and neither should cultural categories in which the gospel is and must be understood.

When given expressions of the gospel in their limitations and possibilities encounter specific local realities with their own limitations and possibilities, both must be allowed to expand and break at the seams. Otherwise, Christian identity will be warped, artificially restricted, and fossilised.

Handled with confident faith in God's Spirit working in and through the Church and in the world in general, the current crisis of uncertainty is a seedbed for potentially fabulous human growth. Through the opaqueness of the experience of the death of the old African and Christian identities, a new, expansive African-Christian spirituality will emerge. Indeed, a new African spirituality and religious synthesis are beacons on the horizon; the search for them is the real and present task.

The Guest

The narrative of the incarnation, death, and resurrection of Jesus on which the Christian faith is anchored shows that the quest will not be easy or its exact contours predictable. There was no such certainty in the pilgrimage of Jesus on earth. At some times, the map as a whole will be fuzzy; at other times, the paths on the map will be crooked, rendering the search for a true African-Christian identity messy and even agonising, familiar as many of us are with the comfort of the seeming theological clarity of yesteryear. But in the inscrutable functioning of the Holy Spirit, this may be the only authentic path in search of ultimate truth. The goal is eschatological, just as Jesus' own was.

While the ambiguities we face should alert us to the possible and even probable pitfalls along our pilgrim road to authentic African-Christian identity, they point also to immense opportunities that can be accessed only through the messy process of "discerning the spirits" (see 1 Corinthians 12). Is it not true, after all, that almost all the doctrines we hold as unquestionable went through a similar route of risk through the untidy dynamics of deconstruction and reconstruction?

At any rate, there is no reason to believe uncertainty is about to be eliminated as the way by which the growth of the Church occurs. With increasing globalisation, the opposite appears to be the case. The question for true and authentic African-Christian identity (or inculturation) is not whether to travel the path of risk but how to handle the risks involved in the journey of how to find one's innate, God-given self-cognition and recognition as an African-Christian. The obligation involves how to make present Christ's message of liberation in Africa without violence and damage to African culture and rationality.

Although globalisation as a movement has many defects, it also serves to reveal, perhaps in a clearer way than ever, the rich, God-given diversity and beauty of the universe in which we find ourselves and in which we must learn to live. Human beings must try to be at home in the world as citizens of specific places even as they are simultaneously citizens of the diverse world. This is obviously not easy on account of the often contradictory demands of each; so, the danger is real that one will neither be local nor global.

However, here is where the responsibility of finding oneself lies. It is only by trailblasing through these apparent contradictions that one can be authentically local as well as global and so avoid a dangerous state of existential dichotomy such as has recently led to much violence and suffering in the world through what is popularly referred to as the clash of civilisations.

Only through deconstruction can we reconstruct who we are and what and how we want to be as African children of God and believers in Christ. Noted American theologian Robert J. Schreiter speaks of this as "the new Catholicity," a child of theological reciprocity "between the global and the local."[9] It is a Catholicity that avoids homogenising tendencies based on a unipolar or unicentric set of experiences that are insufficiently sensitive to different local conditions and needs. This situation is challenged by the theology of liberating inculturation and the pastoral need for self-identity. Both theology and pastoral planning must be situated in a local context. If the universal can obviously not be rejected without detriment to the local, it must judiciously be incorporated into the local without running roughshod over it so that as a result, both become new.

The skill lies in the manner of integrating the local and the global for the creation of new horizons. Syncretism, which is fundamental to the process, should not necessarily be perceived as a theological and pastoral deviation. Syncretism is negative only when cultural meanings and values are not integrated and internally expanded but merely superimposed upon one another without inner coherence; it is the forced assimilation of contradictory spiritual and theological cosmologies without any attempt at fundamentally synthesising their underlying understandings and meanings, or, on the other hand, refusing to recognise the impossibility of doing so.

However, an approach to evangelisation disregarding the necessary synthesis of Christian and African cultural values and meanings will, in the long run, be hugely damaging to both Africanness and Christianity in the search for an African-Christian identity. As Jesus in Matthew's gospel puts it, "Every scribe who has been instructed in the kingdom of heaven is like the head of a household who brings from his storeroom both the new and the old" (Matthew 13:52).

Attention to the old and new or the global and the local is what Schreiter describes as "glocalisation."[10] It demands a different way of proceeding (i.e., deconstruction) for the emergence (i.e., reconstruction) of a new, more humanising culture. In terms of evangelisation, the result is a new Catholicity, the outcome of a creative tension between the two. It is a result of mutual centripetal movements of values and meanings, processes of mutual fertilisation between and among different cultures, understandings, and practices of natural revelation in Africa and special revelation through the gospel of Christ.[11]

The process involves various elements and paths. I have space to sketch only two among them, namely, language and ritual.

Beyond Information to Communication

A very enlightening article by George A. De Napoli makes the fundamental point that culture is not a "reified" object existing by itself, "something that can be seen, touched, and manipulated"; rather, culture exists only in people. It is the foundation of understandings, meanings, and values whence human behaviors flow. Culture is thus primarily "in the mind and hearts of people."[12] Strictly speaking, understood as such, this should be the target of evangelisation or inculturation towards transformation or conversion. The most important carrier of culture in this sense is language in its larger sense as "art, literature, music, artifacts, rituals, etc."[13]

Human beings identify themselves culturally because they employ language in these forms to communicate. Thus, people distinguish themselves from one another as individuals or groups specifically by the kinds of stories they tell and, in terms of cultural identity, what meanings their stories carry for a kindred group. Here the groups' foundational narratives, which may include any or all combination of the above-mentioned dimensions of language, take pride of place. Such narratives represent and shape the groups' identities and spiritualities and their relationship to one another and to God. Shifts in these stories/narratives, particularly also in how they are told, induce change in social and spiritual behaviour. An indicator of the labour pains of the new spiritual creation we seek lies, therefore, in the linguistic dimension of human existence. How and for what purpose we use theological language are, therefore, questions we must pose. How do we tell God's story and, of course, as Christians, the story of Jesus in relation to our location?

Religious discourse in sub-Saharan Africa has for a long time remained unrelated to African experiential story. This accounts for the malaise of the dichotomy between Africanness and Christianity. Theological language in Africa that is incapable of following to its internal conclusion the logic and spirituality of witchcraft, polygamy, divination, traditional healing practices, and so on except to condemn these beliefs and practices fails miserably to engage with the African person holistically. It addresses culture as a theoretical object outside the person. But the Bible should indicate the way: the Bible's is the language of "evil spirits," "demons," "angels," and "dreams"; of "sons of God and daughters of men," and so on (see Genesis 6:1–4). A literal application of a Bultmannian "demythologisation" principle might not serve us well.

The verbal and other symbols classically employed to explain and give meaning and direction to Africans' life aspirations inspired by the above-mentioned realities are unable to communicate, even though they may inform. Current Christian theological language abstracts itself from fundamental African experience, which is marked by a loathing of extremes that are antithetical to harmony. In particular, even as it proposes to explain it, Christian religious and theological discourse in Africa appears to pay scant attention to the breadth and depth, the complexity, of the African person's attempt to relate to the divine self-revelation in an African context. Instead of being elastic, as surely befits the complexity of God speech because it addresses an ultimately incomprehensible infinite reality, theological discourse in Africa has for the most part remained rigid and inflexible, seeing as its main purpose the streamlining, *ad extra,* of African divine-human encounters into certain predetermined categories of thought and structures of ritual called dogma. On account of this, theological discourse and the life it seeks to influence and shape have lost much of their African aesthetic character.[14]

But theology that is instrumental for holistic growth must be a form of aesthetics, one that shapes people's lives from within toward that beauty we call God. Therefore, not only logic and dogma are to be cultivated and accorded theological dignity but also art, music, religious artifacts, rituals, meditation, and contemplation. Walter J. Hollenweger alerts us to this imperative when he writes that "Conceptual language" and logical "theological arguments" are not the exclusive means of communication, nor are dogmatic "definitions" or "hermeneutical analysis." Important also in Africa are "stories," "testimonies," "participatory dance," "songs," and ritual such as deliverance and "healing."[15] These are the approaches to God, expressed supremely in ritual, that most endure. Ritual is the "speechless speech" that evokes wonder and awe before what Rudolf Otto characterised as the *mysterium tremendum et fascinans,* the awe-inspiring but fascinating mystery that is God.

Scriptural language should serve as a paradigm. The Bible is predominantly a portrait, a picture of hope and laughter or disappointment and tears because this is the experience of all humanity. The story or narrative is the preferred method of theological communication there. The Bible contains simple, straightforward stories of redemption and betrayal, of faithfulness and faithlessness. It contains no mechanistic, how-to prescriptions or directives but a chain of songs of invitation to fidelity, of emotions of disappointment, and of bursts of frustration and anger.

The Bible is unique not because it is particular but because the feelings it evokes are of universal recognition and application; its narratives intimately touch the core of every man and woman – the need for liberation, healing, and other favors humans long for. One is impressed by the magnitude and gratuitousness of divine love just as one is equally disgusted with the human ingratitude and betrayal one encounters there. The Bible addresses the heart of everyone's elementary sense of common humanity in a very accessible manner. Biblical language is a language of Pentecost, recognizable by the most disparate of individuals and communities: "Each of us hears them in our native language!" (see Acts 2:7–11 NIV).

For the purpose of achieving an authentic African Christian spirituality, revelational and dialogical models of theology do not stand as opposites or competitors but as complementary approaches. As Hollenweger puts it, the dimensions of contemplation, participation, and compassionate solidarity "constitute a pastoral triage as old as the Acts of the Apostles but as fresh as any alert Christian community today." These comprise the essence of spiritual growth: "Where [these are] alive and well, there is hope for faith in spite of the complexity of the culture. ... [and] we are well on the way to recreating a living [African-]Christian culture for our time."[16]

Sacred "Games" We Play

Contemplation, participation, and compassionate solidarity are acted out in ritual and worship. Ritual constitutes the sacred games (or relationships of affection) people play for the creator or other invisible forces with power over humanity. Their importance as symbols for African people and societies cannot be overemphasised.

> Members of an African society feel their unity and perceive their common interests in symbols, and it is their attachment to those symbols which, more than anything else, gives their society cohesion and persistence.[17]

Here, rituals play a special role as part of life-giving sacred language.

The African worldview of the omnipresence of forces and interrelationship between them and humanity necessitates ritual as the essence of harmony in existence. Life can be sustained only by maintaining internal harmony among the various elements of visible and invisible powers of existence through ritual performance. There are rituals to revere good powers, to appease evil or angry ones, and always to try to preserve universal harmony. Still prevalent in Africa are:

> Rituals that celebrate the cosmic cycle of birth, death and new life; the unity of the visible with the invisible world; the sacredness of the earth; and healing rituals form part not only of indigenous people's worship but of popular religiosity.[18]

To be effective, rituals have to exude or communicate meaning in the present for the people concerned. Thus, as Ignatius Pambe cautions, "To try to formulate a symbol or ritual meaningful to all people, at all times, in all places is a form of pride that anyone interested in communication cannot afford."[19]

Rituals are theology *in* or *as* action. As the venerable Latin axiom has it, *Lex credendi lex orandi lex vivendi* (As we believe so we worship, so we live). It shortchanges African spirituality when ritual is relegated only to predetermined official settings and times, such as in a church on Sunday or even to just liturgical occasions and functions, thus separating them from their place and role as the daily bedrock of the possibility of human and universal existence, unity, and harmony. In healthcare, for example,

> the African does not believe in unconsecrated "medicine," wherever and however dispensed. So, an object [medicine] which lacks the "official" and "trusted" manipulator is reduced to a secular state and the sacred symbol is pushed to oblivion.[20]

The rituals accompanying quotidian human callings such as family care, work, salutations, socialisation, and so on, which African spirituality perceives as fundamentally sacred, must not be trivialised. If the home is not the primary temple where human communion is forged through everyday cognition that life is lived under divine and ancestral power, no other temple will succeed in conveying the message. From the African worldview, these activities not only connect human persons with one another to construct the greater humanity, *ubuntu*; they also underline the sacred vocation of the human person to connect with the entire universe and God.

Renowned African theologian Elochukwu E. Uzukwu makes an important point drawn from the experience of some African initiated churches (AICs) of West Africa: "In times of need, [African] Christians do not ask the theoretical question about the identity of the health generating *spirit*."[21] With gratitude, they accept healing wherever they can get it. AICs act upon this and thus expand and deepen the function of African healers in the Christian belief in the power of God the Holy Spirit by "successfully [replicating and] integrat[ing] the ministry of diviner-healers into the structures of the church."[22] In this reconstructive approach, the action of the Holy Spirit is allowed its true biblical freedom on the one hand, while the putative autonomous or autochthonous power of spirits in African cosmology is reined in and placed under the overarching power of the Holy Spirit. A form of Christianity, simultaneously true to Africa and to the inspiration of the gospel, is thereby born.

Conclusion

According to Michael Paul Gallagher, "Christian spirituality has to do with building daily bridges between the gift of God in Christ and the limited realities of each one's life-situation." That is why, as he puts it, "spirituality is the essential link between faith and culture.... It is the zone where ... [Christians] opt to give attention or not to the calls of the Spirit, where they shape the quality of their Christian journey, where they protect the freedom of their hearts, and where they learn to discern wisely amid the pressures of the culture."[23] As such, spirituality is "a practical human art, for a more than human adventure [and goal]."[24] In the adventure, both culture and dogma must not be allowed to "remain 'trapped at the surface level,' alienated from the deepest languages of our humanity." The quest towards authentic African-Christian identity calls, rather, for balance to be struck between "excessive fear" of the limitations of culture and "excessive innocence" or the uncritical trust in the accuracy of human linguistic formulations of faith in God. It calls for a "new cultural-religious synthesis."

Endnotes

1   David Tracy, *On Naming the Present: God, Hermeneutics, and Church* (Mary-knoll, N.Y.: Orbis, 1994), 3.

2   See Wayne Ellwood, *The No-Nonsense Guide to Globalisation* (London: New Internationalist, 2001).

3   A question by African feminist theologian Mercy Amba Oduyoye as a rejoinder to this presentation on August 16, 2013 at the Hekima Institute of Peace Studies and International Relations (HIPSIR), Nairobi, Kenya.

4   For a collection of extracts of some of the major papal pronouncements on this issue, see http://afrikaworld.net/afrel/atr-popes.html.

5   A query by one of the participants in the colloquium in which this presentation was given, on August 16, 2013 at HIPSIR.

6   In a homily preached at Hekima Jesuit School of Theology, Nairobi, Kenya on Sunday April 28, 2013, Deacon Ablam Atsikin, referring to Revelation 21:1, distinguished between the biblical usage of the terms *kainos* and *neos* to imply qualitative newness and newness as though *ex nihilo* respectively. According to Atsikin, the seer's vision of "a new heaven and a new earth" means that "Despite the discontinuities, the new cosmos will be an identifiable counterpart ... [of] the old cosmos and a renewal of it, just as the body will be raised without losing its former identity ... But renewal does not mean that there will be no literal destruction of the old cosmos, just as the renewed resurrection-body does not exclude a similar destruction of the old."

7   For this fundamental distinction in Christian identity, see (with reference to Asia) Aloysius Pieris, "The New Quest for Asian Christian Identity: Guidelines from the Pioneers of the Past," *Third Millennium: Indian Journal of Evangelisation*, XII, no. 3 (July-September 2009): 9–28.

8   John C. Sivalon, *God's Mission and Postmodern Culture: The Gift of Uncertainty* (Maryknoll, N.Y.: Orbis, 2012), 17.

9   See Robert J. Schreiter, *The New Catholicity: Theology between the Global and the Local* (Maryknoll, N.Y.: Orbis, 1997).

10   See Schreiter, *The New Catholicity,* 12.

11   Some light has been shed from the East on this; see Michael Amaladoss, "Attaining Harmony as a Hindu Christian," in *In Search of the Whole: Twelve Essays on Faith and Academic Life,* ed. John C. Haughey (Washington, D.C.: Georgetown University Press, 2011): 99–110, and Peter C. Phan, *Being Religious Interreligiously: Asian Perspectives on Interfaith Dialogue* (Maryknoll, N.Y.: Orbis, 2008).

12   George A. De Napoli, "Inculturation as Communication," in *Inculturation: Working Papers on Living Faith and Cultures,* ed., Arij A. Roest Crollius (Rome: Centre "Cultures and Religions" – Pontifical Gregorian University, 1987), 74.

13   See ibid., 73–73.

14   Who could blame the Shilluk people of Sudan, therefore, for running away from missionaries who went around wearing a figure of a man fixed on a tree, a sign to the Shilluk of ultimate cruelty? See R. G. Lienhardt, "The Dinka and Catholicism," in *Religious Organisation and Religious Experience*. AMA Monograph 21, ed., J. Davis (London: Academic Press, 1982).

15   Walter J. Hollenweger, "Foreword, " in John S. Pobee and Gabriel Ositelu II, *African Initiatives in Christianity* (Geneva: WWC, 1998), ix.

16   Ibid, "Foreword," 139–45.

17   Ignatius M. Pambe, "Religious Symbols, Inter Culture Communication and Change in Africa," in *Service* 5&6 (1980), 20.

18   Margaret Shanthi, "Worship/Rituals," in *Dictionary of Third World Theologies,* ed., Virginia Fabella and R. S. Sugirtharajah (Maryknoll, N.Y.: Orbis, 2000), 238.

19   Pambe, "Religious Symbols," 36. Original in italics. He adds, "The tendency to static formulations [in the Catholic Church] by drawing symbols from medieval Christianity of Europe will be redundant antiquarianism which would not serve effective culture communication in relation to African religion and symbols."

20   Ibid., 26.

21   Elochukwu Eugene Uzukwu, *God, Spirit, and Human Wholeness: Appropriating Faith and Culture in West African Style* (Eugene, Ore.: Pickwick, 2012), 177.

22   Ibid., 177–78.

23   Michael Paul Gallagher, *Clashing Symbols: An Introduction to Faith and Culture* (New York: Paulist Press, 1998), 138.

24   Ibid.

How African is African Theology?

Teresa Okure

Preliminary Observations

T he "Theological Colloquium on Church, Religion and Society in
Africa" by nature requires a colloquial style of engagement. The
main dimensions of this project – the theological colloquium and
church, religion, and society in Africa – are worth noting. My observations
may not touch on them all, but it is important we keep them in focus because in conversation, we critically engage each other and exchange ideas.

First, I noticed that the word "culture" is missing from the project title.
This may be because culture is so endemic in every aspect of human life that
it is taken for granted. In Africa, as elsewhere, one cannot go far towards
effective life-giving, life-transforming endeavours in church, religion, and
society without explicitly addressing culture. Because culture is endemic
and irresistibly operative in all we do, we need to be aware of its pervasive influence in our thinking and theological discourses. We are all slices
of our cultures or multicultures (if we go beyond the culture of our birth
and upbringing). Culture is the basic denominator that identifies, defines,
unites, and divides us as Africans, depending on what we do with our rich
cultural diversity from Cape to Cairo. Our diverse cultural perspectives
are inevitably at work as we engage one another even in this colloquium.

Second, theology (from the Greek *theos*, God, and *logos*, word) is
traditionally defined as faith seeking understanding through philosophical
discourse. This definition attributed to Anselm of Canterbury has become
the classic definition of theology. From African and biblical perspectives,
we may need to redefine theology as God's word about humans and creation. God spoke creation into being (Genesis 1:1–2:4a; my translation from
the Hebrew), and deliberatively spoke humanity into existence: "Let us
make *adam* [humanity] in our image and likeness" (Genesis 1:26–27).[1]
God named the humanity created in the divine image and likeness "*adam*
when he created them" (Genesis 5:1–2). In the "new creation," God more

wonderfully recreated humanity (male and female) as God's children in Christ, God-Word incarnate (John 1:1–2, 14), the new humanity (*kainos anthropos*). As a result, all discrimination based on race/ethnicity ("Jew or Gentile"), class ("slave or free") and sex ("male and female"), the heritage of unevangelised cultures, ceases to exist (Galatians 3:26–29). In Christ, each is "a new creation" (2 Corinthians 5:17) that becomes one in him. African and other Christian theologies find in this divine, creative word their true identity and mission.

It is essential that we consciously conduct our theological colloquium from the primary standpoint of God's word about us and creation. The nature and scope of a product are determined by its manufacturer. Whom does God say we are and what does God say creation is? Whom do we say we are because of whom God says we are? In a typical African way, we are because God says we are, and because God says we are, each of us is.

How do we carry this awareness into conversing theologically on Church, religion, and society in Africa? "Word" (*logos*; *iko* in Ibibio [Nigeria]), especially in traditional Africa, is not mere sound; like God's word, the human word affects at its own level what it says, because humans are in God's image and likeness.[2] When faith seeks to understand God's word about humans, our seeking to understand God through our philosophical (human) discourse makes truer, fuller sense. Our identity is not determined through encounters with others but uniquely by whom God says we are.

My task, to determine how African is African theology, can be approached from many directions, but ultimately, the idea is to take critical stock of African theology in its present-day context, noting established traditions and addressing gaps. I have taken seriously this freedom to approach the topic as I think fit. This free rein meant I did not have to wade through volumes of works by African theologians before I could write what I think African theology is or should be doing. My reflection, therefore, is not an attempt to note established traditions and address gaps on the basis of the works of others. Rather, I share in this chapter what I think African theology and we African theologians should focus on if our theologising is to meet the real-life needs of people in the teeming multicultural, multiethnic, multireligious, and greatly diversified population of this great and vast continent, Mama Africa.

The rationale and inspiration for this project, specifically my topic on how African is African theology, deserve attention. I address them one by one. First, given that – as mentioned by the series editor – "globalisation and postmodernity hold strong influence on all forms of contemporary scholarship, including theological scholarship" in Africa as elsewhere, "Can we still claim and affirm the existence of a pristine body of theological knowledge and research christened 'African'?"

Insofar as Africa exists and God has a word about it, we can speak of African theology. That said, other questions arise; as a typical Nigerian who answers questions by asking questions (Jesus habitually did the same), I ask, "Who needs this 'pristine body of theological knowledge' and for what purpose? For whom is this question important and why? Should we be concerned with theological knowledge or theological life, life that is rooted in God and seeks to appropriate and live to the full our divinely endowed identity as God's children?" Knowledge undoubtedly comes to play in this, but is not the organising principle. "Knowledge puffs up but love [God] builds up" (1 Corinthians 8:1).

Some of the current factors influencing, shaping, and defining theological reflection and scholarship in Africa come to my mind in the form of questions. Are the current influencing factors largely our desire to be heard, appreciated, and applauded, especially overseas? Are we motivated to do African theology because other Third World constituencies and marginalised peoples (Asian, Latin American, South African, and North American blacks) also do theirs? Who and what does our theology serve? Are we motivated by the need to have a market for our theological products, obtain funding to publish them and for further research, seminars, and symposia? Are we hired to theologise for export, or do we theologise for home consumption, the nourishment of our theologically hungry and starving people who are exposed daily to "Mama put" ("roadside food") theologies and spiritualities? In cultivating other people's theological gardens and serving their interests, have we left our own gardens uncultivated (cf. Songs 1:6)?[3]

I shared with my African sisters at the inaugural conference of The Circle Accra in 1992 that if such are the factors that influence and shape our doing theology as African women, we are wasting our time, God's precious time, and the time of our expectant people.[4]

Are the categories that inspire, impact, and energise our theologising those of the theological club that is always one step ahead, the club to which we attach ourselves as perpetual disciples? Or is our theologising informed by the multifaceted life questions of our people such as growing militancy, violence of all types, joblessness, loss of cultural identity in the bid to be current ("Americana")? How do we theologise to meet our people's way of knowing and searching for God and their fear of evil spirits? How does our theology address the growing ills in our African and global society, including corruption, embezzlement (terms that do not exist in my Ibibio language), lying as an acceptable way of conducting business, and the exploitation and marginalisation of women even in the Church?

Does the pure desire to proclaim the gospel inspire, energise, and drive our theological endeavours? Since Vatican II, the Church has passionately urged that all fields of study be conducted from the perspective of Scripture, which gets its meaning from Jesus (Romans 1:1 -16; John 5:39).

"The study of the sacred page should be, as it were, the very soul of theology"; this quotation from the dogmatic constitution _Dei Verbum_ has become increasingly familiar over the years. Care must be taken to ensure that the study of Scripture is truly the soul of theology inasmuch as it is acknowledged as the Word of God addressed to today's world, to the Church, and to each of us personally. The notion of scholarly theological research that is neutral with regard to Scripture should not be encouraged.[5]

This may be the time for African theologians to pay serious attention to cultivating their own gardens and using God's Word, of which our people are so enamored today, as a guide. This entails asking our own theological questions from scratch, not by first finding out how we fit into the categories and the theological questions and answers of others and their expectations of us. Third World theologies, spearheaded by Ecumenical Association of Third World Theologians (EATWOT), drew their origins from the dawning awareness of Oscar Bimwenyi of Zaire, a theology student at Louvain in the early seventies, that he was spending his time learning answers to other people's theological questions while his own questions were not even being asked.[6]

Only after we have toured foreign theological methodologies and interests, after we have responded to what others expect of African theologians, and after we have secured admission into the theological club can we return home to cultivate our own gardens with our own African natural (not genetically produced) theological seeds and crops.[7] The native instincts, wisdom, morals, religious beliefs, and traditions of our people[8] are wasted, mostly untapped because they do not serve the interests of external sponsors and Western readers. Have we been too busy searching for theological inspiration and nourishment in foreign ideas and categories in a bid to be relevant to notice the superabundant wealth of theological resources God has given us in Mama Africa?

We can learn here from Jesus' disciples.[9] They complained of inadequate resources to feed the people. Common sense dictated that Jesus send them away to buy food for themselves; did he want them to gather all their meager resources to go to town (go abroad, where there is plenty) and buy food for the people? Even that would not suffice. Jesus said, "No! You give them something to eat from your own resources. Revisit your perceived insufficiency."

"Well, there is a little boy here with five loaves and two fish; but what is that among so many?"

"Bring them to me, in the ways of the child, with perfect trust and faith. I will do the rest."

They brought Jesus what they had obtained from a little boy; it was perhaps his day's ration packed by his mother. Jesus gave thanks, blessed, broke, and gave it to them to distribute. They did. The miracle happened in the sharing of a common vision, purpose, and resources, in a spirit of gratitude, with utter confidence in the one who was directing their theologising and mission of feeding the people.

What of us? Do we tap the richness of the theological works by our African brothers and sisters, especially the sisters? Or do we consider such works insufficiently and inadequately scientific? Do we groom our students to read only foreign works because otherwise they, like us, will not be considered learned? The task of developing a life-oriented African theology for the nourishment of Africans appears daunting, especially given Africa's vastness; its multiplicity of social, religious, political, and economic problems; and its diversity of cultures, traditions, and languages (native and colonial). What hope is there on a continent considered the most poverty stricken and disease ridden in the world? "Unless you become like little children, open, childlike, and self-assured in me, with a mind that believes what its parents [your God] say, you cannot make it." Teresa of Avila used to say, "Teresa and two pence are nothing. But Teresa, God, and two pence can accomplish much."

Approaching African theology this way requires faith, moving from the periphery and launching into the depths (*duc in altum*) of African reality and cultures, where life is in abundance.[10] It requires relocating to the margins where the people live but where normally we do not think we can get inspiration for our theologising. It requires rethinking our notion of theology and in prayer plunging into the depths of God's ever-faithful and inexhaustible love and word about us, our continent, and our world.

Concerning faith, we learn from the little girl who listened to a conversation (colloquium) between her aunt and a visitor while the little girl played with her toys on the floor, seemingly oblivious to their conversation. In the course of it, the aunt said, "Me, I'm afraid, very afraid!" After the visitor had left, the little niece, still playing with her toys, asked, "Auntie Ceci, did I hear you say you are afraid? Don't you believe in God?"

Is our theological reflection rooted and founded on faith? Does faith have a place in theological discourse at all, or is that for ordinary pious people? Are we too afraid of our previous masters to chart original, God-inspired ways of doing theology in Africa?

Commemorating the fiftieth anniversary of the Second Vatican Council, the Church inaugurated the year of faith and a new evangelisation. The council called for opening windows in all aspects of church life, letting in fresh air, and admitting people hitherto treated as outsiders (the laity and women). While significant progress has been made in the *aggiornamento* the council desired, the challenge to revisit exclusivist theological presuppositions and penetrate them with the light of the gospel still remains.[11]

I ask African theologians: "What windows have our theologising opened in the Church since the council? Who does it need to admit into discourse to make it more inclusive? Besides using African categories, we dialogue critically with all received theologies and with biblical (*Dei Verbum* 15), patriarchal, and other cultures to ensure our theologising is built on the solid rock of God's Word about us and creation and on God's gospel, Jesus of Nazareth. We tap into the philosophical, moral, religious, and sociocultural treasures of Africa, not for the sake of increasing theological literature or proving we have such treasures but because we want our theology to be grounded in African reality to ensure that the gospel takes flesh and dwells in our land, that it impacts and transforms our cultures and the lives of our people.

What historical values, methods, approaches, and contents do African theologians need to retain? Here I may (at the risk of appearing selfish) cite in the first place African women's life-giving, life-centred, constructive criticism of culture, Church, and tradition, and their liberating and all-inclusive theology.[12] An African male theologian described African women's theology as the cutting edge of African theology that "tired male theology" needs to seriously engage for refreshment.

African male theology appears to have lost its passion, its compassion, and its prophetic urge. African theology is bewildered and confused by the dismantling of apartheid; increased globalisation; the forceful emergence of issues of gender, ecology, and human rights; and the advent of a new world order. Admittedly, some male theologians have been trying to respond to the new situation, but many of their responses lack the freshness, enthusiasm, creativity, and sharpness that one senses in the writings of African women. A striking feature of much current and allegedly innovative African male theology is its inability to dialogue with and engage the ideas and thoughts of African women.[13]

In addition to engaging with African women's theology, we need to develop what I may call a "roundtable" theology, a collaborative or communal way of doing theology. I mentioned this before as a way forward in my previous works and lately in my reading of the story of the woman with the haemorrhage in the context of fifty years after the independence of many African states.[14] I may expand the concept a little further.

I am thinking of an approach in which people would pair up to study a given issue from different perspectives, cultures, and locations, not simply sending essays to peer referees. The pairing could take diverse forms in terms of gender, nationality, race, colour, ethnicity, scholars, "ordinary people,"[15] denomination, and creed. This way of doing theology fits that of the church-family of God. Jesus sent his disciples in pairs (Matthew 10:1–7) for effective witness. Do we share our theological insights and dreams while they are in the making, or are we afraid to share because others may steal our ideas? The miracle happens in the sharing (as in the miracle of the loaves), not in the hoarding (as in the case of the rich fool; Luke 12:13–21).

The Word by nature grows and expands as it is shared and spoken. If our theologising is in service of the gospel, we will not fear if others (with the same mind and heart) take and develop, not steal, our ideas.

Another model is the "bread for life" way of doing theology, which African mothers do daily. What would be its dynamics, approach, content? Who would participate in it? A eucharistic and a good-shepherd theology is at the heart of "bread for life" theology; the theologian lives for and leads the sheep to green pastures so they can feed themselves.

In our theological discourse, we listen to, draw from, connect with, and respond to the real needs and concerns of our people. Most of Jesus' and the apostles' theologising was based on the life concerns of the people, not on abstract discourses of their scribes and rabbis.

To update African theology in contemporary contexts, we must ensure that it is life centred. If it is, it will constantly update itself by keeping pace with life. The Bible is the record of a people's constant theological updating of the demands of their covenant relationship with God based on their experiences in Israel and in exile. Each theologian needs to ask: "Why and for what purpose am I doing theology? What is its value or relevance for God's people?" Unless theologians theologise from the depths of their faith commitment and convictions, such theologising means little. In academia, scholars may devise, update, and change methods at will, but in the Church, theology is or should be in service to the gospel.

When it comes to reporting on new theological approaches in the postmodern and globalised Africa, I lack the resources to do so, but I have a fundamental problem with methodology as a starting point in theological discourse; this may be related to the tension between inductive, deductive, and intuitive approaches to life. At the Society of Biblical Literature (SBL) ongoing seminar in Atlanta (USA) on contextual biblical interpretation (CBI), women scholars noted that obsession with methodology was essentially a male "thing." I may add that it is a Western rather than an African "male thing," as I discovered in my select literary survey of readings of the Bible in Africa.[16] Intriguingly, the men in the group did not protest. Africans seem to act first and then reflect, if asked, on how they did it.

Does this mean that new methods are not emerging in African theology? By no means.[17] The concern is that African theology should aim more at being life-giving than in abstractly designing acceptable theological methodologies. Concern with method can be derailing.

A recent study has shown that the historical critical method that reigned supreme in biblical studies since the Reformation was designed by German scholars to ensure their national interests and supremacy. This rigorous scientific method derailed if not killed biblical scholarship as scholars worldwide took to it like gospel until Third World and women scholars came from their experiences on the underside of history to ask the texts life-related questions. So doing they brought Scripture back to the realm of life and of the Church, where it properly belongs.[18]

4

But has God died permanently in Africa with no hope of resurrection and renewal? This question generates others: Is this question in reference to God as God or to how some Africans (maybe foreigners) perceive God? Would an African left to himself or herself think of God dying? If we take religion away from the African, what is left? The African finds in God ultimate meaning in life. Globalisation and postmodernity cannot kill this native instinct, not even among the African elite who feel emancipated by material wealth. If they ever thought God was dead, pastors eager to make money will relocate them in their African roots by citing as their enemies evil spirits and ancestral curses, thus driving fear into their hearts. Clients are made to believe that unless they pay the pastor heavily to pray for their protection, their ruin is certain.[19] If African theology relates to the African psyche, it would never consider God as dead. The majority if not all Africans do theology in their daily relationships with God.

From the standpoint of religion, the discourse on God dying has its source in globalisation and postmodernity. Modernism at least had a place for God, but postmodernity finds God irrelevant in life; it has the attitude that God should be grateful for any acknowledgment received. This mindset frees humans to enact laws – whether or not such laws fit in with God's word about creation and humanity. The God-is-dying talk recalls Jean Paul Satre's *En Attendant Godot*. One waits in vain for Godot (a code name for God?) and then realises the imperative of taking one's destiny into one's hands and forgetting about God. The ideology that drives globalisation is the concept that money is everything; it gives power and seeks to build a new world order at God's expense with the death of Africa as integral to its success.

From the scriptural perspective, when the God who created and sustains heaven and earth has died, we are left with the foolishness of our human philosophies (1 Corinthians 1:18–30). If God in Christ became incarnate to destroy death for us, rose from the dead to give us new life and make us "a new creation" (2 Corinthians 5:17), commissioned us to proclaim the good news to the world with the assurance that God is with us till the end of time, and promised a new heaven and new earth (Revelation 21:1–2), can theology rooted in faith in this God seriously perceive him as dead?

To repeat the question: has God died permanently in Africa with no hope of resurrection and renewal? The feeling that God is absent in Africa is not without foundation. The reasons are abundant; a few will suffice. How can God be alive in Africa yet see the continent exploited left, right, and centre in its human, animal, and natural resources? How can God be alive and watch the escalating human trafficking on the continent? How can God be alive yet tolerate the exploitation of the poor by their greedy political and religious leaders (men and women) of God? How can God relish the reduction of Africa to slavery and refugee status on its own soil?[20] How can God be alive yet see the teeming masses of African youth socialised and brainwashed into embracing religious militancy as a way of life and being conscripted by selfish politicians and foreign arms dealers who instigate Africans to war to divert attention from their reckless looting of the continent? How can God be alive yet see the recent, mind-chilling land grabbing by foreigners with the willing collaboration of African leaders though our ancestors used to say, "We do not lend land to our children, we borrow it from them?"[21]

What then is the way forward for African theology in the twenty first century? I recall here the points that emerged from my previous studies on this issue. First, African theologians (men and women) need to take seriously African women's theology; failure to do so will deprive everyone of precious, God-given resources and the continued impoverishment of Africa. To ignore women, half of humanity, is to think with one side of the brain, see with one eye, or walk with one leg.

Politically, Africa has made significant moves in the inclusion of women with two women heads of state, many deputy governors, and as in Nigeria, ministers of important parastatals. What about the Church, family of God, and our theological organisations? Pope Francis has called for the development of a theology of women. The foundation for this would be a sound theology of humanity rooted in God's creation and in a Christology in which man and woman are one in Christ.

Second, we need to adopt sustainable measures to overcome our lack of faith in our theological reflections that is proven by our preference for foreign authors. EATWOT refused to publish works of its members who did not engage seriously with the works of other members, using the EAT-WOT methodology of praxis (action, reflection, action). Cultivating other people's gardens and leaving uncultivated our own lush green gardens will no longer do. One of the greatest damages colonialism did to the African psyche was to colonise and socialise it into looking down on itself and on things African and mediating the same to one another. In honesty, we admit that we almost have to do violence to instinct to cite each other's works. African theology must deliberately tackle this problem and decolonise the mind by celebrating, even if critically, African authors, using the gospel as the antidote to the import-oriented mentality and mindset.

Third, the human being is the route to travel in evangelisation. Humans are the root cause of all of Africa's ills, chief among them being bad government.[22] Human beings too are agents of change and transformation. How people-centered is African theology? Does it empower people to reject death-dealing forces, embrace gospel values, and choose life for themselves and their communities? Does it reach and impact African politicians and Church leaders? Traveling the human route requires patience and deliberate, step-by-step progression.

Fourth, theology for empowerment needs to go beyond the classroom. Jesus taught in towns, villages, synagogues, and private homes. Today, Pentecostal preachers operate in buses and motor parks and through rallies; they conduct door-to-door evangelisation in villages while our established Church waits for people to come. The gap between the altar and the pew, between the theologians and the people, is huge. People touched Jesus, ate with him, and invited him to their homes. He did some of his most memorable theologising in private homes (e.g., John 11). Pope Francis has highlighted the need to smell the odor of the sheep if we are to be good shepherds and theologians to them. The search for new paths in African theology impels us to return to our life-centred African and gospel roots after over two thousand years of getting off-track.[23]

I have cited elsewhere the use of parable as a gospel-based biblical hermeneutics; parables were Jesus' preferred method of speaking to the people.[24] Parables invite people to reflect, draw objective conclusions, and apply those solutions to their real-life situations. The method invests great faith in people's ability to reason and discover correct answers to their problems. This parabolic way of speaking is typically African; people communicate naturally in proverbs.[25] Parabolic discourse makes the people subjects, not objects, of theological reflection.

Further, Jesus habitually asked those he cured what they wanted from him, though he knew. After the cure, he praised them for doing it themselves, through their faith. We normally do not consider Jesus a theologian. The rabbis persecuted him for breaking the rules of traditional orthodoxy, supposedly demonstrating thereby that he was not from God. The ordinary people hung on his words spoken with authority (enabling power) because his teaching liberated and gave them new status in life.

Scripture, God's Word about us, is the soul of all theology. Jesus, God's Word incarnate, is the heart of Scripture. If we school ourselves to let him continue doing theology in and through us, our theology will be in the service of life. In our theologising, we set our hearts to discover, accept, and live by God's gift for us in Christ; our theologising becomes good news that helps people take up their lives and live in Jesus and to accept in faith God's gift on God's terms, not on those of quack pastors or their miracle-hungry adherents.

I mentioned at the beginning of this chapter the need to showcase culture in our effort to reevaluate African theology. The Church recognises that it is impossible to proclaim the gospel effectively without addressing the cultures of the evangelised. Culture permeates all human undertakings. The hesitation of male theology to engage African women's theology has its roots in culture reinforced by the colonial socialisation into self-rejection mentioned above. Culturally, African men do not learn from women. A theology that wants to help Africa stand on its own feet, as the second African synod encouraged, must infuse with gospel values the culture in persons and systems as in Scripture and traditional theologies and practices.

African theology is African because it is conducted by Africans to addresses the needs of Africans. We need to see our theologising as a ministry to people in service to the Church's missionary mandate to proclaim the good news. We must reject the notion that reaching out to the people is lowering our academic standards. We must strive to transcend with freedom the urge to the win approval or fear criticism of our former teachers. Colonial and postcolonial categories and theologies cease to drive our theologising. Through our theologising, the forces of globalisation and postmodernity yield to the dynamism of the gospel that transforms all humans, their systems, and their endeavours.

Endnotes

1   *adam* is not emphasis, but the Hebrew word used for "humanity" in Genesis 1:26, 27; 5:1-2. It is in italics to show that this is not an English word.

2   On the human word being akin to God's Word, see Teresa Okure, "Alive and Active: Images of the Word of God in the Nigerian Context," in *Alive and Active: Images of the Word of God in the Bible*; Acts of the Catholic Biblical Association of Nigeria, Maiden Edition (Port Harcourt: CABAN Publications, 2012), 1–26.

3   The bride speaking here is an African (perhaps the groom too), though scholars debate her identity.

4   Teresa Okure, "The Will to Arise: Reflections on Luke 8:40–65," in *The Will to Arise: Women, Tradition and* the *Church in Africa,* ed. Mercy Amba Oduyoye and Musimbi R. Kanyoro (Maryknoll, N.Y.: Orbis, 1992), 221–30.

5   Benedict XVI, *Verbum Domini*, Post-synodal Apostolic Exhortation on the Word of God in the Life and Mission of the Church (Vatican City: Libreria Editrice Vaticana, 2010), nos. 31, 47. The pope cites *Dei Verbum* 24, *Providentisimus Deus, Divino Aflante Spiritu,* and *Spiritus Paraclitus* as predecessors.

6   See Sergio Torres and Virgin Fabella, eds., *Irruption of the Third World: Challenges to Theology* (Maryknoll, N.Y.: Orbis, 1983).

7   My mother loved to cite to us the Ibibio proverb, *Se eka anie k'aben okongo eyen,* "Whatever the mother has, that is what she puts on the child," thus forming us to be satisfied with what we have.

8   See for instance Laurenti Magesa, *African Religion: The Moral Traditions of Abundant Life* (Maryknoll, N.Y.: Orbis, 1977).

9   The accounts of this are in Matthew 14:13–21, Mark 6:32–44, Luke 9:10–17, and John 6:1–15.

10   The phrase *duc in altum* is the leitmotif of John Paul II, *Novo Millennio Ineunte,* "At the Dawn of the Third Millennium" (Vatican City: Libreria Editrice Vaticana, 2001).

11   *Lumen Gentium* defined the Church as "the people of God." The first African synod adopted the notion of "Church as family of God." Fifty years after the council and over ten after the synod, we are yet to fully explore and apply these beautiful concepts in our self-understanding as Church.

12   My review of African women's theological hermeneutics in "Covenanted with Life: Invitation to African Women's Hermeneutics" gives the main features of their theology. Originally given at the SNTS Post Conference in Hammaskraal, South Africa, in 2000, it has been published as "Invitation to African Women's Hermeneutical Concerns" in *Interpreting the New Testament in Africa,* ed. Mary N. Getui, Tinyiko Maluleke, and Justin Ukpong (Biblical Studies in African Scholarship; Nairobi: Acton, 2001), 42–67, and in the *African Journal of Biblical Studies* 19, no. 2 (2003): 71–95.

13   Tinyiko S. Maluleke, "African 'Ruths,' Ruthless Africans. Reflections of an African Mordecai" in *Other Ways of Reading,* ed. Dube W. Musa (Atlanta: SBL; Geneva: WCC, 2001), 237–51, especially 237–38.

14   Teresa Okure, "The Challenge of the Woman with the Hemorrhage (Mark 5:24–34) for African States Fifty Years after Independence" in *The Church in Africa 50 Years after States' Independence;* Association of African Theologians (Abidjan: Editions ATA, 2013), 391–409, especially 405–09; for the select literary survey, see note 16 below.

15   Gerard West of the University of Kwa-Zulu Natal in Pietermaritzburg has been doing this for years. What is envisaged here is moving this exercise out of

academic institution to wherever "ordinary people" live their lives and relate spontaneously with God.

16 Teresa Okure, "Readings of the Bible in Africa: A select literary survey," in *Yearbook of Contextual Theologies 2002* (MWI, IKO, Aachen, 2002), 174–209. Though the topic was on the Bible, the principles discovered in the survey grew from the African way of approaching life generally.

17 See for instance, J. S Ukpong, *African Theology: A Profile*; Spearhead 80 (Eldoret: AMECEA Gaba Publications, 1984); Augustine A. Nabachukwu, "Third Word Theologies and the Recovery of African Identity," *Journal of Inculturation Theology* 2, no. 1 (1995): 17–27.

18 Michael Legaspi, *The Death of Scripture and the Rise of Biblical Studies;* Oxford Studies in Historical Theology (Oxford: Oxford University Press, 2010).

19 For a documentation on this, see issue Anthony Iffen Umoren, *Paul and Power Christology: Exegesis and Theology in Romans 1:1–3 in Relation to Popular Power Christology in an African Context*, New Testament Studies in Contextual Exegesis vol. 4 (Frankfurt: Peter Lang, 2008).

20 Teresa Okure, "Africa: A Refugee Camp Experience," in *Migrants and Refugees, Concilium* no. 4 (1993): 12–21. Writing a commissioned paper on "Africa's refugee camps," I discovered that the continent itself has been reduced to a refugee camp on its own soil. Since then, the situation has gotten worse. Impoverished and exploited Kenyans serve as watchmen of the rich estates or holiday resorts of their absentee foreign landlords.

21 Aniedi Okure, OP, Executive Director of Africa Faith and Justice Network (AFJN) in Washington, D.C., presented a chilling documentary on land grabbing in Africa at the SECAM Forum on Culture and Development in Africa (Dar es Salaam, Tanzania, November 2012). Huge numbers of hectares of fertile land are being leased out by political leaders with certificates of occupancy lasting over a hundred years; *www.Afjn.org* gives links to other websites (e.g., Oxfam) on this issue.

22 Good governance is the concern of SECAM, a dimension of the three-year project of the Association of African Theologians and of Africa Faith and Justice Network; see the SECAM Pastoral Letter on "Governance, Common Good, and Democratic Transitions in Africa" announced on the SECAM Website; also, Aniedi Okure, "The Economic and Development Problem of Africa: A Problem of Governance": A Presentation from Africa Faith & Justice Network (AFJN) to Africa Europe Faith and Justice Network (AEFJN) on the Occasion of the 25th Anniversary of AEFJN, Brussels, April 22–25, 2013.

23 John Paul II drew attention to our "deviations from the gospel" even as he urged launching into the deep.

24 See note 17 above.

25 In TV shows, e.g., *The Village Headmaster,* in Nigeria, the characters speak in proverbs peculiar to their environment; for example, "The lizard does not penetrate the wall if there is no crack in it."

Sense and Nonsense of an African Theology

Eloi Messi Metogo

Almost thirty years ago, I focused my first work of theology on methodological problems in African theology.[1] This study drew attention to a double misunderstanding concerning Africa and its evangelisation and Christianity. On the one hand, the Africa that was spoken about was reduced to the one described by ethnologists whereas African societies were changing. On the other hand, despite the discourse on incarnation and inculturation, African theologians continued to refer to a missionary Christianity that was bourgeois, individualistic, and meticulous about rites and "doctrine." Has this theological method changed?

In many areas of research, especially perhaps in theology, there continues to be a defense of an immutable identity of the African. Young students take up this discourse, whereas they do not even know how to speak their mother tongues! Yet, for more than forty years, we have had philosophers who constantly warned us about a static conception of identity.[2] All living beings' identities involve change, continuous self-transformation. One cannot live without changing the forces acting on oneself (air, moisture, etc.) in parts of one's own subsistence and growth. For a living being, continual change is

> the only way to remain oneself, to maintain one's identity, because stopping the self-transformation process means death, degradation, the release of elements with which one was composed of, the permanent loss of identity.

What is thus observed in the biological process is also observed in social and cultural life.

> A society, a cultural totality is alive as long as it struggles to ensure its survival and development, not only against the elements but also against hostile social and cultural forces: aggression, opposition, corruption … The renewal that it imposes on itself, far from destroying it, is on the contrary, the very condition of its preservation and development. It dies as soon as she stops and freezes.[3]

Cultural identity is dynamic. Tradition, be it African or other, is never the mechanical transmission of identity but a creative interpretation of its content depending on the situation and needs.[4] Africa has undergone and will still go through several other changes. For Paulin Hountondji,

> the alleged acculturation, the alleged "encounter" of African civilisation with that of Europe, is in fact an additional mutation carried on by the African civilisation itself, a mutation posterior to many others that we know probably imperfectly, a mutation which also announces many others to come, perhaps even more radical.[5]

Africa has never been a metaphysical entity outside history; it is not an island, and it has long embarked on what we now call globalisation. One imagines that the values considered to be specifically African (the sense of the sacred, respect for life, solidarity, hospitality, and so on) can exist without material bases. However, we are witnessing today the disappearance or the perversion of these values in a context of poverty and misery for many: solidarity and hospitality become patronage and parasitism, and we record more induced abortions and heinous crimes. Africa will certainly not be restored in its being and dignity without solving its economic problems and without building a physical power base capable of resisting colonialism in all forms. Those who dominate us physically dominate us spiritually by imposing on us their books, their films, their ways of dressing, eating, making love, and so on. We must realise that Africa was colonised because of its material inferiority. It is for the same reason, in my opinion, that Africans are despised, not because of the colour of their skin.

Finally, it is dangerous to believe that the misfortunes of Africa come from outside, from the West, which was responsible for slavery and colonisation. The dignity and rights of Africans today are denied by other Africans; this is, in the words of the Kenyan writer Ngugi wa Thiong'o, "the *summum* of irony" from those who have suffered slavery and colonisation. The reduction of culture to disembodied African values of civilisation risks hiding this fact and making sport of the current dictatorships that people have so much trouble getting rid of.

The identity of the African person is not given once and for all; it results from the integration of physical and economic conditioning and political and spiritual variations of existence. It derives from a project clearly defined by himself or herself. Traditional values must be transposed into modernity, and the inculturation of Christianity assumes knowledge of Africa today, in the church and in society.

Inculturation also supposes knowledge of the living Christian tradition and serious theological reflection. However, the other pole of inculturation is often overlooked in favour of wild imaginings of traditional societies. We restrict ourselves by simply repeating the catechism of Trent or manuals of scholastic theology whose content we adapt. Africa is still in dire need of specialists in Scripture, Patristics, Church History, Dogmatics, Moral Theology, and so on.

In international colloquia and specialist journals, the contributions requested of Africans are hardly ever on the fundamental issues in the theological disciplines cited; they appear as exotic illustrations of others' research when they do not sink into folkloric exhibitionism. We cannot inculturate Christianity without knowing its founding texts, doctrines, and institutions. The theological task is to read the Word of God and the tradition of the Church fathers from the questions and concerns of men and women of our time, and each generation must engage in this exercise on its own account. African theology must also remain in dialogue with other theologies; failing to do so isolates it and prevents it from being Catholic, that is to say, not bringing anything to the universal effort of inculturation in a world that has become a global village.

We can roughly distinguish two major trends of African theology: the cultural-religious trend and sociopolitical trend which, while incorporating traditional values duly criticised with regard to the requirements of the present focus on economic and political issues.

The first missionaries did not speak of inculturation but the salvation of souls and the establishment of the church. They led a serious crusade against the manners and customs of the indigenous people. Africans were pagans and glorified infants who needed to be evangelised and educated. Their customs had to give way to Christianity and Western civilisation. The criticism of missionary evangelisation and the affirmation of the African personality will constitute the first major themes of African theology.

The theology of adaptation and stepping stones, less brutal than the establishment of the church, developed after Vatican II. This seeks in African cultures those values and practices that are close to Christianity to make them points of departure for preaching and catechesis. But it risks imposing a model of Christianity imported from elsewhere, complete with all its aberrations and eccentricities, and fusing them with values of indigenous cultures considered as stepping stones of Christianity. The bishops of Africa and Madagascar rejected this approach in the Roman synod of 1974 in favor of the theology of incarnation: Africans have the right and duty to read the gospel and to live it in their own sociocultural context. Today we hear much about inculturation and contextualisation.

In addition to this (more widespread) first trend concerned with the rehabilitation of cultural values and African spiritual traditions and their insertion in the work of evangelisation, there is the sociopolitical trend mainly represented by Jean-Marc Éla. It tries to read the gospel through the eyes of African peasants "facing famine, drought, and disease." He presents the gospel as the power of liberation of the poor and the fight for respect of human rights as an essential dimension of evangelisation.

Theological and pastoral problems in Africa are not reduced to the issues related to traditions, rites, and customs. I mention briefly those that seem to me most important and urgent.

Religious ignorance is largely responsible for the success of new churches, sects, and secret societies. Many Christians do not know about their religion apart from the catechism of their first communion if they have not forgotten that. It is urgent to present the revelation, in the line of Exodus, as being at the heart of biblical faith, as the active manifestation of God's liberating action in history in favour of the oppressed. There is no need to offer recipes for happiness – medals, effective prayers, exorcisms, and so on – to block the new churches and sects. Pastors must ensure greater biblical, theological, and spiritual formation of the faithful to help them discover the gospel's power of social transformation.

Many still believe that the Church is the pope, bishops, priests, and male and female religious, but Vatican II reminded us that the Church is the community of the baptised, that is, the people of God. There can be no Church without the participation of faithful Christians. Ecclesiology and the ministries must become important chapters in the story of African theology so the priesthood can cease to be considered a social promotion, or a source of income, or the origin of magical power by which the weak and ignorant are terrorised; this will help the laity to become more mature, take the initiative, and assume responsibilities under the disinterested conduct and caring of their pastors.

It is in this context that the question of relations between Rome and local churches arises. Theological and liturgical creativity, the pastoral dynamism of local churches, should be encouraged and respected.

What are the role and meaning of prayer, the sacraments, and sacramentals (the use of holy water, various blessings, etc.) in a general context of belief in occult powers and magic? The belief in witchcraft and magic are perhaps the foremost pastoral problems in Africa today. Religious "entrepreneurs" of all stripes use these methods to escape economic hardship. Accusations of witchcraft cause migration, distrust, and hatred in families. Patients who could have been saved if they had been taken in time to the hospital die at the hands of charlatans unable to cure them, and death reinforces people's belief in the power of witches. Instead of freeing the people of God from such beliefs by reminding them of their baptism in the name of Jesus Christ, victor over all principalities and powers (Colossians 2:10–16), some priests and religious are engaged in disconcerting practices, sometimes sacrilegious, for example, when goat's blood is mixed with the wine in the Eucharist and given to the faithful.

We see the urgency of catechesis on prayer and the sacraments: Christian prayer is not reduced to making demands; it respects the freedom of God. Sacramental gestures should not be cut off from the Word of God, which gives them meaning, or the ethical requirements to which they direct worshippers.

Finally, in a context in which every disease and death is caused by witches, pastors must help Christians face suffering and death, which are simply part of the human condition. Once we have done what is in our power to push them back, we offer others the possibility of living differently, in union with Christ on the cross in the hope of resurrection.

We now know that human promotion and development are not prerequisites or consequences of the mission but an integral part of the work of evangelisation. The theology of "anthropological poverty," according to which the humanity of African people was denied and caused the loss of their cultural identity, and that one wishes to oppose to Latin American liberation theology risks forgetting that today, Africans suffer above all from material poverty, injustice, and oppression. Here, as in Latin America, the Churches must clarify their position in relation to the power to reassess the impact of their apostolic social charities. These Churches cannot demonstrate the relevance of Christianity in the present situation without denouncing the political violence that paralyses the mind and imagination and without forming the Christian to analyse the mechanisms of domination. Few Churches seem prepared to cope with the rapid changes currently occurring on the African political scene.

How far has the dialogue between separated Christians gone? It is urgent to study and clarify the practical ecumenism that has existed for a long time and go further, to a more credible Christian witness. This dialogue cannot ignore the independent or African Christian churches, and another dialogue must be engaged with traditional religions and Islam. The rivalries between the various Christian denominations and religions undermine the work of evangelisation and social peace.

Men and women in Africa today have distanced themselves from religion because they do not see its relevance. Some say they are agnostics or atheists. We must take them seriously instead of continuing to say they are believers who are unaware, because Africans are "incurably religious." And contrary to popular belief, religious indifference and unbelief are not only the effect of Western influence.[6] All Africans have not always believed in a supreme God, and the belief in an afterlife is not as widespread as has been said. Some adults in traditional societies have ceased to believe in the myths and rituals of their communities. The study of initiation rites and of secret societies leads to a nuancing of their religious character that is so often affirmed. They include performances that are "sacred lies" designed to impress the uninitiated, women, and children; masquerades; masked voices attributed to ancestors; etc. We are in the presence of a strategy of political power: the new initiates admitted to the association now participate in the government of the tribe or ethnicity and enjoy a number of advantages on condition of their silence. Witchcraft is held to account for death sentences decided and executed by secret societies in communities in which there is no prison. This shows the extreme precaution with which pastors must address issues related to witchcraft.

It is appropriate to recall the wise reflection of Leon Merssi, an old Cameroonian priest now deceased about traditional beliefs: "The less of it we know, the more we believe in it." It is important to read the huge anthropological literature on witchcraft in questioning its psychological, economic, and political functions in traditional societies if we do not want to reduce Christianity to magic and drive more Christians to popular credulity that is being skillfully exploited by a growing number of charlatans.

The search for wealth consumes the energies of the pastors at the expense of their authentic Christion vocation and ministries. The material dependence of the churches *vis-à-vis* outsiders limits their freedom of inquiry and speech, and inculturation is severely compromised. We can see how urgent it is for Christians in Africa to provide the means for the needs of their churches. This requires clear information about incomes and their distribution, strict management at all levels, attention to fair distribution of resources, and investing in the essential.

The term "African theology" must cease to point to the theology of an unchanging African person outside history. The epithet "African" shall designate the place of production of a theology from what Jean-Marc Éla called "African banality," that is to say, the real problems and needs of men and women of the continent.

Translated from French by
Christophère Ngolele, SJ, and
Kpanie Addy, SJ

Endnotes

1   Eloi Messi Metogo, *Théologie africaine et ethnophilosophie, Problèmes de méthode en théologie africaine* (Paris: L'Harmattan, 1985).

2   Séverine Kodjo-Grandvaux, *Philosophies africaines* (Paris: Présence Africaine, 2012).

3   Marcien Towa, "Civilisation industrielle et négritude," *Abbia* 19 (1968): 31–45.

4   Fabien Eboussi Boulaga, *La crise du Muntu, Authenticité africaine et philosophie* (Paris: Présence Africaine, 1977), 155–58.

5   Paulin J. Hountondji, *Sur la "philosophie africaine," Critique de l'ethnophilosophie* (Paris: Maspero, 1976), 233.

6   Eloi Messi Metogo, *Dieu peut-il mourir en Afrique? Essai sur l'indifférence religieuse et l'incroyance en Afrique noire* (Paris-Yaoundé: Karthala-Presses de l'UCAC, 1997).

Scripture Studies and African Theology: A Critical Overview from an OT Perspective

Paul Béré

Some years ago, I had an informal conversation with two renowned theologians: David Schultenover, SJ, editor of the American journal *Theological Studies,* and Bénézet Bujo, a leading African moral theologian. My question to the first was about the use of Scripture by theologians. His answer at the time (2008) was that almost nobody to his knowledge began his or her theological discourse with an exegetical study of a relevant biblical text.

I asked Bujo a broader question about how African theologians used the Bible in their theologising. The problem I felt at the time was the gap between some principles Vatican II formulated in the constitution on divine revelation, *Dei Verbum,* in order to facilitate radical ecclesial renewal by reaching deep to its roots (*ad fontes*) and the way those principles have actually been carried out in theology in general, considering Africa as a case in point.[1]

This chapter intentionally narrows the scope to the field of African OT studies in Catholic theology for two reasons. First, we know that by tradition, Protestant theologising usually stems from Scripture studies. A well-known case in point is David Bosch[2] and his mission theology. Second, the contribution of African New Testament scholar Chantal Nsongisa to this volume provides the NT perspective.

My perspective will be twofold. Under "The Road Traveled Thus Far," I will discuss the situation of Bible studies in African theology. After that, I will suggest a few steps to help move on the way forward.

Before I step into the arena, some cautions might be useful. The biblical apostolate has been extensively promoted by BICAM (the Biblical Center for Africa and Madagascar). It certainly makes the Word of God nourishment for the people of God whose *sensus fidei* remains the main source of any genuine theology. But whenever I use the phrase "African theology" in this conversation, I will always be referring to what has been produced in and for the academy.

1. The Road Traveled Thus Far

1.1 Principle and Reality: Views of Theologians

African theology is marked by two features that could be identified from its beginning:[3] a reflexive attitude[4] and a conversation.[5] These two events set the agenda for what developed after Vatican II. A few terms will be coined to encapsulate the task: adaptation, inculturation, liberation, contextualisation, construction, and so on. A close look at the theological outcome of these trends shows, from a biblical vantage point, that the Bible as a foundational dimension of Catholic systematic theology is a question. As a matter of fact, Charles Nyamiti, notes that:

> The subject of African theology is closely linked with the question of its sources. This topic was particularly discussed in the late 1960s and early 1970s. Some suggested that the sources of African theology are the Bible and African traditional religions. Others – especially Catholic writers – claimed that its sources were Christian revelation and African philosophy. Another opinion held that the analysis of sermons by African and non-African preachers in Africa, or the translation of the Bible into African vernaculars, were the right sources.[6]

Nyamiti made his own conclusion and wrote there were two sources. The first was the Christian: the Bible, which is the soul of all theology, and the authentic tradition of the entire Church – with particular stress on the official teaching of the Church, the Magisterium. The other source was the African sociocultural situation seen in its relation to its past, present, and future, the non-Christian source for African theology.[7]

Emmanuel Ntakaturimana, another African theologian, looking back critically at African theology in its relation to the Bible, writes,

> Wherever African Theology was quite dependent on Western philosophical debates, it becomes important for us now to look back at Scripture and its translation into African idioms, in order to rethink the first experience of the encounter with the God who comes to lead us through Jesus Christ to a fulfilling Christification (emphasis mine).[8]

The strength of this judgment rests on *Ad Gentes*, a decree of Vatican II that boosted theological work in Africa. The same document has long called for a theological reflection on "deeds and values revealed by

God, and *kept in Holy Scriptures* and explained by the Church and the Magisterium" (n. 22; emphasis mine).

The impression one gets from these witnesses is that in spite of its centrality, the Bible as a key source of theology has simply been left out of African theology. A question arises from this statement: "Is the scholarly work on the Bible in Africa part of 'African theology?'" In Protestant theology, we would probably get a straightforward answer, for Scripture in Protestant theology is its fundamental soul. In the Catholic scholarly environment, the sharp distinction between exegesis and biblical theology has fueled passionate debates. The creation of a specialised institution in 1909[9] with the aim of engaging the Bible scientifically may have been one of the main sources. There is no doubt that the work of those trained by the so-called exegetical programs nourished the mind and judgment of church leaders until Vatican II and beyond. Hence, the call for a theology rooted in "the study of the sacred page" (*Dei Verbum* no. 24).

1.2 Looking at the Issue from an African Biblical Scholars' Perspective

In his recent publication on the Word of God in the plurality of the scholarly readings, Paulin Poucouta, a biblical theologian,[10] discussed the relationship between biblical theology and exegesis. He rightly stated that they should not be separated. Biblical scholars were named under the same appellation, "biblicists," an overriding category that allows Poucouta to discuss the relationship between biblicists and theologians and to conclude,

> In Africa, the rediscovery of the relationship between the Bible and theology was very felicitous. It helps bridge the gap between biblical scholars and theologians. It makes possible for us a cross-fertilisation between biblical studies and theology, a cross-fertilisation that facilitates the emergence of African readings of the Bible and African theologies.[11]

This statement is more of a wish than a reality. Indeed, it tells us what should be done and not what has been done. Biblical scholars have been producing substantial works,[12] but it seems that no consistent theological piece of work in African theology has begun with an in-depth study of the sacred page or an in-depth reading of African exegetical studies on a given issue. The concern has long been expressed and kept on display.[13] André Kabasele, an OT biblical theologian, sounds more radical; he believes that "one must register the quest for African Bible reading in the wider horizon of African theology."[14]

Knut Holter, a Norwegian scholar, has dealt with Old Testament scholars of Africa as a topic of research. His studies[15] reveal a striking fact: the first generation of African OT scholars are in conversation with their peers in their respective institutions of training, and the hermeneutical principles they use often simply replicate those of the places where they themselves were educated. One would expect the second generation to dialogue with the first. Unfortunately, this is not the case. As a consequence, a gap appears between African OT scholars themselves and also between all of them and African theologians in their respective fields, including biblical theology, dogmatic and systematic theology, moral theology, and so on.

1.3 Summary

To sum up the ongoing overview on the relation between Bible study and African theology, I point out a few facts:

1. African theology may sometimes use biblical texts in quotes but not a systematic study of the Bible as points of departure. An amazing material fact is the lack of indexes of biblical citations. Very few African theological works with a scholarly brand provide such an index for their readers. Instead, we find indexes on authors and themes.

2. Biblical studies by Africans are well developed, and the work of the Pan-African Association of Catholic Exegetes (PACE) may serve as a case in point. No systematic methodology has so far proven operational for theologians to use, since most African OT scholars – the exceptions are few – work with well-established or mainstream methods.[16]

3. The guild of African OT scholars is made up of two generations, but no conversation seems to be taking place between them. I even doubt that it happens within the same generation. It suffices to check the references.

The awareness we have reached in reviewing African theology from the perspective of the role of the Bible should not leave us lamenting. We should rather devise means of bridging the gaps and hearing the call from *Dei Verbum* to not only quote the Bible here and there to back up this or that idea but also to better let the deep study of the sacred page permeate our theological discourse. We will thus move from a dichotomous perspective on Bible and theology in Africa to a multidimensional understanding of their relationship.

2. What Does the Expression "Word of God" Refer To?

Some of the unsettled issues in the current theological discussion may come from our struggle to clarify the fact that Scripture studies are the soul of theology. What do we refer to when we use the expression "Word of God?" As we know, the word "theology" itself, *theou* and *logos*, may etymologically point to the Word of God through a human, self-disclosing discourse on God. Taken in a subjective sense, we may say that the Word of God refers to any place that one finds God speaking to his people. Where then do we hear divine utterances? A popular and straightforward answer usually given narrows the scope of the Word of God to the Bible. The Word cannot be reduced to a book. Happily, in the Post-synodal Apostolic Exhortation *Verbum Domini*, following the 2008 synod on the Word of God in the Life and Mission of the Church, an effort has been made to "unpack" the expression and clarify what it stands for or refers to. There we learn that God speaks through various channels: Jesus Christ, Scripture, tradition, cosmos, and conscience.[17]

- *Jesus Christ:* In the proper sense, Jesus is the Word made flesh (see John 1:1ff). Not only does he reveal by his words and deeds what God has long been telling us (see Hebrews 1:1ff), but he also explains in human terms, by his whole life, the mystery of God. Through him we hear God speaking.

- *Scripture:* Access to God's words through Jesus is made possible thanks to the written word of the witnesses who lived with him (cf. 1 John), listened to him, and experienced his salvific power in his compassionate ministry. Scripture therefore is the main gate to the person of Jesus, and through him to the unique face of his God. For that reason, Scripture plays a special role in Christian life and theology.

- *Tradition:* The concept of tradition points foremost to the soul of a community. What the Church has long called tradition has a double understanding: the apostolic tradition, which came down to us exclusively from the apostles (see for instance Paul's reference to tradition in 1 Corinthians 11:2; 2 Thessalonians 2:15, 3:6; 2 Timothy 2:2), and the ecclesiastical tradition, which carries with it the effort made by various Christian communities to make the gospel message their own and let it transform and recreate its cultures.[18]

- *Cosmos:* Nature as God's handiwork speaks on his behalf: "The heavens are telling the glory of God; and the firmament proclaims his handiwork" (Psalm 19:1 NRSV). Therefore, nobody would find any excuse for not believing in God, as Paul said to the Romans,

> For what can be known about God is plain to them, because God has shown it to them. Ever since the creation of the world his eternal power and divine nature, invisible though they are, have been understood and seen through the things he has made. So they are without excuse (Romans 1:19–20 NRSV).

- *Conscience:* Finally, human conscience should not be forgotten as we explore places where God's voice can be heard. In accordance with the long theological tradition of the Catholic Church, Henry Newman defined conscience as "the aboriginal Vicar of Christ."[19] The mediatory function of the community through the magisterium should not erase the ultimate place where God's Word becomes a personal calling. The story of Samuel (1 Samuel 3) can be a scriptural case in point.

These five instances, which are not exhaustive, are all sources in which we can hear God speaking. The theological discourse that understands the Word of God as a wide reality that goes beyond the material biblical text can draw from them to make the faith intelligible. The starting point for such a discourse need not necessarily be the Bible; it can be any of the other four elements explained above.

Does Scripture therefore lose its specific role? The main function of Scripture in the view so far explained could be simply called "canonical" in its etymological sense. It serves as a rule; it portrays for us Jesus, the man who came from God. It equips us with a measure to discriminate right from wrong in the community (discernment). It teaches us divine grammar so we can decode and interpret God's words through the cosmos or our consciences. If a theological discourse finds God speaking through a particular community experience, it can develop that very word against the witness of Scripture, for the God of Jesus cannot contradict himself. It is also true for the mystic who finds no word to express his or her experience of the divine being.

For the Bible to play such an important role, we have to do more than simply read it; we have to study it in depth. By so doing, the world of the Bible will mold and shape the theologian's world view and thinking.[20]

3. The Way Forward

If we want theology in Africa and elsewhere to be molded by an in-depth study of the sacred page, some distinctions have to be made and some cautions respected. The elements I list below are not exhaustive; they are meant to launch the conversation.

3.1 Distinction between Biblical Theology and Exegesis

The debate on exegesis and biblical theology has long been fueled in the Catholic Church.[21] Indeed, it would be counterproductive to separate them. On the other hand, it appears irrelevant in today's world of inter-disciplinary approaches to reality. We should nevertheless keep sharp the distinction between biblical theology and exegesis; each has its own way of proceeding. We may consider them as steps in the process of receiving the biblical message. Thus exegesis, by "drawing out" of the text the mean-ing intended by the human author in his or her culture and society, leads to biblical theology, whose task it is to highlight the divine component, namely, that which makes its message a Word of God. This will result in providing some responses to faith seeking understanding in dogmatic theology or right being and acting in moral theology.

Exegetical methods are cultural products of a given society.[22] Unless our exegesis is in tune with our cultural and social mindset, we will not be capable of paving the road for a theology rooted in Scripture studies that also speaks to the hearts and minds of our contemporary audience.

3.2 Accuracy in the Exegesis of Dei Verbum's Often-Quoted Phrase, "Let the study of the sacred page be like the soul of sacred theology"

The avatars of this statement tend to equate the phrase "the study of the sacred page" with other expressions such as "the Word of God" or "the Bible."[23] This lack of precision in itself tells a lot about our way of using the Bible. In spite of the strong affinities the OT has with the African world in many aspects (anthropological, social, linguistic, theological, etc.), we should remind ourselves that our Western training gave us Western cultural and hermeneutical lenses with which we read the Bible. We need to deconstruct that mindset to uncover the specifics on the Bible beyond these cultural conditionings or better, in a cross-cultural move.[24]

3.3 Relevant Exegetical Methods

We need to review the methods we have been using to engage the biblical texts with the questions generated by the exegetical or theological problems we have identified. The relevance I have in mind presupposes that criticism in biblical exegesis applies to the reader of the text and to the text itself. For example, Genesis 2:24 says the man will leave his parents and cling to his wife. It makes perfectly sense in some societies in Africa and elsewhere, but in others, the wife should leave her parents and cling to her man. Depending on where one belongs in a social setting, exegesis may require moving first out of one's mindset to properly draw out of the text what it means.

3.4 Conversation between Exegetes, Biblical Theologians, and Theologians in Other Areas

This conversation is badly needed first of all in our respective academic papers, and second, in meetings organised around the theme. The Pan-African Association of Catholic Exegetes (PACE) has managed to convene its members every two years to reflect on and discuss the same broad theme. The results of all these studies should be considered by theologians in their respective fields and with their proper methods.

Conclusion

This chapter started with a quest: to find out the way African theology used the Bible, particularly the OT. I narrowed the scope to the dialogue between African theologians involved in African OT scholarship. I have reached the conclusion that even the dialogue between African theologians with the Bible in general as requested by Vatican II in *Dei Verbum* 24 has not yet started.

African OT scholarship has benefited from a special attention outside Africa, and it became clear to me that many issues have to be clarified first. I have outlined some of them in the second part of this chapter. The task that now faces African theologians and exegetes is to recognise the special character of exegesis and biblical theology and devise creative ways of initiating conversation between biblical scholars and theologians in Africa.

Endnotes

1   For the sake of this chapter, I focus on Africa, but a careful assessment of the situation worldwide would show that the problem is universal in the Catholic Church.

2   See David Bosch's masterpiece, *Transforming Mission: Paradigm Shifts in Theology of Mission* (Maryknoll, N.Y.: Orbis, 1991, 2011); it starts from the NT (Part I), moves to history (Part II), and ends with context (Part III).

3   See the very extensive bibliography provided by Josée Ngalula, *Production théologique africaine, 1956–2010: Bibliographie sélective de 6000 ouvrages et articles des théologiens/nes africains* (Kinshasa: Editions Mont Sinaï, 2011); see a thematic treatment of African theology in the Anglophone Africa by Benoît Awazi Mbambi Kungua, *Panorama des théologies négro-africaines anglophones* (Paris: L'Harmattan, 2008). An insightful assessment of African theology is provided by Emmanuel Ntakarutimana, "Où en est la théologie africaine?" in Léonard Santedi Kinkupu (dir.), *La théologie et l'avenir des societes. Colloque du Cinquantenaire de la Faculté de théologie de Kinshasa (Avril 2007)* (Paris: Karthala, 2010), 231–47.

4   *Les Prêtres noirs s'interrogent* (Paris: Cerf, 1956).

5   Tarcisse Tshibangu and Alfred Vanneste, "Débat sur la Théologie Africaine," in *Revue du Clergé Africain* 15 (1960), 333–52.

6   Charles Nyamiti, "Jesus Christ, the Ancestor of Humankind: Methodological and Trinitarian Foundations," in *Studies in African Christian Theology*, vol. 1 (Nairobi: CUEA, 2005) 7.

7   Ibid.

8   Emmanuel Ntakarutimana, "Où en est la théologie africaine?," 247: *"Là où la théologie africaine a été assez tributaire des querelles philosophiques occidentales, il devient important aujourd'hui de faire un retour sur l'Ecriture et sa traduction en langes africaines pour repenser l'expérience première de la rencontre avec le Dieu qui vient en Jésus-Christ pour nous conduire à un accomplissement de christification."* He further remarks that: *"Les instituts de formation théologique en Afrique se trouvent devant le défi de repenser leurs sources, de revoir leurs bibliothèques, de réarticuler leurs programmes, de reconsidérer leurs langes d'enseignement en fonction des communautés qu'ils ont à servir."*

9   See M. Gilbert, *L'Institut Biblique: Un siècle d'histoire 1909–2009* (Rome: Pontificio Istituto Biblico, 2009).

10   Paulin Poucouta, *Quand la parole de Dieu visite l'Afrique: Lecture plurielle de la Bible* (Paris: Karthala, 2011) 226–31.

11   Ibid., 231.

12   See PACE.

13   See N. Soede Yaovi, *Théologie africaine: Origine, évolution et méthodes* (Abidjan: ICAO, 1995), 54–55; R. L. M. Mika, "Repères éthiques pour un bon usage de l'Ecriture Sainte en théologie morale," in A. Kabasele Mukenge

(dir.), *Bible et promotion humaine. Mélanges en l'honneur du professeur P. M. Buetubela Balembo* (Kinshasa: Mediaspaul, 2010).

14 André Kabasele Mukenge, "La théologie africaine à l'aube d'un nouveau siècle," in *Afrikanistik online* (2005); www.afrikanistik-online.de/archiv/2005/79, 2 (emphasis mine).

15 See Knut Holter, *Let my People Stay! Researching the Old Testament in Africa* (Nairobi: Acton Publishers, 2006); K. Holter, *Old Testament Research for Africa: A Critical Analysis and Annotated Bibliography of African Old Testament Dissertations, 1967–2000* (Bible and Theology in Africa 3; New York: Peter Lang, 2002).

16 See PBC, *The Interpretation of the Bible in the Catholic Church* (1993).

17 This fifth element was not mentioned, but it comes from the theological tradition and has been taken up into the *Catechism of the Catholic Church*, no. 1778, where one reads that the human conscience is the first vicar of Christ. An insight taken from Henry Newman's letter to the Duke of Norfolk, section 5: "Conscience is the aboriginal Vicar of Christ, a prophet in its informations, a monarch in its peremptoriness, a priest in its blessings and anathemas."

18 If we look at cultures as the mold that shapes humanity, one can hardly separate the experience of God from a genuine process of becoming human. "Long ago," reads Hebrews 1:1, "God spoke to our ancestors in many and various ways" (NRSV); this does not hold true only for Israel's ancestors; it is universal. Indeed, each of us can say, "God spoke to my ancestors." The divine words our ancestors have handed to us have been considered stepping stones. Therefore, through Jesus, we believe that God has fully revealed himself.

19 See Henry Newman, "Letter to the Duke of Norfolk," section 5. This sentence has made its way into the *Catechism of the Catholic Church*, § 1778.

20 At some stage in African theology, African traditional religion was considered the "OT" of African Christians. We should not forget that the OT is important for us because it provides us with the mental frame of mind and symbols to understand the salvific message of Jesus and to walk in his footsteps. Jesus thus remains the real Word of God in the proper sense.

21 See Joseph Fitzmyer, *The Interpretation of Scripture: In Defense of the Historical Critical Method* (Mahwah, N.J.: Paulist Press, 2008); M. Gilbert, *L'Institut Biblique: Un siècle d'histoire 1909–2009* (Rome: Pontificio Istituto Biblico, 2009).

22 See Joseph G. Prior, *The Historical Critical Method in Catholic Exegesis* (Rome: PUG, 2001); John Barton, *The Nature of Biblical Criticism* (Louisville, Ky.: Westminster John Knox Press, 2007).

23 See for instance in Poucouta, *Quand la parole*, 230, he quotes *Dei Verbum* no. 24, and on p. 231, one reads, "si la Parole de Dieu est l'âme de la théologie."

24 See Albert Nolan, *Jesus Before Christianity* (London: Darton, Longman & Todd, 1994); Ernest R. Wendland and Jean-Claude Loba-Mkole, *Biblical Texts & African Audiences* (Nairobi: Acton Publishers, 2004).

The Role of the Scriptures:
The New Testament in African Theology

Chantal Nsongisa

Introduction

The question this chapter seeks to respond to is the role Scripture, especially the New Testament, plays in African theology. By asking ourselves this question, we seek to clarify the relationship that must exist between the Word of God and theology.

In the perspective of the project of theological research envisaged by the Theological Colloquium on Church, Religion, and Society in Africa (TCCRSA), which promotes a new method of theological reflection in Africa, I believe it is timely to reconsider or, better still, to revisit the relationship between Scripture and theology in a specifically African context.

In an attempt to take an intelligent approach to this issue, I will deal with four points. The first will focus on a presentation of the intrinsic link between the Scripture and the Christian experience as an experience of faith. The second point will focus on the role or the place of the Scripture in theological discourses in regard to the hermeneutical task of understanding this experience of faith. The third point deals with the place the Scripture occupy in theological research and scholarship in Africa, with particular attention to exegetical research. The fourth and final point deals with the relationship between exegesis and other theological disciplines. A few suggestions on new perspectives in theological research in Africa will conclude this chapter.

1. The Relationship Between the Holy Scriptures and the Christian Experience

There is an intrinsic relationship between the Christian experience as an experience of faith and the Scripture, because all faith experiences –

with the Christian experience being one such experience – are based on the Scripture, are nourished by the Scripture, and are understood in the light of the Scripture.

The Word of God in the Scripture instructs believers concerning a God who revealed God's self to humanity and communicated God's plan of salvation for humanity to all women and men. God always takes part in the happy and unhappy events that make up the fabric of human existence. Indeed, the Old Testament constitutes a rich tableau of the quality of the multifaceted relationships existing between God, the Creator, and humanity, God's creation. This rich relational portrait is fully manifested by Jesus Christ in the New Testament. In effect, the experience of faith is nothing but a relationship with God.

The economy of salvation of humanity as conceived by the Creator is realised and continues to be realised today for all humanity through the mediation of Jesus Christ, whose advent was announced in the Old Testament. This mediation is made possible by means of a comprehensive dialogue as a trusting relationship and love between humanity and God.

In addition, thanks to the revealing and illuminating light of the Word of God, we can know ourselves and understand what God wants and expects of us and better appreciate the quality of our relationships with God. In doing so, we learn through God's Word that God is the only one who enables and empowers us to give an appropriate response to God's offer of fullness of life.

The value and the importance of knowing the Scripture were highly perceived and highlighted by the fathers of the Church. St Jerome especially felt that ignorance of Scripture amounted to ignorance of God.[1] One cannot claim to do theology as an intelligent and intelligible study of God without the knowledge of the revealed Word. Thus, if the Word nourishes and maintains the experience of faith, faith itself helps us adhere to the Scripture by serving as a lamp for our path (cf. Psalm 118). There is therefore a dialogical relationship between Scripture and faith.

Similarly, St Thomas, in line with St Augustine, insisted on the importance of faith in understanding of the Scripture. He recommended faith in Christ as a prerequisite for the action of the Word in believers. Without the grace of faith, "even the words of the Gospel kill."[2] Without faith, theologians will not be objective and will be tempted to project their own thoughts into the texts. Theological study without the dimension of faith nourished by the knowledge of the Scripture will be only an attempt to satisfy curiosity.

Thus the Scripture should play an important role in any theological discourse worth its name. What is the role of the Scripture in the theological discourse as a hermeneutic of the experience of faith?

2. The Role of the Scripture in the Theological Discourse as a Hermeneutic of the Experience of Faith

By its very nature, theology draws upon the Word of God as its preferred foundation because the Word is the written form of divine self-revelation to humanity. Theology receives data about God, the subject of its study, from the Scripture. It must not use the Scripture as an instrument at the service of theological discipline, whose purpose is simply to confirm doctrinal theses[3] but as a study.[4] The latter will lead to knowledge of God, generate faith, and guide Christian life.

The use of the Word of God is fundamental because, according to the Magisterium of the Church, it is "the soul of theology."[5] In that role, it operates in a manner similar to the human soul. The soul and the body are different elements that coexist. We can say that a person is dead when the two elements that constitute the person separate. Thus, the Word of God and the study of humanity about God (theology) are two separate elements that coexist harmoniously.

The Word of God is not the only source for theology, [6] but it is its main source, its "soul." Christian reflection on God must make use the Word to better clarify its theological assertions. In addition, theological research and scholarship aims for a better knowledge of God, which is acquired only from the Scripture; theology, deprived of its soul, its body – which becomes a human formulation – loses its quintessence. It is a dead and foundation-less theology.

As the human soul is the principle of thought and the principle of the will, the Word of God is the principle or the basis of reflection for a theologian. To make an abstraction of the Word of God for a theological work would be to develop a theology with only superficial consistency and therefore without any impact on the lives of its audience.

What then is the place and the impact of Scripture in the work of African theologians? Is the Scripture used as the basis of theological reflection?

3. The Role of the Scripture in Theological Research in Africa: Biblical Exegesis

Based on the works of the continent's specialists, the Word of God has been used effectively but also in superficial ways. Some theologians refer simply to the Scripture to support their assertions; the Word does not constitute the basis for their work. I do not perceive a thorough study of the Word of God that allows us to realise its full spiritual wealth and to arrive at a better understanding of the topic under consideration.

Although these theologians have addressed interesting questions in an African context, they fall short when it comes to a close, deep relationship with the Scripture. The Scripture does not play the role of being the soul of theology, that which gives form to the thought. By way of example, Bishop Desmond Tutu approached the topic of apartheid but did not base it sufficiently on the Bible. He wrote of the theology of liberation, "black theology,"[7] and aimed to give meaning to the suffering of his people,[8] to justify the goodness of God, and to refuse to admit their suffering comes from God.

The work of the bishop fits well into the desire of African theologians to engage in theological study based on the reality of the continent, but it would have been better to base this reflection on a precise passage that describes how the people of Israel suffered oppression but continued to believe in God and recognise God's goodness. This would have allowed a biblical text to give effective form to the reflection.

Tutu is, of course, among the first generation of African theologians who have paved the path of African theological thinking; so, it is understandable that his was not an exhaustive work. It is up to the new generation of theologians to take into consideration the role of the Scripture in their theological reflections.

African writers have also made use of the Scripture as the basis of their thoughts. Some begin from an African cultural fact and reexamine it in the light of Christ. Others begin with a biblical text and apply it to the African reality. They make comparative studies between African culture and tradition and the Christian faith and draw similarities and dissimilarities. By doing so, they arrive at a better understanding of Christ for the African people.

In this regard, theologian Bénézet Bujo deserves special attention; he has made the Word of God the main source of his reflection. In his article "The theology of the Ancestors as the point of departure for a new theology,"[9] he bases his argument on the biblical passage of the Last Supper in John 13. This event, according to Bujo, recounted the action of a traditional African ancestor, the last hour a parent spends with his or her children. He examines the African tradition of the ancestor in the light of Christ.

Bujo's study enables Africans to see Jesus in their own context. Jesus is not just any ancestor; he is the protoancestor or the ancestor par excellence, judging from the fact that he has achieved the ideal of authentic, God-fearing African ancestors and transcended them by doing so.

The second trend of those who begin their theological reflection from the Scripture is the understanding of the message of a biblical text in order to illuminate African reality. In his study, Emmanuel Katongole begins with the episode of Zacchaeus narrated in Luke 19:1–10 to urge all to an authentic, practical, and effective appropriation of the Word of God.[10] The author invites all to take up the challenge of theology in combatting what he calls the Zacchaeus syndrome. He was anxious to see Jesus, but due to his small size, that seemed impossible until he climbed a tree. According to the author, Zacchaeus's approach is a temptation to see reality from above. Thus, this approach fails to see situations as they arise in the ordinary context of human life.

There is evidence of some African theologians' attempts to incorporate the Word of God in their writings.[11] However, the study of the biblical texts that forms the bases of their work is not thorough. They would have achieved very significant results if they had begun with an exegetical analysis of the text. This would have offered them a well-developed theological sense that would have allowed them to present believers with the spiritual meaning of the text. Nevertheless, their theologies are very much in the spirit of the magisterium in using the Word of God as the soul of theology. What role should Scripture play in all facets of theological reflection?

4. The Relationship between Exegesis and Other Theological Disciplines

Collaboration between biblical theology and other theological disciplines is a strong recommendation of the magisterium.[12] Emeritus Pope Benedict XVI affirmed that the effectiveness of the Church's pastoral action and of the faithful's spiritual life depends to a large extent on the fruitful relationship between exegesis and theology.[13] Thus, African theologians in particular are invited to a fruitful relationship with the study of the Bible and a love for Scripture in all its dimensions. This promotes an effective pastoral life in our African Christian communities.

In addition, Benedict insisted that the biblical hermeneutics of the Church ought to be pivotal in order to avoid a certain dualism of secularised hermeneutics.[14] The latter would provide the opportunity for fundamentalist or spiritualised interpretations of the Word of God. The Church recommends hermeneutical orientation, which requires the complementarity of the literal and spiritual meaning, a harmony between faith and reason.[15]

The Scripture as presented by the Church to believers is already an interpretation. The later authors reread ancient texts in the light of the passion, death, and resurrection of Christ. By relying on the ancient texts, new texts have created new understandings from these ancient texts that sometimes differ from their original sense.[16]

To encourage faith and to guide the ecclesial life, this work of interpretation continues in the Church. This is the task of exegetes in collaboration with other disciples of theology because exegesis is a theological discipline. It studies the scriptural form of divine revelation to derive theological sense from it. However, Catholic exegetes in particular approach the Scripture with the biases they receive especially from systematic theology. This kind of understanding or approach is found at the level of the certainties of faith, according to which the biblical writings are inspired by God and entrusted to the church to awaken faith and orient the Christian life. However, each theological discipline has a different approach to the Bible.

Exegetes are able to uncover the theological sense of the Bible through a careful examination of the texts. They place them in their historical and literary context and in the context of the canon of the biblical texts.[17]

They engage in historical and descriptive analysis and do not see only what is written. Theologians make use of the exegetical data to develop the spiritual sense in their fields of study. This implies that the exegetes must orient their research so as to highlight the religious message of the biblical writings[18] that will serve as the basis for theologians. In doing so, the study of the Scripture effectively becomes the "soul" of theology.[19] Thus theologians will refute that false charge of extremist tendencies such as dualism and fundamentalism that can easily slide into their reflections.[20]

Dualism leads to the separation of doctrinal truth of the Scripture from their linguistic expressions.[21] However, for the Scripture to arouse the faith of people of every age and culture, it should be approached by paying critical attention to values and principles present in different cultural contexts where the Word of God is proclaimed. Once again, it is up to the exegetes to detach, to a certain extent, the Word of God from its historical context to insert it into a modern historical context to arrive at the theological sense of the Word. Theologians must begin from bases established by the exegetes while obviously taking into account other theological sources. In doing so, they will arrive at theological and specific assertions proper to each discipline of theology in which the spiritual meaning of the Word is highlighted.

Used in this perspective, the Scripture will play its full role as the soul of theology, that which gives form to the ecclesial reflection on God.

Conclusion

The aim of this chapter was to explore the role played by the Scripture in any effort to reflect the divine self-manifestation. This experience is communicated to us in the two testaments through various characters, particularly the person of Jesus Christ. To be credible, the Christian experience of faith must revitalise itself by the Scripture, the soul of this experience.

All theological discourses in general and African Christian theology in particular are called upon to use the Scripture in its role as the soul of theology. The studies of African theologians can contribute to the awakening and maturing of the faith of Christians and therefore the effective accomplishment of the mission of African Churches. To do this, the analyses African theologians should be applied to refresh the message of the biblical texts in current African circumstances and to express this message in a renewed language, notably through cross-referencing the situations experienced by Africans with the images and events in the Scripture.[22]

Promoting biblical exegesis in African theology will curb the threat that a superficial knowledge of the Scripture poses to the Church and its believers in Africa; that superficial knowledge is the consequence of the practice of the members of certain religious movements in Africa that offer tendentious and fanciful interpretations of the Word of God to their followers.

In terms of pastoral care, such a use of Scripture could show how God listens to Africans in their specific contexts and responds to their needs through God's Word, just as our ancestors did. Africans would thus better understand the incarnation of Christ.

St Bonaventure was right in affirming that the Scripture has "fullness of the everlasting bliss" as their fruit.[23] It invites us to believe and to possess eternal life, because it is in the latter that the desires of women and men will be fulfilled. To do this, faith in Jesus Christ constitutes an indispensable dimension of the Christian experience. It allows one to understand the Scripture.[24] It cannot be otherwise, and it will be advantageous to Africans who, by reason of their conception of human existence as founded on the principle of fullness of life, desire to live fulfilled lives.[25]

Rethinking the practice of African theology in this new perspective is possible because of the fullness of the meaning of the Word,[26] which is valid for people of all ages and cultures (Isaiah 40:8, 66:18–21; Matthew 28:19–20). This hermeneutical task requires a close collaboration between African exegetes and theologians.

Translated from French by
Andrew Setsoafia, SJ

Endnotes

1   Cf. St. Jerome, *Commentariorum in Isaiam Libri, Prol; PL 24.17 B*; Benedict XVI, the postsynodal exhortation *Verbum Domini*, no. 129.

2   Cf. Thomas Aquinas, *Ia Summa Theologiae II–II, q. 106, art. 2;* Benedict XVI, *Verbum Domini*, 55.

3   Cf. Pontifical Biblical Commission, _The interpretation of the Bible_, 102.

4   Cf. Vatican II, _Dei Verbum (Dogmatic Constitution on the Revelation)_, no. 6, nos. 24, 143.

5   It is an expression used by Leo XIII (_Providentissimus Deus, 1893_), Benedict XV (_Spiritus Paraclitus_, 1920), Vatican II (_Dei Verbum_), and Benedict XVI (_Verbum Domini_).

6   It considers a lot of other data such as patristic writings, conciliar definitions, other documents of the magisterium, liturgy, philosophical systems, the cultural situation, and social and contemporary policy.

7   Cf. Cf. D. Tutu, "The Theology of Liberation in Africa" in _African Theology En Route,_ ed. Kofi Appiah-Kubi-Sergio Torres (Maryknoll, New York: Orbis, 1979), 162–68.

8   Cf. Ibid., 164.

9   Cf. B. B. Bujo, _African Theology in its Social Context_ (Paulines Publications Africa, Nairobi 1992), 75–91.

10   Cf. E. Katongole, "'African Renaissance' and the Challenge of Narrative Theology in Africa" in _African Theology Today_, ed. E. Katongole (Scranton, PA: University of Scranton Press, 2002), 212–14.

11   The Scripture and the Word of God may be interchangeable. This is due to the fact that the Holy Scriptures are inspired by God. Because of this, they exist because of the Word of God. Otherwise, the Word of God is found in the Scriptures. However, they have been used interchangeably a few times to mean the same reality: Word of God expressed in human language.

12   Cf. Leo XIII, _Providentissimus Deus_; Benedict XV, _Spiritus Paraclitus;_ Pius XII, _Divino afflante Spiritu;_ Vatican _Dei Verbum_; Benedict XVI, _Verbum Domini_.

13   Cf. Benedict XVI, _Verbum Domini_, no. 59.

14   Cf. Ibid., no. 66.

15   Cf. Vatican II, _Dei Verbum_, no. 68.

16   The positions taken by Jesus during his public ministry as evidenced by the sermon on the mount (Mt 5:21–48), the observance of the Sabbath (Mk 2:27–28), the precepts of ritual purity (Mk 7:1–23), and the radical requirement of Jesus in other areas (see Mt 10:2–12, 17–27). There is a clear difference between the interpretation received from its era which was the one of the scribes and Pharisees (cf. Mt 5:20), his critical stance towards publicans and sinners (cf. Mk 2:15–17), and personal interpretation. The behaviour of Jesus translated its fidelity to the will of God expressed in Scripture (cf. Mt 5:17, 9:13; Mk 7:8–13, 10.5–9, etc.).

17   Pontifical Biblical Commission, _The interpretation of the Bible_, nos. 61–64.

18   Exegesis, through its methodologies, must launch challenges to theologians and remind them of the important aspects of divine revelation in their work of

systematisation. The theological disciplines are called to enlighten exegesis by their theological research so that it can pose "important questions to the biblical texts and better discover their whole scope and fertility." It is important for those who are engaged in the scientific study of the Bible to be in connection with theological research, spiritual experience, and the discernment of the Church. The context of the living faith of the Christian community is the appropriate framework for best results in Bible study because the faith of this community seeks the salvation of humankind. Pontifical Biblical Commission, *The interpretation of the Bible*, nos. 97–98.

19   Vatican II, *Dei Verbum*, no. 24.

20   Pontifical Biblical Commission, *The interpretation of the Bible*.

21   On one hand, one can estimate that the linguistic expressions or the rational dimension of the Scripture are not necessary, and one adopts a fideist approach to the Word of God because it is only what comes from feelings that is important for faith. On the other hand, value is given to reason in the understanding of the Word. Therefore, attention is focused simply on what is meaningful. This leads to a rationalist approach to the Word of God. The fundamentalist understanding of the Scripture stems from a confusion of two inherent aspects present the Word of God: the human and the divine. The proponents of this trend make no difference between what is casual and what is doctrinal truth. They recognise only the literal meaning and are opposed to or ignorant of the historical and scientific interpretations. Faced with these two trends in using the Word of God, the Church recommends a distinction and not a separation between the human and divine dimensions that make up the Word of God. In effect, God expresses God's self to humanity through human thought and words. The Scripture is at the same time from God – as an inspirer – and from humanity, as inspired.

22   V. Mulago, *Un visage africain du Christianisme. L'union vitale bantu face à l'unité ecclésiale* (Paris: Présence Africaine,1965).

23   Cf. Bonaventure, *Breviloquium, Prol. Opera Omnia, V*, 201–02.

24   Cf. Ibid.

25   Cf. P. Temples, *Philosophie bantu* (Kinshasa: A.J. Smet, 1945, 1979).

26   Cf. Pontifical Biblical Commission, *The interpretation of the Bible*, no. 102.

No Longer Truly African, but Not Fully Christian: In Search of a New African Spirituality and Religious Synthesis

Eunice Karanja Kamaara

Introduction

According to John S. Mbiti, "Christianity in Africa is so old that it can rightly be described as an indigenous traditional and African religion."[1] Mbiti is accurate; Christianity was in Africa, specifically North Africa, in its first few centuries. Indeed, among the people present at the Pentecost event recorded in Acts 1 were Africans, albeit it there was no name for Africa or Africans then.

Yet, nineteenth-century Christian missionaries assumed that "African" and "Christian" identities are not only separate; tension also exists between them. Indeed, to become a Christian, indigenous peoples of Africa were largely required to let go of their ways of life, an impossible task for any human individual or community. Thus the struggle for African identity in the context of western Christianity has dominated the continent for a long time.

Since the first Ecumenical Council held in Nicaea in AD 325, the Catholic Church has had at least two scores of ecumenical councils (exclusive meetings of patriarchs, cardinals, bishops, abbots, and male heads of religious orders and any other persons nominated by the bishop of Rome) called to settle doctrinal issues. In 1869, Pope Pius convened the first Vatican Council, which marked a break in the history of the Church in that papal infallibility was defined and declared. It was expected therefore that after 1870, the Roman pontiff would, by his word, settle any doctrinal issue. So, when Pope John XXXIII announced the convocation of the Second Vatican Council (Vatican II) in January 1959, many people in and outside the Church were surprised. But this turned out to be the most significant council for the Church, not only in contemporary times but through time.

This latest Church ecumenical council has significant bearing on this chapter; but for Vatican II, I probably would not be writing it. Before this council, the Church operated as an other-worldly phenomenon. It would seem that Vatican II brought the Church down to earth. Today, fifty years after Vatican II emphasised that the Church is in the world and not against the world, the question of what it means to be African, to be Christian, and to be African and Christian at the same time, especially in the postcolonial African contexts, remains unanswered.

Three categories on understanding of this identity exist. First, to some, to be truly African is to return to indigenous beliefs and practices as exemplified by The Tent of the Living God in Kenya founded by Ngonya wa Gakonya. It was registered in 1987 but dates back to the early 1960s, when Ngonya started questioning Christianity as professed by his parents.[2] Second, to others, to be Christian, an African has to leave behind all indigenous African beliefs and practices and embrace Christian values and European culture propagated by European missionaries. My mother, as do many members of the Presbyterian Church of East Africa, belongs to this category. Her parents were first-generation Christian converts of the Church of Scotland. While we were growing up, my mother would "beat the devil out of us" if she found out that we had disobeyed her by participating in traditional dances for national music festivals.[3] Third, to yet others, to be African and Christian is to embrace Christian values but express these in African practices and thought forms. J.N.K. Mugambi used the allegory of fish and water to explain that for Christianity to survive, it must swim in cultural "waters." Those in the latter category belong to the inculturation school, of which Ayward Shorter, Charles Nyamiti, and Laurenti Magesa, to mention but a few, are renowned members.

Against the various understandings, I hold that the issue of African-Christian identity is yet to be resolved. Thus, in this chapter, I seek to raise controversy and in the process provoke continued reflection and discussion on what it means to be African and Christian at the same time by introducing a fourth category of understanding. In this fourth category, I propound a paradigm shift from thinking of African and Christian identities as separate to presenting them as one and the same. I wrestle with the question of the identity of Christians in postcolonial Africa to argue that a person who is truly African is fully Christian and vice versa. I argue that human identity (unlike that of objects and perhaps animals) based on external manifestations such as human colour, language, dress, and practices, among others, is a cosmetic identity that disappears once the true human identity is revealed.

Against this understanding, I suggest that it is time to move beyond external manifestations of the identity of Christians of Africa to focus on bringing out the identity of Christians in Africa by their internal values. Further, I argue that this authentic African identity is synonymous with authentic Christian identity; fifty years after Vatican II, the term "African Christian" is tautological.

The Meaning of Identity

In discussing the identity of Christians in Africa, a brief exposition on identity suffices. Identity may be defined as the distinguishing characteristic of reality that distinguishes it from other realities. Thus, philosophers define identity as "sameness with self" so that all other reality is distinguished by this sameness. The identity of a specific reality may be objective (as is) so that every person identifies the reality by the same definition. But the identity of reality is often dependent on the person defining it. When reality is defined as is, we get the objective truth accessible to all. While this is often possible with natural objects (hence the phrase "objective truth") when dealing with objects made by humans, identity becomes elusive as each human defines the object in relation to its functionality. The interpretation of an empty Coca-Cola bottle as a gift sent by the gods from the "skies" in the film, *The Gods Must Be Crazy* (1980), comes to mind as an example of how humans define the same objects differently. Identity is much more complicated when referring to human reality than to objects, given the complexity of human beings.

African Identity

Who is an African? What is the defining characteristic of Africans that makes Africans the same and therefore different from non-Africans? These two questions bring out the idea of individual identity (African) and group identity (Africans). Individual identity applies to all humans regardless of colour since every human is unique. Group identity suggests that a certain group has a defining characteristic. An objective identity of African either as an individual or as a group is nonexistent since Africans as individuals are unique, just as are all other persons, and as a group, Africans have nothing special that differentiates them from other human beings. Often, we take it for granted that black is what defines an African objectively, but this is no longer viable; with intensive human migrations and interactions, colour no longer defines nationality.

Human identity is a social construct; a subjective identity constructed by the self or by others for self or for others. Thus, a white man may be African regardless of where he was born depending on how he perceives himself and how he is perceived by those who call him African. Consider this: one Briton empathised with indigenous Kenyans over the colonial period and was commonly found in their company in "black-only" neighbourhoods. One day, a Kenyan saw the Briton in the midst of black Kenyans and switching to local, coded language, asked, *"Nikii mukaburu areka guku?"* "What is a white man doing here?" One of the black Kenyans in the company of the white man said, *"Uyu ti mukaburu. Uyu ni John,"* "This is not a white man. He is John."

What then defines authentic Africanness is not so much the colour of skin, language, or culture in general but rather character. In Kenya alone, there are over forty-two ethnic groups, each with distinct languages, histories, and sociocultural, political, and economic practices, not to mention subethnic groups or emerging cultures. While it may have been possible to distinguish between ethnic groups in Africa before colonialism because each group was largely autonomous with little or no contact with the others, at the dawn of twenty-first century, interactions, including intermarriages across ethnic groups, have blurred the line between one group and another.

The objective truth is that Africans are human beings with dignity, rationality, free will, and spirituality. But Africans, like any other human beings, are often defined in relation to constructed and dynamic specifics such as time and space – spatial, social, cultural, economic, historical, and political, among others.

For example, Africans, as are other peoples, are at times defined in relation to the poor leadership that characterises many a government on the continent, while at other times, they are defined in relation to poverty and hunger, and yet at other times, they are defined in relation to cultural attributes. However, unlike other human societies that are constantly and consistently developing, Africans are defined as if they were static and therefore live in the twenty-first century as they lived in the first century. If any change is envisaged, it is a change for the worse.

To understand how we are where we are, questioning our identities in terms of how we perceive ourselves and how we are perceived by others calls for an understanding of the history of Africa. I am aware of the argument that Africans unnecessarily blame the West and the past for all their woes, but for me, in line with postcolonial theory and as Chinua Achebe would say, we cannot tell where we dried our bodies if we cannot tell where the rain began to beat us.[4]

Two phases mark the history of Africa. The primitive phase refers to the period before Africa was named, a phase when human life was elementary, original, fundamental, and pristine. This phase is not unique to Africa as it existed or continues to exist in all human societies. I have already indicated the heterogeneity of Africa and Africans, but for the purposes of this chapter, I focus on what was common across societies to emphasise unity in diversity to refer to the African society in singular. I acknowledge that some whole societies and some individuals in Africa continue to adhere to indigenous beliefs and practices and so refer to the traditional African society in the present.

In indigenous African society, to be truly African is to be guided by the *utu* philosophy, to appreciate the dignity of human persons, communitarian and ethical living, and the centrality of relationships. If a person acts contrary to this, he or she is not considered African. In nearly all societies, a person who has seriously violated these ethics is not considered human anymore and would be excommunicated. For example, in many indigenous societies, a person who violates the dignity of human life by deliberately killing another is considered more or less an animal. But as has already been noted, Africa is not static – every society is dynamic.

The imperialist interlude, the beginning of which was marked by slavery/slave trade and colonialism and the attendant process of Christianising the native, now labeled African, was responsible for the brokenness, hopelessness, and confusion that characterise many an African's mind. Specifically, Christianity operated as a colonising agent that largely dismissed indigenous beliefs and practices as savage and backward. To be a Christian, a native was expected to give up all these indigenous beliefs and practices. Since these were integrated into all departments of life, to be a Christian was to discard the whole way of life – to cease to be African.

Christianity was presented as a European religion, and Africans were expected to take it up complete with the European cultural garbs in which it was preached. But we all know it is not possible for humans to give up their ways of life overnight, so many Africans converted to Christianity but retained their traditional beliefs and practices. Surprisingly for Africans, it was possible to adopt this attitude towards a new religion, since Christianity was not presented as a way of life but as a kind of club that met once a week in designated places.[5] Since then, religious hypocrisy has flourished as Africans continually attempt to be African and Christian at the same time. As postcolonial theorists[6] observe, colonialism has had so adverse and long-lasting an impact on the African continent that the contemporary situation cannot be understood without reference to the process. According to Crawford Young, "Overall colonial legacy cast its shadow over the emergent African state system to a degree unique among the major world regions."[7]

The phase that emerged from the interlude may be regarded as the modern phase, the neocolonial phase marked by globalisation with competition for economic profits as its central value. This phase is defined by neoliberal capitalism, which is largely characterised by materialism, individualism, and consumerism oiled by competition for profits.

Christian Identity

To understand what it means to be fully Christian, we need to understand Christian identity, a concept, like many others, we take for granted. But "the trouble with concepts … is that we think we understand them too well. We may define them in different ways, assume different political or moral positions in relation to them, but they seem 'natural' to us."[8]

Christian identity is identity in Jesus Christ. To be fully Christian is to be fully Christlike. But who is Jesus? Who is Christ? Perhaps the identity of Jesus has been the most controversial doctrine of the Church. Well before the advent of the Church as an institution, Jesus put the question to his disciples: "Who do the crowds say I am? But who do you say I am?"(Luke 9:18–21 ESV). These questions bring out the relational aspects of human identity. Jesus appropriately expected that the disciples, having had close relationships with him, would have a different understanding of him from that of other people.

In biblical times, Christian identity was not so much a profession as a way of life. In the absence of churches as places of formal worship, Christians met in each other's houses to share and encourage one another in unity. The only way one could tell they were Christians was by their actions of love for one another. Love is a universal reality that can be expressed in only one way: sharing.

The subject of Jesus' identity was the single doctrine that attracted the highest number of ecumenical councils in the early Church. The Council of Chalcedon held in 451 under Pope Leo, the second council of Constantinople in 553 under Pope Vigilius, and the third council of Constantinople (680–681) presided by Pope Agatho were called to settle matters on the nature of Jesus Christ. From my perspective, Vatican II is not only a continuation of this debate but also a major step in the Church's understanding of Christ as it sought to reconcile incarnated identities to the divine identity of Christ.

African/Christian Identity

African theologians have come a long way in seeking to manifest African identity in the context of Christianity on the continent. As early as 1956, Africans in the Roman Catholic Church in Africa were calling in their writings for the adaptation and Africanisation of Christianity. For example, there was a collection of articles written by African Catholic priests titled *Des prêtres noirs s'interrogent*.

By the early 1960s, African theologians were writing to affirm that Africans had systematic religious beliefs and practices well before the coming of any Christian missionaries and that these could form a basis for expression of Christianity in the continent. Mbiti's book, *African Religions and Philosophy*, first published in 1969, is one of the classic examples of these. To date, hundreds of books have been written on the subject as it evolved from adaptation and Africanisation through incarnation to inculturation.

But Vatican II was the most significant landmark in the development of Christianity in Africa. This council marked the official recognition of African identity as an integral part of Christian practice in Africa. Soon after the council, Pope Paul VI affirmed this at the occasion of the canonisation of the Ugandan martyrs in 1969 when he declared to Roman Catholic bishops, "You may and you must have an African Christianity." This was echoed by Pope John Paul II in his 1980 visit to Africa.[9]

Lumen Gentium invites all persons to holiness regardless of their sociocultural identities:

It follows that though there are many nations there is but one people of God, which takes its citizens from every race, making them citizens of a kingdom which is of a heavenly rather than of an earthly nature. All the faithful, scattered though they be throughout the world, are in communion with each other in the Holy Spirit, and so, he who dwells in Rome knows that the people of India are his members". Since the kingdom of Christ is not of this world, the Church or people of God in establishing that kingdom takes nothing away from the temporal welfare of any people. On the contrary it fosters and takes to itself, insofar as they are good, the ability, riches and customs in which the genius of each people expresses itself. Taking them to itself it purifies, strengthens, elevates and ennobles them. The Church in this is mindful that she must bring together the nations for that king to whom they were given as an inheritance, and to whose city they bring gifts and offerings (13).

In this statement, Vatican II declared that the universality of the Church does not negate cultural diversity and pluralism but rather affirms these, for through them, Christ may be manifest.

Since Vatican II, African theologians have appropriately and effectively reflected on how to emulate Christ in the context of African cultures and situations. The theology of "adaptation" was first propounded and popularised but sooner than later criticised as inadequate. By the early 1970s, there was already a paradigm shift, and in 1974, the Symposium of Episcopal Conferences of Africa and Madagascar (SECAM) officially adopted the shift to embrace the theology of incarnation.[10]

This reflection is commendable, and indeed, it has left its mark. As observed first by Franz Fanon[11] and later by Ngugi wa Thiongo[12] among others and echoed by Sabine Jell-Bahisen.

When Christians or others who have abandoned their ancient cultural beliefs and practices go to the extreme of demolishing their traditional religious effigies, they expressed a tremendous disdain for the creations of their own culture, a denial of their indigenous history and identity and ultimately self-hatred. Psychologically, such self destructive behaviour is associated with a "colonised mind", widespread throughout independent world.[13]

I appreciate and applaud the great work done by theologians in Africa especially in terms of reaffirming the self-value of Africans as human created in the image of God. Indeed, this was necessary to give Africans a sense of pride in their ways of life following distortions through the process of colonialism and the attendant Christianisation of the native.

Close to forty years ago, Aylward Shorter acknowledged that there had been a lot of talk about "adaptation" and "Africanisation" since Vatican II, but this has translated only into "the production of vernacular liturgical texts and the creation of local musical settings for these texts."[14] We appreciate vernacular liturgical texts, liturgical dances, the sound of drums, and other local music settings, but fifty years after Vatican II, it is time to make the next step to emphasise indigenous values and ethos.

Fifty years after Vatican Council II, the Church should take to itself not only the mere external manifestations of African culture but much more important, it should purify, strengthen, and elevate the internal African values to strengthen the whole Church toward fullness in unity. I propose a shift beyond inculturation, which has been associated with external manifestations of African identity, to unification – a unity of Christian identity and African identity into a whole that is manifested by the internal value of love made evident externally in acts of sharing. An analysis of African values and Christian values provides for such unification.

To be fully Christian is to be like Jesus, Christlike. To be Christ is an ideal that cannot be lived in human cultural contexts, but it is an ideal we can aspire to. To be truly African is to be truly human, which is to be born in time and space as Jesus was. The two major values of Christlike identity are love and justice, in which justice is the minimum requirement of love. The greatest commandment incorporates love for God, which translates into love for neighbour and for all elements of the created order. This is what aspiring to be like Christ is about.

The two major values in African identity are human dignity and oneness of all creation and therefore the value of relationships in the ethical community. These values are institutionalised in social systems and practices such as the extended family and charity. This is unlike what we have today as philanthropy, where we stand on rooftops to announce what we give back to society when it is only a small fraction of what we should be giving back. The extended family, which continues to be a characterising feature of African societies, is the antithesis of the individualism and consumerism that characterise modern life. The concept of extended family calls for sharing in love and care with others; it presupposes interdependence. Contrasting African and Western cultures, Ikenye Ndungu JB observes that, "The core values of self-reliance and self-independence in America and Europe and interdependence as the African core are held as different core values of these two cultures, yet valued by their communities of embeddedness."[15]

A comparative analysis of the values of Christianity and of Africa suggests that to be truly African is to be fully Christian regardless of time and space. The Wafipa of Tanzania appropriately say, "Where the elders pray, there is the God of the Door and the God of the Door is the Christian God also."[16] Thus, to be Christian is to be African and vice versa; it is to aspire to follow Christ in word and deed in context, a specific time and space.

To insist on African identity as unique is to miss the truth that human beings are one and the same and that it is not possible to distinguish one from the other in the context of Christ. As observed, Africa is not homogeneous; so, if we insist on the uniqueness of African identity on the basis of external manifestations, we will be giving weight to division of Africans and ultimately of humanity. Maria Crosz-Ngaté and Kokole argue against persistent identification of Africa with clearly distinguishable and separatist tribalism.

> The identification of Africa with distinct people and primordial loyalties is not confined to the popular imagination but extends to thinking in government and academic circles as well. Even anthropology departments still frequently list introductory courses on Africa as "people and cultures of Africa" in titles that evoke multiplicity but also separation and boundedness, certain visions of Afrocentricity, on other hand reify … cultural particularity than evaluate it to an "African" universal. The long standing debate on ethnicity in Africa further enhanced by Africanist research and writing with and without Africa continue to emphasise the interplay of culture and history and the permeability of boundaries.[17]

Indeed, as *Lumen Gentium* declares, Christ may be manifest through various cultures.

We must rethink and reconsider our emphasis on African languages and dress as this may separate us from the rest of humanity. However, focusing on values unites Africans with humanity, for indeed, as archeological studies indicate, all societies began as indigenous with more or less the same values as Africans claim: the value of human dignity and the oneness of all creation and therefore the value of relationships in the ethical community. As mentioned above, these are comparable to Christian values of love and justice.

Way Forward: Reconstruction for Unification of African and Christian Identities

Giving a Walter Rodney Lecture, Stuart Hall observed,

> No cultural identity is produced out of thin air. It is produced out of those historical experiences, those cultural traditions, those lost and marginal languages, those marginalised experiences, those peoples and histories that remain unwritten. Those are the specific roots of identity. On the other hand, identity itself is not the rediscovery of them but what they as cultural resources allow a people to produce. Identity is not in the past to be found but in the future to be constructed. And I say that not because I think therefore that Caribbean people can ever give up the symbolic activity of trying to know more about the past from which they come, for only in that way can they discover and rediscover the resources through which identity can be constructed. But I remain profoundly convinced that their identities for the twenty-first century do not lie in taking old identities literally but in using the enormously rich and complex cultural heritages, to which history has made them heir, as the different musics out of which a Caribbean sound might one day be produced.[18]

Hall was speaking in reference to the Caribbean, but his words apply to Africa as well. In propounding a way forward for Christian identity in Africa in the twenty-first century, I agree with him that though identity is grounded on the past, it is not confined to the past but oriented towards the future. Unlike Hall, who uses the word "construct," I prefer the word "reconstruction" by Jesse Mugambi[19] in agreement with his contention that the starting point for African theology must be Africa and African culture. I advocate for a process that begins with an affirmation of African values rather than one that begins with Western Christianity that integrates African values. I propound another step forward to conceptualise and propose the reconstruction of African indigenous values and Christian values to bring out a whole that unites the two into one identity not only African but also universal.

The process builds on what has already been done from adaptation to inculturation since it necessarily starts from the reconstruction of African self-value and self-identity; these two attributes will lead to the reconstruction of relational identity, which, in turn, will lead to the reconstruction of identity as perceived by others.

We have appropriately and effectively reflected on African/Christian identity for more than fifty years now; it is time to declare our identity by action. In this, we need to reclaim our identity by acknowledging indigenous values across societies but also to appreciate human dynamism and overcoming the effects of postcolonialism. Following this, we will embrace and evangelise African identity not so much by word as by deed. Yes, they will know we are African by our practice of love and justice. Andre Karamaga buttresses my argument for unity.

> There is no single human being who chooses to be born in one or the other ethnic group. No one chooses physical or linguistic particularities for a given group, therefore no one has to bear consequences or be discriminated or be mistreated because of his/her ethnic belonging. Moreover, when a given ethnic group uses its particularities selfishly against the other, it becomes a prisoner with consequences of hatred, war and destruction … but the Bible reminds us that we have received freely what we have and who we are, "what have you that you did not receive, if then you have received it, why do you boast as if it were not a gift?" (1 Corinthians 4:7).[20]

Africa is at crossroads. A theology that addresses this situation is required. Aylward Shorter observes,

> An African Theology will derive from an African reading of Scripture. Clearly, if African theologians are to enjoy any originality, they must go themselves to the source of revelation, and must make the Word of God the key to their understanding of their own problems and priorities as Africans.[21]

The following section presents a theological justification for unification using an Old Testament story and a New Testament story.

United in Sharing: a Reflection on the Story of Ruth and the Miracle of Sharing

Running away from a serious famine, Elimelech, Naomi, and their sons Mahlon and Chilion left their land for Moab. In Moab, the two sons married Moabite women, Orpa and Ruth. But more tragedy struck when Elimelech and his two sons died, leaving Naomi with her two daughters-in-law. In hopelessness and helplessness, Naomi released her daughters to go their way. At that point, there was no hope for justice and no hope for life; Naomi told her daughters that even if she were to remarry and have more sons, they definitely would not wait for them to be big enough to marry them. Orpa went her way, but Ruth stayed with Naomi, a helpless old woman. "Do not urge me to leave you or to return from following you. For where you go I will go, and where you lodge I will lodge. Your people shall be my people, and your God my God" (Ruth 1:18, ESV).

Eventually, God delivered justice and life for Ruth, blessing her not only with a husband and a son but with a royal line. Ruth's son, Obed, was the father of Jesse, the father of David, the ancestor of Jesus Christ.

The story of Ruth is the story of Africa. Hopelessness, brokenness, and helplessness characterise post-colonial Africa. In a new context of globalisation characterised by individualism and consumerism, will Africa stay with Naomi (traditional values that seem to increase our vulnerability), or will it choose to go its own way like Orpa?

The Miracle of Sharing: A Reflection on John 6:1-15 (Jesus Feeds the Five Thousand)

The miracle began when Jesus recognised that the big crowd before him was hungry, so he asked his disciples, "Where are we to buy bread so that these people may eat?" Of course, Jesus knew his disciples did not have enough money to buy food for so big a crowd. Could it be that the generosity of a small boy would drive others to share their food and thereby feed everyone? In the context of neoliberal capitalism, the greatest miracle required for the world today is the miracle of sharing. As a popular *cliché* puts it, there is enough in the world to satisfy human need, but there will never be enough to satisfy human greed.

Will Africans lead the way in sharing? Africans have the resources. Shall we share, or shall we claim a special identity? In the context of neoliberal global capitalism, Africans have the option to join in greed or to draw from indigenous human values, as did Ruth, and unite them with Christian values to lead the world in sharing in justice and love to feed the world.

Endnotes

1 John S. Mbiti, *African Religions and Philosophy* (Nairobi: Heinemann, 1990), 223.

2 Grace Nyatugah Wamue, "Revisiting our indigenous shrines through Mungiki" in *African Affairs*, 100 (2001): 453–67.

3 National music festivals are events in which students from all over Kenya compete in singing and dancing.

4 Achebe Chinua, *Things Fall Apart* (New York: Anchor Books, 1994), cited in www3.dbu.edu/mitchell/achebequ.html.

5   Mbiti: *African Religions and Philosophy.*

6   See, for example, C. Leys, *The Rise and Fall of Development Theory* (Bloomington: Indiana University Press, 1996); M. Mamdani, *Citizen and Subject: Contemporary Africa and the Legacy of Late Colonialism* (Kampala: Fountain Publishers, 1996); Crawford Young, "The Heritage of Colonialism," in *Africa in World Politics: Post-War Challenges,* ed., J. W. Harbeson and D. Rothchild (Boulder, San Francisco, and Oxford: Westview Press, 1995).

7   Crawford Young, "Africa's Colonial Legacy," in *Strategies for African Development,* ed., R. J. Berg and J. S. Whitaker (Berkeley: University of California Press, 1986).

8   Homi Bhabha, *The Location of Culture* (London–New York: Routledge, 1994).

9   See afrikaworld.net/afrel/atr-popes.html.

10   For a clear discussion on the distinction between adaptation and incarnation, see Aylward Shorter, *African Christian Theology* (London: Geoffrey Chapman, 1975).

11   Frantz Fanon, *Wretched of the Earth* (New York: Grove Books, 1965).

12   Ngũgĩ wa Thiong'o, *Decolonising the Mind,* 1986, apracticalpolicy. org/2009/04/02/ngugi-wa-thiong%E2%80%99o-decolonising-the-mind.

13   Sabine Jell Bahlsen, "Slaughter for the Gods – Who will remember the Igbo story? Owu Masquerade as an important repository of indigenous knowledge, culture and history," in *Africa After Fifty Years: Retrospections and Reflections,* ed., Toyin Falola, Maurice Amutabi, and Sylvester Gundona (London: Africa World press, 2013), 55–77.

14   Shorter, *African Christian Theology,* 146.

15   Ikenye, Ndun'gu JB, "Pastoral Care and Counseling g in the African ethnic Context," in *Our Burning Issues: A Pan African Response,* ed., Edison M. Kalengyo, James N. Amanze, and Isaac Deji Ayegboyin (Nairobi: AACC, 2013), 221–43.

16   R. Willis, *There Was a Certain Man: Spoken Art of the Fipa* (London: Oxford University Press, 1978), 98.

17   Maria Crosz-Ngaté and H. Kokole Omari, eds., *Gendered Encounters: Challenging Cultural Boundaries and Social Hierarchies in Africa* (New York: Routledge, 1997), 1.

18   Stuart Hall, "Negotiating Caribbean Identities," in *New Caribbean Thought: A Reader,* ed., Brian Meeks and Folke Lindahl (Kingston, Jamaica: The University of the West Indies Press, 2001), 37-38.

19   J.N.K. Mugambi, *From Liberation to Reconstruction: African Christian Theology After the Cold War* (Nairobi: East African Publishers, 1995).

20   Andre Karamaga, "Ethnicity in Africa: An Overview" in Kalengyo et al., *Our Burning Issues,* 177–84.

21   Shorter, *African Christian Theology,* 30.

Christ in the *'Argànona Màryàm*: Theology in the Ethiopian Christian Tradition

Daniel Assefa

This chapter aims at showing the significance of Christology[1] in a fifteenth-century text entitled *'Argānona Māryām (AM)*.[2] Written in classical Ethiopic by Giorgis of Gasiccha, an Ethiopian monk,[3] the *AM* is a series of prayers and praises addressed to Mary, the mother of Christ. The word *'Argānon* means the "organ" or "harp" (of Mary).

My choice of such a text might lead to the following questions: Why look for Christological themes in a devotional text that praises mainly Mary? Why not take an Ethiopian work dedicated solely to Christ? The Ethiopian devotion to Mary, who has several feasts throughout the year, seems in the eyes of an outside observer to be exaggerated. A close study of Ethiopian Marian texts shows, however, that the mystery of Christ is indeed given a central place in Ethiopian Mariology. The *AM* has the advantage of combining theological richness and popularity,[4] unlike some texts that, despite their significant theological content, are read by only a few scholars.[5]

Even though the author of the *AM* constantly addresses Mary, Christ is omnipresent throughout the text. According to the author, Mary is great because Christ is more than great. Thus the choice is made, among other things, to show that many Ethiopian Marian texts are deeply Christological.[6]

This chapter has two parts; the first deals with the literary characteristics of the *AM*, and the second focuses on the Christian teachings we can draw from the text.

1. The Literary Aspects of the *AM*

The *AM* is a poetic text with sections assigned to each day of the week.[7] For the most part, transitions from one week to the next are marked by concluding doxologies and introductions to the following section or week.

These introductions and conclusions are of a Trinitarian character. The introduction of the *AM* of Saturday (p. 341) is a good example.

> In the name of God the Father who loved your purity,
> In the name of the God the Son who dwelled in your womb,
> In the name of God the Holy Spirit who liked your shade.

Although the author speaks most of the time to Mary throughout the book, from time to time, he also invokes the persons of the Trinity (cf. pp. 109–20). The prayer can also be more specific and directed to Christ (e.g., pp. 125ff), in which he confesses that the Son of God existed before the creation of the world and that he is the Son of God the Father and a human being (son of Man) in his incarnation. The author raises his hands to heaven and implores Christ with a long prayer in the *AM* of Sunday (pp. 379ff). Mary, mother of Christ, is mother of God (*Theotokos;* cf. pp. 369, 386).

1.1 The Style of the AM

The *AM* is poetic. The sentences follow by and large a regular rhythm. Many sentences are parallel, starting in similar ways or even with similar words, especially accompanied with exclamatory terms. Throughout the text, there are numerous sentences that start with the words "O! Virgin," "Oh! Lady" or "O! Mary" (e.g., pp. 41ff).[8] On the *AM* of Wednesday, the author repeatedly starts several sentences with the word *amān'kē*, meaning "truly";[9] then comes the word *laki*, meaning "to you,"[10] to introduce a series of new sentences. This is followed by a string of new sentences beginning with the word *'ebel*, "I say."[11] Then comes a group of sentences introduced by the expression *tazakarani'egzio*, "remember me, O Lord."[12]

On the *AM* of Thursday (pp. 225–26), the author shows the huge gap that exists between his little stature and the greatness of Mary through twenty-four successive sentences, each of which is introduced by the word *wasōba*, meaning "and when". All this and more examples of intense repetitions of words and exclamations make the *AM* a very solemn text.

1.2 Rhymes

Although written in prose, the *AM* contains an impressive number of sentences or phrases with rhymes, difficult to notice in other versions in

Amharic or any other language. The *AM* of Sunday, for instance, makes a start with three sentences that rhyme while describing the actions of each person of the Holy Trinity (cf. p. 378):

> In the name of God who strengthened (Anha) the power of your (Mary's) reign (…ha)
> In the name of God the Son who was carried in your womb for nine months (awraha)
> In the name of the Holy Spirit who made your path (zasarha)

1.3 Personification

The earth and the mountains revere Mary because she embraced the one who makes them stay firm, the one who stretched them out. The seas and the rivers tell the greatness of Mary because she carried in her narrow womb the one who broadens the cleft of the waters (p. 43). Fire, flame, and thunders confess the glory of Mary, for she touched with her hands Christ, whereas the seraphim (made of fire) angels tremble (p. 44).

1.4 A Metaphorical Language[13]

The author keeps on admiring the mystery of incarnation; he does not find enough words to describe it. He therefore uses all kinds of examples, metaphors, and images to exalt what God did through Christ and through Mary.

Therefore, Mary, a blessed plant with extraordinary fragrance, is also compared with different kinds of plants.[14] Nevertheless, the metaphors are almost always Christocentric. They are not so much inspired by what Mary did by herself or who Mary is in herself; they are rather about what Mary did and who she is in connection with Christ. According to the *AM* of Monday, Mary is a mandrake,[15] olive tree,[16] fig tree,[17] almond tree,[18] lily (Song of Songs 2:2), vine,[19] and the burning bush.[20]

Besides these connections with plants, one finds an impressive amount of other metaphors. Mary is the golden chalice that keeps Jesus, the sacramental wine (p. 230ff). She is the golden censer that keeps Jesus, the divine, live coal.[21] Mary is heaven, giving birth to Jesus, the Sun of righteousness.[22] The expression "Sun of righteousness," found in Malachi 4:2, has been interpreted both by a number of Church fathers and the traditional Ethiopian biblical commentary as a reference to Christ.[23]

Mary is called the holy place of Horeb, where a rock on which God stood is found. And that rock was Christ (p. 296). This is inspired by 1 Corinthians 10:4. Mary is Zion, the tabernacle of the God of Israel; in other words, Christ is the God of Israel (p. 296). Mary is perfumed oil by which Jesus Christ, the High Priest and the King of kings, has been anointed since he took her flesh (p. 298). At this point, the definition of "Christos" as the anointed One is given and reference is made to Cyril of Alexandria.

1.5 Paradoxes

The mystery of incarnation is underlined through paradoxical language. Mary, a creature, has carried Jesus, who carries everything; Jesus is the rain of mercy. Mary has fed Jesus, who nourishes all life. Mary, a human being, has contained in her womb Jesus, a terrible fire. The author affirms that angels praise Mary because she gave birth to the one who created them. Human beings and animals praise Mary because she fed with milk the one who feeds all living beings (p. 43).

A contrast between three births that did not satisfy the author and the birth of Christ, the incarnation, is made at the beginning of the *AM* (cf. p. 4ff). Neither the birth of Adam from the earth (cf. 1 Enoch 85) nor the birth of Eve from Adam's side, nor the birth of Cain were of benefit for the author. But the birth of Christ brought about salvation to the author and to nations.

The birth of Christ deserves praise and adoration, exaltation, chant, power, submission, hymn, acclaim, (pp. 17–18); the author admires the mystery of the incarnation: fire and water are united in Mary; Christ, the ruler of the world, has been laid in the manger; Christ, whom heaven cannot carry, has been contained in the manger; on page 19ff, the crib is praised because Christ, the Lord of the powerful ones, was born in it. According to the author, the crib surpasses respectively the chariot and the throne seen by the prophets Ezekiel and Daniel.

The city of Bethlehem became like heaven (p. 20); instead of the natural sun, there came out Christ, the Sun of righteousness; the natural sun sets, but Christ is a Sun that never sets; it shines always on the saints.

1.6 A Remarkable Trio

In several metaphors or perhaps allegories, the author, Mary, and Christ form a trio. The author affirms he is someone who is thirsty, while Mary is a golden jar, and her Son a well of life-giving water. Here the Christian, through the example of the poet, can assert that he thirsts for Christ; (pp. 223ff). Christ is also a pearl, whereas the author is a pilgrim (a traveler) looking to purchase a divine pearl, and Mary is the ark (ship) that facilitates the travel. Christ, Mary's Son, is a place of profit in which the treasures of all good things are found. Again here, the author considers himself like any Christian, a pilgrim in search of a treasure. Christ is the target from whom treasures are drawn.

The treasure is not material because the pearl sought after by the pilgrim is connected with divinity (*malakot*). The motif is inspired by Jesus teaching or parables on the kingdom of heaven in Matthew 13:45–46. The author situates himself in the place of the character of the parable; he applies the more general features of a given individual to a personal situation.

One may say he identifies Jesus with the kingdom of heaven when he affirms that Mary's Son is the seat or source of that treasure. Finally, he inserts a person in that parable, that is, Mary, the means by which he attains the treasure.

One new element is also the motif of sea travel. In Matthew 13:46, it is not clear by which means (sea or land) the merchant in search of fine pearls was traveling. The *AM* imagines a merchant who travels by sea and presents the ship, the means of transportation, as a symbol of Mary.

The poet is eager to reach the dwelling place of light. Mary is the bridge, and Jesus is that dwelling of happiness and the consolation of the oppressed. The author is a poor person willing to receive the wealth of the Holy Spirit; Mary, the coffer of all glory; and Christ, the beauty of all ornament, glory, and splendor.

Giorghis is the one who asks Mary, the one who offers the prayers, and Jesus, the one who forgives the sins and bestows grace. He is wounded while Mary is the vessel of medicine and Jesus is the physician. He is rotten because of sins and seeking the perfume of the saints, whereas Mary is a bottle of perfume and Jesus the divine oil with more fragrance than any sweet-smelling perfume. He is naked while Mary is the loom and Christ the cloth of faith, which is incorruptible.[24]

In this trio, a huge contrast is depicted between the prayer, who speaks in the first person, and Christ. The author describes himself as the worst sinner, the perpetrator of all kinds of transgressions, but he also affirms there is no greater merciful Lord, far from punishing, abundant in forgiveness, and righteous as the Son of Mary.

1.7 Foils for Christ (pp. 232ff)

Christ's superiority is repeatedly underlined in the *AM* through a comparison with OT figures. Despite their greatness, they lack something that is found in Christ only; they are just foils for Christ. Abel was killed mischievously by his brother Cain, but his blood did not give power to anybody, whereas Christ's blood (the fruit of Mary's womb) redeemed Adam and his children. Enoch pleased God and escaped death; he received life on account of his own justice; however, his justice was not sufficient to give life to others. But Jesus tasted death and brought about life; he was the Savior through his death, which gave life to the dead.

Noah was loved by God and escaped with his family from the danger of death, but he did not save any others from the flood. Jesus, however, saves nations through the power of the cross. Abraham is found faithful; he was called the father of many. He was given the sign of circumcision; despite so many blessings and privileges, he was not able to save people from Sheol. On the contrary, Mary's Son saved many through his death.

Isaac was given as sacrifice, but he did not save others except that he himself was replaced by a lamb of sacrifice; but the Son of Mary, becoming the Lamb of sacrifice, saved many through the shedding of his blood.

Moses was exalted among the children of Israel; God spoke to him face to face (Exodus 33:11); although he stood in front of the glory of God, he was not able to save himself and others from the power of death; but the Savior and helper of whom Moses prophesied dwelt among us.

Aaron was high priest who received much wealth from God; He became a portion for his Creator, endowed and embellished with religious garments; he was like a star who offered sacrifices. But Mary's Son willingly sacrificed himself and saved many through the shedding of his blood.

Neither the manna from heaven nor the water that gushed out from the rock saved the people (cf. John 6), but greatness, beauty, and salvation came from Christ. Those who listened to the oracle of the prophet Jonah (pp. 247–48) and repented escaped from the punishment of this world, but they did not escape from the punishment coming from heaven. Christ remained for three days in the "belly" of the earth, preached to the souls of Sheol, and liberated them from the power of death.

The prophets Zechariah, Habakkuk, Daniel, and many other biblical figures and prophets also are contrasted to the surpassing grace accomplished through Christ. Toward the end of the *AM* of Thursday (p. 256), one finds a summary of all the comparisons somewhat close to Pauline theology (cf. Romans 5:14ff and Galatians 3) but also reminiscent of the letter to the Hebrews, which enumerates a number of remarkable people of faith who still needed the coming of Christ to receive what was promised (cf. Hebrews 11:39). The text of the *AM* reads,

> From Adam to Moses no one was supposed to subdue himself to God since the Law was not given. From Moses up to John the Baptist people were called to abide by the Torah. Nevertheless no one was able to save himself from the power of Sheol. This was until Mary's Son came in the image of human beings, and took flesh which is corruptible in order to introduce in it incorruptibility.

2. A Creed: Christ, God the Father, and Mary

In the *AM*, one finds something close to the creed but in a form of a prayer addressed to Christ by the author (pp. 115–17). Thus, the author confesses,

> I believed (Oh) Lord that You are source from Source, Divine Nature from Divine Nature, Lord from Lord, Life from Life; I believed Oh Lord that You are the begotten from the one who begets, Splendor from Light, Wisdom from the Sea of Knowledge; I believed in You (Oh) Lord that You are the First-born for the One (God the Father) and for the other (Mary) who begot You; the Only begotten for the One who begot You. Your birth from above is different from your birth from below. Your birth in Heaven is different from your birth on Earth. Your first birth is Fire of Life (found from fire of Life). Your later birth remains the Word born of a Woman. Your first birth is hidden from the world. Your later birth is from a Virgin, through the Announcing. Your first birth is Power derived from Power. Your later birth is divine power from a Daughter. I tried to grasp your first birth but I could not find it. I considered your later birth and I admired it. I praised your first birth while unable to reach it. And I invoked your later birth through genuflection and prostration. Your first birth came to be known through your later birth. Your divine birth was praised by your virginal birth. When you were born from a Virgin, your birth form the Father became revealed.

2.1 Mutual Knowledge of the Persons of the Holy Trinity

No one knows the Father except the Son and the Holy Spirit; no one knows the Son except the Father and the Holy Spirit; no one knows the Holy Spirit except the Son and the Father (cf. p. 381). The text continues: there is no council of the one of the persons of the Holy Trinity hidden to the other two persons of the Trinity (381ff). Moreover, the Father does not precede the Son because he begot Him. The Son does not come after the Father because He is born from Him.

No one knows how the Father begot the Son, and no one knows how Jesus was born. How do we know the Holy Spirit is a person? We know it because Christ (you) promised the apostles he will send another "Paraclete," the Holy Spirit (p. 383).

The Holy Spirit comforts those who are in chains for the love of Christ. The Father loved Mary. The Son became flesh; the Holy Spirit covered her. The author asks for Mary's intercession so her Son may send him the Holy Spirit; that would allow him to practice righteousness (pp. 310–11). He thus wishes to be the dwelling place of the Holy Spirit, having his soul purified and his body sanctified.

2.2 References to Christ's Earthly Life and Ministry

The author implores for blessings in the name of Mary and of the deeds of Christ on earth, like the miracle of Cana, the cleansing of the man who had leprosy, the chasing away of the evil spirits, the healing of the paralytic, the opening of the eyes of the man who was blind, his passion, his crucifixion, the entrusting of Mary to the beloved disciple at the cross, his drinking of myrrh, his death (the leaving of his soul), his burial, his ascension, his sitting at the right of the Father, and the eschatological wedding prepared by Christ, who is the bridegroom (pp. 304–08).

Christ used to change his color in the womb of Mary, and due to that, Mary's appearance was also changing (p. 94). That is an interpretation of Matthew 1:24–25. Joseph did not know her until she had born a son. This would mean, according to the author, "he did not recognise her" until she gave birth. Once the child was born, Joseph did not have a problem in the sense that her appearance stopped to change as it had when the child was in her womb.

2.3 Titles of Christ in the AM

Without being exhaustive, the following titles illustrate well the Christo-centric character of the *AM*. The author affirms that Christ is Lord (p. 10), a Savior, a cure for the souls who are in Sheol (p. 33), the God of the "God of Daniel who tames lions" (p. 220), the lamb of sacrifice (Isaiah 53:7; cf. p. 49), a heavenly lamb (p. 51), lamb and priest (pp. 177–78), a heavenly high priest (p. 187), the fountain of mercy (p. 174), the Word (p. 292), the Emmanuel, the fragrance of saints (p. 175),[25] the ruler of all the world (p. 187), "our God who became man," the one who fills the whole world (p. 299), the one who breathed into the nostrils of Adam (p. 300), and a heavenly star (178).

2.4 The Uniqueness of Christ's Blood

Christ sacrificed himself on the cross; he sprinkled with his blood the faithful; he sealed them with the pouring of his blood (p. 97). The blood of Christ is different from that of Abel, who accused his brother for vengeance (Genesis 4:10). The blood of Christ brought about forgiveness and an end to all vengeance (p. 98). The Eucharistic blood is different from the blood of Naboth (1 Kings 21:13); it is rather the divine blood sacrificed for his sheep (cf. John 10; p. 98). Christ's blood is different from the blood of lambs sacrificed by Aaron's children; that blood was unable to cancel sin; it was rather the blood of the Lamb of God that carried the sinners of the world (p. 98; Hebrews 10:4–5). Christ's blood has been poured out at Calvary at the time of Jewish Passover (cf. John's gospel). The blood is poured perpetually (99).

2.5 Mary and the Eucharist

Mary is a golden *Masob* (a round basket table around which a family sits for meals and upon which the food is put; p. 177). The food on the golden *Masob* is the Eucharist. The author asks Mary to help him be ready to receive fittingly the Eucharist, the manna, the eternal food of righteousness, the offering of salvation. Mary is also the golden chalice that contains the wine, sacrament of the saints mixed with the fragrance of the Holy Spirit (pp. 177, 230).

The author poetically expresses his admiration for what the priest does when he touches and offers the divine host (p. 50). The body of Christ is fire, and it is amazing to have a priest who touches all this with his hand. The priestly ministry is praised, especially due to Eucharistic overtones. The priest is touching the untouchable (p. 51). Christ united himself with the faithful by offering and sharing his body and blood; thus, he sanctified our bodies and allowed us to receive the Holy Spirit (Epiclesis; pp. 95–96). The one who eats from Christ will not die; the one who drinks from his blood is not corrupted (p. 49).

Christ is of the same nature of the Father and the Holy Spirit; one without separation, equal face (aspect or appearance, equal divinity; p. 184); one without addition, one without subtraction, one without precedence, one without being afterward, whose nature is beyond comprehension; which cannot be described by saying: "from here up to here"; first without beginning; last without end, from ever and ever. Amen.

2.6 Eschatology

Two exceptional births are admired. A unique birth took place before the beginning from the God the Father (p. 358); and in the last days, a unique birth happened from the virgin. The author prays Mary to help him lead a good Christian life "Until your Son comes in the glory of his Father and the Holy Spirit" (p. 287). Jesus says, "When the Son of man comes in his glory" (cf. Matthew 27:31). Unlike the gospel, the author refers to the glory of the Father and the Holy Spirit.

On page 312, more-detailed reference is made to the eschatological banquet prepared by Christ. The author wishes to enter in the wedding house of heaven through the intercession of Mary (p. 89).

2.7 Christ and the Church

The passion of Christ is connected with the birth of the Church. Moreover, the birth of the faithful from the Church, which is taken as a bride by Christ, is underlined. Christ is thus the bridegroom of the Church (p. 32). The Church, adorned and protected by Mary, is the bride of Christ (p. 37). The gate of the Church has been sprinkled with the blood of Christ

(p. 38). The Church came to be thanks to the death of Christ and obtains consolation through the resurrection of Christ (p. 38). It praises Mary, for she is baptised by the water that came out from the side of her Son and was sealed by his blood (pp. 38–39). The Church, spouse of Emmanuel, the lamb of the Highest God, praises Mary (p. 39). Angels too are invited to join the author in his praise of Mary (pp. 190–99).

Christ mixed his highness with the lowness of the Church. He took the death of the Church and gave it his life. Christ came down from above for the love of the Church. Christ suffered for her sake (p. 40). Through his resurrection, Christ gave her eternal life. Through his ascension, Christ exalted her and united her to himself. He offered her to his Father. Therefore, the Church burns with the love of Christ (pp. 40–41).

Similarly, the author connects the cross and the pierced side of Christ with the sacramental water of baptism, the source of salvation (p. 32). The idea itself is presented as an antitype to the covering of Adam by a leaf from God ("And the LORD God made for Adam and for his wife garments of skins, and clothed them" Genesis 3:21 RSV).

2.8 Spirituality

Ghiorgis repeatedly confesses he is a big sinner and needs divine mercy through the intercession of Mary. He affirms how little, imperfect, and weak he is. He contrasts his misconduct with Mary's sanctity and Christ's greatness. The Word of God is choked by the thorn of sins (cf. Mark 4:7) because of love of money, luxury, and deceitfulness (p. 323).The author enumerates a number of vices such as killing, calumny, lying, sorcery (or adultery), empty words, and going astray from the teaching of the apostles, from which he wants Marian protection (pp. 394–95).

The author prays so that the Spirit of Christ may reside in him and transform him (p. 324). He wants to be his temple (cf. 1 Corinthians 3, 6). He wishes Christ to sanctify his mouth so he may praise Mary. He is vivified by the offering of the body and blood of the Christ, beloved to Mary (pp. 328–29). He is sanctified with the blood of Christ, which is poured from his pierced side. A strong connection is made between the crucified and the Eucharist.

Mary is implored so that the blood of her Son may not be in vain (p. 232). Christ has redeemed the author by his blood, and Mary should pray so the precious work of Christ may not be futile. Mary is the mother of the Christ, the physician, and the author is wounded by sin. He prays to be healed of his wounds (p. 349).

With a very humble attitude, the author makes a long prayer of confession of sin. He borrows the expression from the Prodigal Son of Luke 15 (p. 389). The author continues by affirming that he is not worthy to enter into God's house (sanctuary) and to stand before the altar before the blood that speaks louder than the blood of Abel the righteous.

The strong Ethiopian reverence for the Eucharist is reflected in the confession of the author, who is afraid to eat the divine fire (the Eucharist) since he is not worthy. The author prays that Christ may receive him, may forgive him, and may introduce him inside the curtain[26] to receive the body and the blood of Christ (p. 391). The author hopes that Christ will make him share from the sacred sacraments that sanctify both body and soul. He wants to be counted among the people to whom Christ said, "the one who eats my body and drink my blood does not taste death. He does not want to be separated from the wedding because of not having a wedding garment" (cf. Matthew 22:11). And, according to the text, the wedding garment is "purple" (*mēlat*) of the righteousness of the saints.

Conclusion

The author of the *AM* cannot but love the Virgin Mary. His love of her is not, though, of his own initiative; it is rather a gift from God (p. 288), something the Lord would have put in his heart. In the *AM*, poetry is so intertwined with Christian doctrine that it is difficult to separate the two without losing something of its vigor and beauty. This chapter has tried to show both in a limited way. The literary splendor of the *AM* is much better experienced when one reads it in its original language.

The option of the author is to make poetry at the service of theology, as one may find in several other Ethiopian Marian texts. Behind the literary masterpiece, one detects a strong desire to reach divine mysteries, a deep sense of gratitude toward the marvels of the incarnation and of the cross, an extraordinary love for Christ and, through and because of Christ, of Mary.

The main source of the *AM* is the Bible.[27] The author derives symbols, images, and metaphors from Scripture. One cannot help admiring the author's outstanding knowledge of the Bible and his command of typological reading of OT figures and events. His Mariology is Christocentric. He situates himself in the trio, where he admires Christ and Mary so close to one another and rather far from him. While humbly confessing constantly his littleness, he expresses his deep longing to draw near to Christ and Mary through conversion, praise, and the Eucharist.

Today, a significant number of Ethiopians pray with the *AM*. Given that much of the text is written in the first person, readers can identify themselves with the humble and generous poet. The author has hence succeeded in delivering a work that touches the hearts of many people.

Endnotes

1   According to Grillmier, Ethiopian Christology has made a synthesis between an interpretation of Christ with Old Testament–Jewish categories, and this with unusual strength; a clear Nicean Christology from above. See A. Grillmeier and T. Hainthaler, 1990 (English translation 1996). *Christ in Christian Tradition: Christ in a New Messianic Kingdom Faith in Christ in Ethiopia.* Vol. 2, part 4, 371.

2   The text is also known by the name *'Argānona Dengel* (organ of the virgin) *or 'Argānona Wuddassē* (organ of praise).

3   There is a debate as to the identity of the author. See Cerulli, 1968. *La letteratura etiopica. L'oriente Cristiano nell'unità delle sue tradizioni.* Roma: Sansoni, 223; Ricci, 1969. "Letterature dell' Etiopia" in *Storie delle Letterature d'Oriente.* Milano, 816. Tadesse Tamrat, 1972. *Church and State in Ethiopia 1270–1527.* Oxford: Clarendon, 222. Concerning the biography of Giorgis, see Colin, 1987. *Vie de Georges de Sagla.* Louvain (CSCO 492, 493) SAe 81, 82; Derat, M-L 1999. *La Sainteté de Gyiorgis de Sagla: une initiative royale?* Warszawskie Studia Teologiczne XII/2/1999, 51–62.

4   There are several texts of this nature in Ethiopian literature. The *Wuddassē Maryam*, literally, "praises of Mary," traditionally attributed to St Ephrem of Syria, is daily recited by most of the Orthodox faithful. For some translations and studies on Ethiopian Marian works, see Grohmann, 1919, *Aethiopische Marienhymnen. Abhandlungen der Philosophisch-historischen Klasse der Saechsischen Akademie der wissenschaften,* Band 33, n. 4. Leipizig: Getachew Haile, 192. The Mariology of Emperor Zera Yaeqof of Ethiopia Text and Translations in *Orientalia Christiana Analecta* 242. Roma: PIO. Tedros Abraha, 2006. "I Canti del tempo dell' Assuntanelrito Etiopico" in *Marianum* 68, 153–206; Pietros Ghebresellassie 2007. *Il Feudo di Maria. Identità Cristiana e devozione mariana del popolo Abissino (Etiopia/Eritrea). Corigliano D'Otranto;* Mroczek, *Il volto Etiopico della Madre di Dio. Un invitodel Santo Padre Giovanni Paolo II a una spiritualità mariana ecumenica.*

5   *Maṣḥāfa Mesṭir*, written by the same author of the *AM* is a case in point.

6   In front of a painting in which Mary is represented alone, the question is put, "Where is her child?" The reader of '*Argānona Māryām* will soon realise that Christological controversies very much common in a number of Ethiopian theological writings are practically absent. For a synthesis of the debates on Christological positions held by various Ethiopian scholars and the corresponding bibliography, see Tesfazghi Uqbit, 1973. *Current Christological Positions of Ethiopian Orthodox Theologians*. Roma: Pont. Institutum Orientalium. One major theme for theological discussions and disputes concerns "Christ as the anointed one"; Grillmeier and Hainthaler, 1990 (English translation 1996). *Christ in Christian Tradition: Christ in a New Messianic Kingdom Faith in Christ in Ethiopia*. Vol. 2 part 4, 341–54. Concerning the interpretation of the episode of Jesus' baptism; ibid, 355ff.

7   I am referring to a published edition entitled *Maṣḥāfa Argānon (ṣalotala Māryam), Book of Argānon (prayers of Mary)*, Addis Abeba: Tensāe, 1996 Ethiopian calendar (2004 Gregorian calendar). The text is rather long; it has 29,800 words. In this book, the prayers of each day of the week are structured as follows. Monday: pages 8–64; Tuesday: 65–128; Wednesday: 129–96; Thursday: 197–272; Friday: 273–334; Saturday: 335–370; Sunday: 371–408. A critical edition of the *AM* was published in 1922 by Leander; cf. Leander, P. 1922. *Arganona Ueddassenach Handschriften in Upsala*. Berlin. A German translation of the parts of the text has been made at different times by Euringer between 1927 and 1931. Cf. Sebastian Euringer, in OrChr 24, 1927 (120–45; 338–55), OrChr 25–26, 1929 (79–108; 248–78), OrChr 27, 1930, (202–31); OrChr 28, 1931 (60–89; 209–39).

8   The expression "The church praises you" reflecting the relationship between Mary and the Church, is found at the beginning of nine sentences (cf. pp. 38–40).

9   For instance, one would read, "Truly, you [Virgin Mary] deserve to be praised."

10   One example is: "To you is due reverence…"

11   I say [about you] that you are more beautiful than the Sun, lovelier than the moon.

12   The technical term for this literary type is "anaphora," which "intensifies expressive efficacy through the repetition of one or more words at the beginning of successive sentences, clauses, phrases, or parts thereof," e.g., Jeremiah 51:20–23; Psalm 29:1–2; cf. Bazylinski, S. 2009. *A Guide to Biblical Research*. Roma: Gregorian and Biblical, 168–69.

13   In the gospel of John, one finds several metaphors: light, water, bread, truth, way, life, vine, door, shepherd, and other elements; they serve to explain the rich identity of Christ. For the symbolic language in John's gospel, see Culpepper, R. A. 1983, *Anatomy of the Fourth Gospel: A Study in Literary Design*. Philadelphia: Fortress, 180–98.

14   After the botanic images, the *AM* compares Mary to precious stones. It is noteworthy that all the botanical and mineral images are drawn from the Scripture.

15   The story of Genesis 30:14–18, especially with the emphasis on the meaning of name Issachar, becomes a type for Mary, the cross, the blood of Christ, and the birth of the church; cf. Daniel Assefa, "Les references bibliques dans l'Arganone Wuddassie" *Transversalités 85*, Janvier-Mars 2003, 77.

16   A link is made between the oil of the olive tree and the chrism of baptism.

17   A connection is made between Adam and Eve, who make themselves aprons (Genesis 3:7–8) and the protection from the shame of the individual thanks to the baptism coming through the Son of Mary.

18   The rod of Aaron that brought forth buds and produced almonds (Numbers 17:8) becomes a type for the virginal birth.

19   Allusion is made to the greetings of Elisabeth in Luke 1:43 (the fruit of Mary's womb) and the blood of the Eucharist (cf. John 6:55).

20   The news of Israel's liberation in Genesis 3 and 6 becomes the type of the salvation of Christians.

21   In the Anaphora of Holy Mary, Mother of God, one reads, "The Father is fire, The Son is fire, the Holy Spirit is fire, but it is one fire of life in the highest heaven."

22   Christ is in fact repeatedly compared with the sun and with light (cf. pp. 1, 44, 170, 230, 364).

23   Some Church fathers make a Christological reading of Malachi 4:2; Ephrem the Syrian (Commentary on Tatian's Diatessaron; ECTD 58–59); Valentine (Letter 216; Valentine to Augustine), Ambrose (Fathers of Church: A New Translation. Washington, D.C: Catholic University of America, 1947, 42:129; Six Days of Creation 4:1.2; Jacob and the Happy Life 7:30–31), Chrysostom (Against the Anomoeans, Homily 7:5–6), Jerome (Homily 94; Fathers of Church, 57:253); John of Damascus (Orthodox Faith Fathers of Church, 37:352–53); Origen (Homilies on Leviticus 9:10.2; Fathers of Church 83:199); Theodoret of Cyr (Commentary on Malachi 4:2; PG 81:1984).

24   In the Anaphora of Holy Mary the Mother of God, one reads, "O virgin, full of glory, with whom and with what likeness shall we liken you? You are the loom from which Emmanuel took his ineffable garment of flesh."

25   A vocabulary reminiscent of Paul's imagery that speaks of God spreading fragrance over the believers through Christ in 2 Corinthians 2:14–15; the author asks Mary to help him become an aroma of holiness (*AM*, p. 175).

26   On the theological significance of the curtain itself as symbol for the body of Christ, cf. Bandrés, J 2008. *A Glance behind the Curtain: Reflections on the Ethiopian Celebration of the Eucharist*. Addis Abeba: Master, 184–97.

27   To appreciate how much Marian hymns written in Ethiopic have a biblical background, see the numerous biblical quotations in the footnotes of Tedros Abraha, 2006, "I Canti del tempo dell' Assuntanelrito Etiopico" in *Marianum* 68, 153–206.

PART TWO

AFRICAN THEOLOGY: METHODS AND MODELS

Methods and Models of African Theology

Stan Chu Ilo

In his postsynodal apostolic exhortation, *Africae Munus*, Pope Benedict XVI called on African theologians to come up with transformative theologies that could give birth to practical ministry in which the great perspectives found in Scripture and tradition find application in the activity of bishops and priests in specific times and places.[1] He further prayed for the birth of new theological schools in Africa that would furnish today's Africa and the universal Church with great theologians and spiritual masters who could contribute to the sanctification of Africa and the Church.[2]

There is the need then to propose some helpful approaches to doing theology in Africa for the renewal of faith and cultures in Africa through the agency of Christianity. Such theologies will significantly depart from defunct Western theologies that are very marginal in the West but still predominant in African theological faculties and Churches.

This chapter argues that cross-cultural currents (African traditional religions and worldviews, missionary factors, African social context, African-initiated churches, African Pentecostalism, and globalisation) shape the development of different approaches to theology in Africa. African theologies are attempts at different levels to account for these cultural currents, to integrate them in shaping the narrative and direction of Christian life and praxis, as well as ecclesial practices and priorities. Theological formulations in Africa thus underlie the narrative of Christianity by African Christians at the specific level of religiocultural experience in a changing and challenging social context.

I will first clarify what one does when one is doing African theology and what I understand by theological method and model. I will propose seven shifts needed in doing African theology today that can enrich current approaches to African theology. I will conclude by laying the outline of a narrative cultural hermeneutical African theological approach and why it should be central to methods in African theology while offering some

propositions on the relevance of African theologies to the most pressing
questions facing African Christianity today.

1. What Am I Doing When I Am Doing African Theology? What Is "Method" in African Theology?

Let me begin by clarifying what I understand by "theological method."
First, a theological method gives an account of the lived faith of the people.
Theology does not exist prior to faith and culture; rather, theology exits
because of faith and leads back to faith and lived life. Thus, a theological
method is conceived in this chapter as a cultural mediation that could provide either a prison or a palace. It could be a prison that shuts me off from
other perspectives when I am locked up in a dogmatic monad or frozen in
a particular theological system. It could, on the other hand, be my palace
in which I find my home because my theological formulations are relevant
to my life and that of my community of faith; theology thus becomes a
channel for gracing my life of faith and for embracing the members of my
faith community in their commitment to the wisdom and ways of God.

Second, a theological method makes intelligible the lived faith of the
church as it crosses different cultural frontiers. Viewed in this light, a theological method is not an invention of a person but the realisation in written
or oral form of a pattern of *intellectus fidei* and performances rooted in the
experience of a faith community as its members respond to the call from
God who reveals God's love in Christ in particular and universal historical
contexts. Theology searches for and identifies in history God's purposes for
humanity and the cosmos as revealed in Christ (*Dei Verbum,* no. 2).

Third, a theological method springs from the heart of faith as its
source, it should be governed by faith as a process, and it transforms
cultures and societies through faith and transmission of faith and life
as its goal. Thus, a theologian without a strong faith will flounder in
developing a theological method, and a theological method that does
not enrich, deepen, and guide the living faith of people is empty. A
theological method shows how God reveals, summons, and enables God's
people to live new lives in Christ with new identities. Thus, a theological
method will offer not a normative *corpus magnum* to be replicated by
rote but a series of processes, activities, practices, and rigorous spiritual,
intellectual, aesthetic, and moral exercises that lead to a deepening of the

understanding of God's Word in the diverse contexts and manifestations of divine revelation in history.

Theological method guides the faith community in discovering the multiple dimensions of the reality of faith that help the believing community interpret and make judgments about what they believe, how they live authentically in the light of Christ, and the hope they have in Christ.

At the heart of any theological method is the explication of the meaning of what we believe, the justification of the reasons for belief, and the verification of the strengths and weaknesses of the rational conditions for our judgments about faith. These help the faith community to revise how doctrines are framed, how the moral inventory meets the ethical demands of the day, and the summons from God to communion with God, with one another, and the created world.

In this regard, theological method is viewed here as a process of accountability of the theologian in a community of faith to both God and the community of believers as to the meaning and relevance of faith to the deepest hunger of the human hearts and the deepest concerns of their daily lives while providing some firm foundations for hope beyond the complexities and joys of today and the pathways for a praxis of transformation through different levels of conversion towards both the proximate and ultimate good.

1.1 Models of African Theology

I understand "model" as a "root metaphor" that informs, influences, and inspires an identifiable pattern or process of doing theology in an attempt to make intelligible the mysteries we believe in and the mysteries we live. Models help us to enter into the "inner logic" of a theological approach or tradition with regard to certain criteria set out by the theological community of a certain region (for instance, Africa) or tradition (for instance, Catholicism) with regard to conformity with Scripture, rootedness in tradition, inner coherence, plausibility structures, illuminative power, practical and theoretical fruitfulness, and suitability for cross-cultural and intercultural dialogue and dialogues outside of its own received and acquired traditions.[3]

The challenge for African theologians and students of theology today is to study and celebrate the works of African theologians and to stand on their shoulders to develop their thoughts and build on what they have started. That is actually how theological methods and models emerge;

they have to be critically and creatively studied, received, appropriated, celebrated, and translated into different academic and pastoral contexts.

A study of specific theological developments in Africa reveals a radical and gradual paradigm shift in both themes and approaches in the search for appropriate models and methods. These shifts have been dictated by historical, theological, social, economic, political, missional, and cultural currents. African theological methodologies could, therefore, be identified and studied from two perspectives, historical (*chronos*) or typological (*topos*). In this regard, one can identify African theological methods and models either by concentrating on the clusters of themes they developed (ancestral Christology, theology of healing, theology of history, African pneumatology, African images of the Church, e.g., family of God, clan, etc). or the historical forces that influence these theologies (the publication of *Africae Terrarum*, colonialism in Africa, the first and second African synods, the genocide in Rwanda, the end of the Cold War, apartheid, the HIV/AIDS pandemic, civil unrest, and so on).[4]

Whichever path one follows in African theology, it is significant to note the constant thread that runs through each method. African theologies of inculturation move more towards typos and systems drawing from methodological formulation, principles, and guidelines for inculturation formulated in Europe or in magisterial sources. There are, however, some theologians such as Laurenti Magesa, Elochukwu Uzukwu, John Waligo, and Patrick Kalilombe who have been very creative in inculturation theologies beyond the narrow confines of normative inculturation and the normative notion of African cultures preferred by the institutional church.

Inculturation theologies in Africa privilege a correspondence-theory approach between an African category and an item in received Christian dogma (for instance, sacramental economy in the Catholic Church). Most inculturation theologies in Africa embrace the synthetic and translation models of contextualisation and operate from the presupposition of a normative notion of African culture. On the other hand, African liberation and reconstructionist theologies as well as African feminist, ecological, and transformational theologies rely heavily on historical and sociocultural analysis and operate from the perspectives of anthropological, countercultural, and praxis models of contextualisation.

While one can identify recurrent themes of liberation from oppression, issues of poverty, integral salvation and liberation, ethnic tension, the condition of African women, and prophetic rejection of structures of sin in African society and even within our ecclesial structures, the themes chosen have often been shaped more by historical forces than any other factors. They are concerned with the role of African Christianity in reversing this condition and shaping African history to conform to God's will and purposes.

My goal is not to examine particular methods in African theology but to offer a general outline for their understanding and analysis. I wish to point out four significant accomplishments of African theologies. The first is that African theological methods are paying attention to the richness, complexities, and ambiguities of unique, African stories. Thus, they show Africans have a voice in a world though that voice tends to be drowned out or distorted by the unequal power relations between Africa and the West, even within Christianity.

Second, African theologies have highlighted the unique mediation of God-in-history in African religiocultural groups and self-understanding as central to interpreting the past, understanding the present, and working toward a better future in Africa.

Third, African theologies place emphasis on the social, cultural, and religious challenges facing Africa and the place of Christianity in the search for transformative praxis for reversing the course of history. Thus, they are privileging African indigenous knowledge, African womanist perspectives, African initiatives in Christianity, and social transformation against the Northern epistemologies that predominate in the received Catholic theology from Rome.

Fourth, African theologies have opened the possibilities for and are actually giving a distinctive African Christian narrative to African worldviews and cultures as well as opening the African maps of the universe through a unique African account of God, evil, good, abundant life, family, the last things, ecology, and images of the church, among other things. There are obvious limitations in doing theology in Africa that I will address in the next sections.

1.2 Theological Method in African Theology

There are three fundamental questions I propose should foreground every African theological method. First, what does it mean to be an African theologian in the unacceptable social context of Africa and in the diversity and pluralistic climate of world Christianity? Second, what does it mean to be an African Catholic theologian in the context of today's Catholic Church with the tension and dynamism between the Roman center and the margins? Third, what is the locus of enunciation of the African theologian; whose voice or voices do I represent? Whose context am I mediating? Whose face or faces do I bear? Am I operating from a position of power and privilege? How do I locate the centre of my discourse at the very heart of the most pressing and relevant questions and challenges facing Africans at each point in time? These questions are seldom posed but seem to me decisive in specifying the path of discovery of the truth in my theological search and the pathways of presenting my theological conclusions to the community of faith broadly conceived.

A preliminary point to consider here is what I mean by African theology[5] before discussing the question of method. I argue that African theologies should be properly understood as African missional theologies because at the present time in African Christian history, theological reflections in Africa deal with the Christian faith crossing different cultural, social, and spiritual frontiers.

African theologies deal with the question of the presence or absence of God in African human and cultural history and the place and fate of Africans in their growing encounters with God through the exponential growth in African Christianity. Africans are doing theology from the margins, at the very edge of reality, and this requires a more expanded view of where God is at work in the social context and the relevance of this organic, human-divine encounter in the exercise of our human freedom.

In this light, theological projects in Africa will deal with a whole variety of realities and issues specific to Africa but potentially appearing irrelevant and even being irreverent to other cultural contexts outside Africa. Issues such as interfaith dialogue, ancestral traditions and curses, funeral rites, the meaning of family life, social and political activism, equity and diversity, the presumed ontological priority of ethnicity over national and Christian identities, poverty eradication, gender rights, and the rights of minorities offer data for theological analysis in African Christianity. This is because they point to where faith and culture intersect in the daily experience of the people who flock to churches in Africa. This is why at the heart of any theological method in Africa will be a narrative of what is going forward within history, how history has moved to this point in Africa, and the place of faith in reversing the course of painful history in Africa and making history in Africa conform to God's plan of abundant life understood as human and cosmic flourishing.

In this light, every good African theologian must be a good African historian who is attentive to the movement of history in Africa and who sensitively listens to and reveres the stories of our people as a way of hearing and knowing what God is revealing for Africa. This goes back beyond the distorted stories of Africa in many cultural, ecclesial, and historical narratives in and outside Africa. African theological engagement with African stories and histories should hark back to the first century, when the Lord Jesus walked the African soil, and even further back to the ancestral past, when God spoke to our fathers and mothers in many signs and languages and in shadows and images that pointed to the full revelation of God in Christ. Pope Benedict XVI also spoke in the same light when he said,

> In Jesus, some two thousand years ago, God himself brought salt and light to Africa. From that time on, the seed of his presence was buried deep within the hearts of the people of this dear continent, and it has blossomed gradually, beyond and within the vicissitudes of its human history.[6]

Many African theologians underlie the importance of a historical turn in African theology and historical forces in the shaping of Christian and cultural identities in Africa today. Mercy Amba Oduyoye, for instance, argues,

> We cannot expect those who cannot tell their story, who do not know where they come from, to hear God's call to his future. We cannot expect a people 'without a history' to respond as responsible human beings living in Africa. If their story is the same as the story of those who live in Europe and America, then they can only echo Euro-American responses.[7]

I emphasise this dimension of listening to the story of our people in the real faith questions of the poor, of the uneducated, of women, of the laity, of the struggling clerics and religious, and of the corrupt or wounded politicians.[8] Henry Okullu agrees with this when he writes,

> When we are looking for African theology we should go first to the fields, to the village church, to Christian homes to listen to those spontaneously uttered prayers before people go to bed. We should go to the schools, to the frontiers where traditional religions meet with Christianity. We must listen to the throbbing drumbeats and the clapping of hands accompanying the impromptu singing in the independent churches. Everywhere in Africa things are happening. Christians are talking, singing, preaching, writing, arguing, discussing. Can it be that this is an empty show? It is impossible. This then is African theology.[9]

The cultural hermeneutical approach in African theology I propose as the theological framework for methods in African theology is concerned with immersion into the narrative of faith and life in the African context that is the necessary starting point for a deeper analysis of ATRs, African histories, cultures, etc. This narrative immersion enables the theologian to "thickly" name, interpret, and understand the hidden cultural grammar and idioms that define African worldviews and influence the present momentum of Christian expansion in Africa. This approach argues that the African theologian must engage the question of conversion in African Christianity, especially seeking for an interpretation of the very flexible and permeable nature of religious affinity and loyalty to denominational ties in Africa.

African theology will be interested in the examination of the perennial culture lag between the material cultures of ATRs (totems, shrines, sacred groves, ancestral sacrifices, etc.) that are disappearing, and the nonmaterial cultures of ATRs (ancestral beliefs, vital force in all reality, the belief that every effect has a spiritual cause, etc.) that, like a hidden cultural grammar, continue to impact contemporary African Christian beliefs and practices. All these are aimed at establishing the nature and meaning of Christian revelation in the cultural universe and religious identity of African Christians and the relevance of the faith to the procurement of abundant life for the people in the social context.

1.3 Seven Shifts Needed in African Theology

The first needed shift is from an uncritical locus of enunciation to a more critical questioning of the ecclesial, cultural, and privileged presuppositions of our theologising to lead African Christians to the authentic exercise of human freedom in the humble search for God's purposes in our concrete historical context. The second is a movement from mainstream theology's focus on what George Lindbeck calls "informative cognitive propositions" to a phenomenological engagement with African Christianity from the perspectives of the lived faith experiences of ordinary African Christians.[10]

Theology in African Catholicism is still very generalised, scholastic, and essentialised. There is a big gap between the abstract theologies of the African academies and the diverse cultural knowledge, artifacts, symbols, behaviors, and worldviews that can be thematised through an immersion in African religiocultural traditions at the grassroots level. The concern should be a cultural-linguistic approach rooted in African narrative theological idioms that make possible "the description of realities, the formulation of beliefs, and the experiencing of inner attitudes, feelings, and sentiments."[11] Such an approach, in the thoughts of Lindbeck, will be attentive to discursive and nondiscursive symbols and communal phenomenon that shapes the subjectivities of individuals and how they make sense of realities.[12]

The fundamental shift here is from systems to stories in which the stories of the people provide the data for theology and in which theology reflects the stories of the people and the immersion of these stories in the continuing stories of God's self-manifestation in personal and group history, especially as revealed in the person of Christ.

Within indigenous knowledge studies, to which African narrative of faith belongs, it is accepted that stories hold within them knowledge while simultaneously reflecting multiple relationships with the past, present, and the future as well as inherited and acquired idioms on common meaning, reality, and the world.[13] In hearing and appropriating the stories of God's mighty deeds in our lives and communities and the limitations of our human response, we will be embracing an appropriate starting point for our theologies.

The third shift is from a narrative of African Christianity driven by functionalist sociologists and scholars of religious studies to a focus on the bigger theological picture beyond demographics. A theological account of the expansion of Christianity in Africa will be more focused on the nature of faith, the fruits of the faith, and the internal stress and strain within the faith life of people. In place of a triumphalist ecclesial theology that glories in the powers and prerogatives of the church and its doctrinal systems, the shift is to a more humble and discerning search for the finger of God in the daily lives of the people.

The fourth shift is one that requires an understanding of African Christianity as a cross-cultural process that will demand an intercultural and interfaith immersion, dialogue, and understanding. This will lead theologians to engage more critically and creatively with such questions as to what is and what is not syncretism, religious intolerance, and religious persecution in Africa; it will also engage them in asking how to deal with the complex African map of the universe with regard to limit situations, witchcraft, sorcery, ancestral curse, sickness, healing (broadly conceived), and the contrasting positions of different churches on marriage, childlessness, and premature and sudden deaths.

The fifth shift is the move from an abstract theological judgment on the faith of African Christians to a more concrete dialogue on the reason for the permeable nature of loyalty to different denominations and faith traditions by African Christians based on the different circumstances they face in life. It is not uncommon to see an African Christian attend a Roman Catholic baptism ceremony for her daughter in the morning, be at an African evangelical church's evening healing service later that day, and consult the next morning with a *sangoma* (witch doctor) to get some protection for her daughter against witchcraft and sorcery.

How can we understand the structure of meaning that shapes this common but contested approach to problem solving and the place of the Christian faith outside a narrow Western conception of the canons of orthodoxy? What canons do we use for judging church expansion?

The sixth shift is from a theology of systems and abstractions to a theology of symbols and embodied experiential meaning, signification, and praxis that shines a light of faith on the poetics of experience of divine-human exchanges in the lives of many Africans. This occurs in the face of suffering, pain, uncertainties about the future, and the search for how to change the unacceptable social conditions through faith's summons to conversion and action.

The seventh and final shift is from an exclusive ecclesial theology, especially in the Roman Catholic tradition, to a more ecumenical theological engagement through an expanded understanding of catholicity as a diverse and vastly extended range of divine-human encounters. These encounters are drawn from community-centered discursive and narrative theology of God's place in people's lives and in the determination of their choices and their construction of meaning and a better future.

2. What is *African* and *Theological* about the Cultural Hermeneutical Method?

The African cultural hermeneutical methodology I propose here is concerned with hermeneutical-phenomenological immersion in religiocultural history and African social context through narration. Its starting point is the stories of God's self-manifestation in African history as appropriated today by African Christians as central to their identity and social context and the construction of a hopeful future. This requires that the African theologian should not be an armchair, speculative practitioner but should be a participant in the multiple events of faith and someone knowledgeable in the use of ethnographic tools for harvesting the data of faith in practice in Africa.

This is significantly different from the predominant, traditional, speculative approach in Catholic theology because in this understanding, the data of theology is seen as a complex of different layers of meaning of diverse faith encounters mediated through African cultural self-appropriation that has to be encountered as a whole. The African theologian enters into this story by immersing himself or herself in stories that convey this judgment in the life of the people who embrace the faith.

This approach is "African" because it is concerned with how to interpret the manner in which the priorities and practices of the Lord Jesus Christ is being appropriated through African religiocultural idioms in the light of the Christian beliefs and practices in Africa. It is also African because this approach incessantly searches for a praxis of action on how to engage and transform the painful African social context through the mediation of African Christianity. This approach is theological because it deals with the search for the divine purposes for Africa and the world through a reflection on the meaning and implications of an appropriated African Christian faith for the cultures and peoples of Africa and the world.

A cultural hermeneutical method in African theology starts from the acceptance of modern science and employs a full range of scientific tools in terms of cultural and social analysis and ethnographic field study that lead the theologian to harvest the cultural knowledge, behaviors and artifacts in African Christianity that help make the Christian faith intelligible. It proceeds by applying a strong, biblical cultural hermeneutic, theological, and anthropological analysis to encounter concrete faith experience of the people to interpret, understand, and evaluate Christian practices in Africa. It presupposes an empirical notion of culture and history. While accepting the revealed truths in church dogma as embodied in history, it will reject the immutable essences of things and utilise diverse tools to appropriate the revealed truth and the faith of the believing community as dynamic in nature.[14]

It further embraces an empirical account whose terms and relations draw as a first step from the understanding of African Christianity as a religiocultural reality that is a new level of African traditional religions. The revelation of the heart of the Trinity can be discovered by any discerning African theologians in the very heart of African religiocultural Christianity as lived and appropriated in contemporary sub-Saharan Africa.

The missional dimension of the cultural hermeneutics is drawn from its proposition that the narratives of faith and life in African Christianity are not simply sociological realities but also manifestations of multiple dimensions of the Word made flesh in African history that point to the presence or absence of the signs of the kingdom of God in the African social context.

The cultural hermeneutical approach will not be satisfied with a fixed meaning but with the common and dynamic meaning embraced by the faith community in its search for abundant life through faith in Christ. The cultural hermeneutical approach is also missional because it studies African Christianity not simply as religious phenomena but as faith's response to God, who reveals the seeds of hope in specific African cultural and social contexts. Thus, a broader perspective on African Christian history requires a broader understanding of the different levels of African religiosity in its encounter with the gospel of Christ and the life of the Church than is common among many modern sociocultural anthropologists. The cultural hermeneutical approach, therefore, constantly engages African Christian religious phenomena whether autochthonous or acquired with a view to showing what they reveal about Africans and how they help them understand themselves, their society, the world, and the direction of history.

In the final analysis, the cultural hermeneutical approach will search for transformation of Africa, using interdisciplinary approaches in the critical, constructive, transformative, and creative harvesting of what it means to be Christian and African and the relevance of faith for the procurement of abundant life for Africans and the world through descriptive, prescriptive, and postulative processes.

By way of description, it seeks a morphological description of the context and content of African Christian history. This immersion in African Christian history opens up the African universe to the theologian whether he or she is an African Christian or a non-African Christian or simply an ethnographer. It furnishes sufficient data for classifying recurrent cultural themes and domains in African religiocultural traditions such as African worldviews, African religiosity, African history, African metaphysics, cosmology, and the moral tradition of abundant life among others.

As a prescriptive interpretative method, the theologian begins to develop norms for understanding the patterns of meaning embedded in

African Christianity. These norms govern the process of accountability of particular religious traits, rituals, spirituality, morality, etc., with regard to the fruits of the eschatological harvest of God's kingdom within particular African Christian communities.

The postulative function fulfills a constitutive function and is concerned with relating faith in African Christianity to African history, culture, and social conditions in the articulation of the ultimate goal of the Christian journey. This aims to build up the community through validating and proposing norms, practices, and transformational praxis that not only hold the community together but also lead people to authentic exercise of their human freedom in their cultural world to bring about the eschatological fruits of God's reign in Africa.

3. What do I Achieve When I Do African Theology?

There are three broad goals to be achieved in any successful African theological reflection that we can use to assess any African theological method. First among these goals is the satisfaction of intellectual thirst for the grounds of faith or the harmony of will and intellect to the divine purposes for the theologian and the Christian community. It is important that my theological reflection and writings as an African give me some sense of spiritual and intellectual satisfaction that fulfills my human quest for meaning and accountability for what I believe, how I live, and what I hope for.

By the same token, our theologies should offer intellectual and spiritual satisfaction to our people that their faith is grounded in something meaningful and eminently fulfilling of their hunger to understand their grounds for faith in the Trinity and their hope for a better future, etc. At the center of every African theology is this embrace of the wisdom of God revealed in history and accountability for the faith.

The second goal is communication; the goal of all theologies should be to communicate God's Word of love in history to people during their earthly pilgrimage to God's house. This is the pastoral dimension of theology, the aspect of correlating theories to practice through appropriate language.

Communication requires listening to God and discerning the voice of God as God speaks in our lives and cultures about who we are though the choices we make as individuals and groups and the documentation, transmission, and appropriation of the fruits of such reflections in pastoral life.

The dissemination of theological works in Africa has been very limited because many African bishops have not taken interest in the theological works of African theologians, and in most cases, many African theologians do not work closely with bishops and episcopal conferences in theologising in the pastoral priorities of Africa. In addition, African theologies have often operated from ivory towers, and sometimes, the cultural categories and materials African theologians use in their reflection are removed from the world of most Africans because of the perennial culture lag that is characteristic of postcolonial societies.

Teaching theology and stimulating African theological reflection at all levels of church life in Africa requires appropriate language and praxis of performance in which our theologies are embraced by our people because they make sense and are meaningful. But meaning is dynamic; meaning is not simply something we discover through memorising catechetical texts or through reproducing by rote the writings of the fathers or theologians or proof-texting magisterial documents. According to Lonergan, meaning is cognitive inasmuch as it crystallises the hidden inner gift of God's love into Christian fellowships; it is affective inasmuch as it directs Christian service to human society to bring about the kingdom of God; and it is communicative inasmuch as it is to be lived, "performed" as an event that has to be incarnated and witnessed to in diverse cultural situations.

> The Christian message is to be communicated to all nations. Such communication presupposes that preachers and teachers enlarge their horizons to include an accurate and intimate understanding of the culture and the language of the people they address. They must use those virtual resources creatively so that the Christian message becomes, not disruptive of the culture, not an alien patch superimposed upon it, but a line of development within the culture.[15]

The third point to make here is that of relevance. I will reformulate the Pauline hymn of love in shaping this final point. If my theological formulation is of no interest or relevance to the people of Africa, I am only a gong booming or a cymbal clashing; if I formulate with great eloquence and in scholastic language inculturation theologies or, in Marxist terms, theologies of liberation, feminist theologies, ecotheology, or theologies of transformation for fellow Africans that are not relevant to their faith and social context, I have accomplished nothing. If I use all kind of indigenous and foreign categories to explain the mysteries of faith that I propose could move mountains and bring down powers and principalities but that have no relevance to ordinary African Christians in their daily lives, my theology will be of no good to Africa.

A relevant African theology will answer the most pressing questions facing Africans today. A relevant African theology will give voice to many voiceless Africans; a relevant African theology will not be a theology of compromise with the powers and principalities in or outside Africa, nor will it be a sheepish imitation of what has happened elsewhere. A relevant African theology will lead African Christians to seize the moment of grace in the present ferment of the faith in Africa and stir the people to higher purpose; a relevant African theology is the most potent weapon for reinventing the future of Africans through a life of faith rooted in hope, hard work, honesty, virtuous living, and humility, among other virtues. It does not matter if it is inculturation, liberation, or a feminist, ecological, or transformative praxis for abundant life. It matters that such theologies matter to Africans because it offers them a pathway to cooperation with God's grace in bringing about a better future and a mirror to see their faces, the faces of their neighbours, and the face of God as well as the face of a hopeful future.

Conclusion

What I have done in this chapter is to present a method and model I propose could help center theological reflections in Africa on God's story in and for Africa by paying attention to the narrative of faith and life in African history, African Christianity, and social context. This chapter argued for a cultural hermeneutical approach to methods in African theologies that is *narrative* because it draws its data from Christian history, especially the Bible, traditions and the teachings of the Church, and the stories of Africans in their daily lives. This cultural hermeneutical approach to methods in African theologies should be *missional* because it is concerned with how the fruits of God's kingdom and the will of God for Africa are being realised in Africa through the agency of African Christianity as the Christian faith crosses different cultural frontiers. It is *transformational* because it is concerned with faith's role in the midst of social changes in Africa and the path to conversion with a view to bringing genuine newness to Africa through daily cultural encounters with Christ and how the faith can be communicated through a relevant theology that speaks to the deepest hunger, desires, and hopes of Africans.

Endnotes

1 Pope Benedict XVI, *Africae Munus*, 10.

2 Ibid., 137.

3 Avery Dulles, *The Craft of Theology* (New York: Crossroad, 1992), 48–50.

4 For the argument on the permeable nature of the boundaries between a histori-cal and a typological study of African theology, see Stephen Munga, *Beyond the Controversy: A Study of African Theologies of Inculturation and Liberation* (Lund: Lund University Press, 1998), 23, 39.

5 When I use the phrase "African theology" in the singular, I am referring in a cognate sense to various theological activities (formal, informal, vernacular, folk, academic, etc.), which is African in content and nature and with specific African interest and concerns. When I use "African theologies" in the plural, I am referring to the manifestations of these theological activities in specific and particular contexts, discourses, and performances as inculturation, liberation, feminist, transformational, praxis-oriented, and so on.

6 Benedict XVI, Address to Members of the Special Council for Africa of the Synod of Bishops (Yaounde, 18 March, 2009): AAS 101 (2009), 310.

7 Mercy Amba Oduyoye, *Hearing and Knowing: Theological Reflections on Christianity in Africa* (Maryknoll, N.Y.: Orbis, 1993), 54.

8 See Albert Nolan, *Hope in an Age of Despair*, Stan Muyebe, ed. (Maryknoll, N.Y.: Orbis, 2010), 19.

9 Henry Okullu, *Church and Politics in East Africa* (Nairobi: Uzima Press, 1974), 54; quoted in Tinyiko Sam Maluleke, "Half a Century of African Christian Theologies: Elements of the Emerging Agenda for the Twenty-First Century," *Journal of Theology for Southern Africa*, 99 (1997), 8.

10 See George Lindbeck, *The Nature of Doctrine: Religion and Theology in a Post Liberal Age* (Philadelphia: The Westminster Press, 1984), 46.

11 Ibid., 33.

12 Ibid.

13 See Margaret Kovach, *Indigenous Methodologies: Characteristics, Conversa-tions, and Contexts* (Toronto: University of Toronto Press, 2012), 94.

14 Justo L. Gonzales makes a distinction between the "old map" and the "new map" in Justo L. Gonzales, *The Changing Shape of Church History* (St. Louis: Chalice Press, 2002), 2–18. See also Bernard Lonergan on the notions of culture and history in *Method in Theology* (Toronto: University of Toronto Press, 1971), 300–306.

15 Lonergan, *Method in Theology*, 362.

A Practice of Theology
at the Service of African Societies:
Some Lessons from the Experience of the Collection
"The Bible and Women in Africa"

Josée Ngalula

"The Bible and Women in Africa" collection (collbifea.blogspot. com) was initiated in Kinshasa (D. R. Congo) in 2003, as a forum for apprenticeship and experimenting a new way of doing theology that would be attentive to the experiences of the Christian communities, and would contribute to the transformation and advancement of society. Through the narration of the motivations and activities of this collection, I will present a case study of a practical theology at the service of African societies through its various aspects and challenges. I will also theorise on the fruits of this experience by proposing aspects of a profile of a theology at the service of African society.

1. Motivation for the Collection's Foundation

The first motivation for establishing the collection was my professional experience and pastoral care in which I found a great distance between African intellectual circles and lay people. African theologians form part of an intellectual elite, and a large number of them are remote from the simple people whom they view from the ivory tower of their theological discourse. They usually have very little interaction with them on an equal basis with a view of mutual enrichment. These attitude prevents theologians from listening sufficiently to questions relating to the lived experiences of the Christian faith of those at the base of society. It constitutes a stumbling block to the development of a theology truly at the service of society.

My second motivation was the thinking of the late Cardinal Malula about African theology. For him, any theologian from Africa who places himself or herself above the real problems of Africa on account of a deficient understanding of the universality of the Church cannot be considered a true African theologian. Theological research and publications must be linked to the present life of the Church in Africa. They must be attentive to the ways African Christians try to live their faith in Jesus Christ and strive to give evangelical responses to the questions raised in their own contexts, especially in Small Christian communities (SCCs).

One must, of course, avoid "canonising" everything happening in Christian communities because from the point of view of living the gospel values they are not perfect communities. Theologians are technicians, and their job is to gather elements of this life, with all its ambiguities, analyse them theologically, and systematise them according to the method proper to each discipline. This is why African theologians must listen to the experiences of Christian communities and dialogue with them. That implies a love for Africa and its peoples: if theologians cannot serve the local, they will not be able to serve the universal.[1]

In light of the foregoing, "The Bible and Women in Africa" stands on three "legs": Bible studies, theological workshops, and popularisation of the fruits of the research to better society. I needed to target a specific audience, so I opted for the members of our Christian communities that constitute the major category – women of simple and poor milieus.

2. Theological Activities of the Collection[2]

The theological activities of the collection cover Bible studies and theological workshops. African exegetes and theologians interested in Bible studies work on a biblical narrative or theme related to the challenges to the Christian faith in African societies today as experienced and expressed by these simple women of our parishes. We discover these challenges by listening, through meetings and dialogues, to these women when they narrate and reflect on their Christian lives at their intellectual levels. These subjects, drawn into the basic Christian experience as represented by the women of simple milieu, are worked on with all scientific seriousness required in theology.

In ten years, this "leg" of biblical studies has produced an anthology, *These women who inhabit the Bible. An anthology of the 250 women of the Bible,*[3] and three exegetical works in booklet form: *The rape of Tamar, the daughter of David (2 Samuel 13): A biblical reflective narrative of our society;*[4] *Women healed and rescued from death by Jesus;*[5] *and The apostle Paul and women.*[6]

These works of exegesis have been disseminated and popularised at three levels, including an intellectual level, so African men learn to be attentive to the critical issues that are paramount for women at grassroots level, and the manner of their engagement with the Bible. For example, the booklet on the rape of Tamar opened up the minds of many men because its exegesis demonstrated that in daily life many African men downplay or ignore the effect rape has on its victims in precisely the same way as Amnon, the rapist, or David, the victim's father did. This book shines a light on the daily sufferings of girls who are victims of incest. To my knowledge, it is the first time the word "incest" was mentioned in an African theological forum, and it opened the eyes of many on the gravity of the crime.

The two other booklets, on the relationship between Jesus and women and on Paul's understanding of the relationship between men and women in Christ, were good complements to this process of questioning traditional prejudices and presumptions.

The second level was a lobbying against silence and the stigmatisation of victims in the Christian milieu and society. The third level involved lobbying with NGOs on the subject of human rights to show that in Catholic doctrine, forgiveness does not mean the absence of justice. I will return to this aspect when talking about the collection's lobbying methods.

The second leg consists of "theological workshops" with poor women of our parishes. The topics covered in the three theological workshops organised in ten years have all been drawn from the daily experiences and questionings of simple, poor women of our Christian communities. The conviction of the collection is that these women are the first competent people to talk about their human and Christian experiences as well as of their creative responses to different societal challenges relating to their faith. They must be listened to when they express their experiences, with their own expressions, in their own consistency, including their attempts to fully apprehend their problems.

Here, interdisciplinary work becomes fundamental; at this level, theologians need the expertise of the liberal arts, especially anthropology and linguistics. With such scientific tools, they help translate into scientific language the basic experiences expressed by women in simple words. We also need sociologists for objective statistics and the systematisation of social experiences. This interaction between the intellectual women and the poor women were very enriching.

The three theological workshops focused on the problem of violence done to women, a burning question for simple and socially disempowered women. The first workshop was on religion and violence against women, what God and the church thought about daily violence against women. Is it "Christian" never to talk about it in reference to our faith or never to denounce the authors of violence in the name of forgiveness? What is the best attitude towards victims of violence in the name of Christ?

The second workshop worked on violence among women, especially in the context of African traditional rituals of purification of widows. Many Christian widows reject traditional rites in the name of their faith, and many pastoral workers create new rites in the name of these women. In some places, sadly, this creativity has generated new forms of violence against widows. Finally, what are the stakes for the widows themselves and for all the church?

The third workshop took on a very delicate topic: the violence women practice on their own bodies to seduce men.

The proceedings of the first workshop have been published: *To dare to defend her in her inviolability: Acts of the workshop "Religion and violence made to the women."*[7] The proceedings of the second workshop have been published as well: *The feminine body, place of unique meeting between Gospel and African customs, Volume I: Rituals of purification of widows.*[8]

The proceedings of the two first workshops show the originality and the force these theological workshops bring to communitarian activities and the interdisciplinary approach of the topics. I work with other scholars (men and women) interested on the topics. Not only is considerable attention given to the monitoring of the women at the grassroots, every problem receives the enrichment of the approaches of different theological disciplines and liberal arts. The proceedings of this third workshop have not yet been published because we are still in the process of listening to the narratives of the simple women.

Some African theologians usually ask me, "When talking about rape and other violence against women, are you doing theology? You feminists are seeing theology everywhere!" I answer, "When talking about abortion, are moralists doing theology? When talking about the passion of Jesus, are we doing theology? When Pope John Paul II writes an encyclical on women's dignity in God, is he a feminist?"

Theology is an activity of intelligence of the faith; because of the mystery of the incarnation, no aspects of the realities that touch human lives, male or female, are foreign to searching for consistency between professed faith, lived or celebrated faith, and testified faith.

3. The Collection at the Service of African Societies

The activities and publications of the collection are at the service of African societies (especially Congolese society) through its lobbying efforts. Working with theological issues drawn from everyday Christian life leads to calls to action for more-effective pastoral care and for the betterment of society as a whole.

Theology in itself is not militant; in fact, the theological training we receive does not make us competent in this area. To put the fruits of the collection's theological research at the service of the world, we must collaborate with experts in the fields of communication, awareness raising, and lobbying. This is why the contributions of social activists have been very important to collection. Here are two examples:

The first one is in the popularisation of the exegesis of the rape of Tamar and the workshop on religion and violence on women. I personally accompanied human rights activists during many conferences and speeches at Catholic parishes and to Catholic women's associations, and I talked with Catholic media. As a medium of communication, I use the local language, Lingala. A good law punishes violence against women in DRC, but many Christian women think it is not good to denounce violators of that law out of respect for ancestral traditions and a desire to "obey" Jesus, who enjoined his followers to forgive!

Because of this lobbying, many women became aware that they usually reacted as Tamar had, by undergoing the violence in silence and locking themselves in feelings of guilt and shame. Through these activities, many women confessed that they educated their daughters by teaching them to be quiet in case of rape to save the family's honour, considering honour to be more important that the victims' suffering, exactly as David the father of Tamar had.

We discussed biblical texts on violence against women during the workshop on religion and violence against women. For the sake of small-group discussion, I had summarised them in a booklet, *God denounces and condemns violence against women.*[9] Many women discovered that God denounces such violence, whereas we women close our eyes to it in the name of family honour. As result of all these exchanges with parish women, many say, "I denounce, because God denounces, because it is the work of the Christian to be on the side of the victims and denounce this violence." The perspectives and reactions are therefore untied, but the big difficulty that remains today is that such "untying" of women's voices happens only in places of security such as the workshop.

The second example is the impact of the booklet *God denounces and condemns violence against women.* To date, many Catholic human-rights activists use this booklet for debates in the media, including in the interior regions of the country. In 2005, an assembly of the United Nations that was to decide on the crime of the use of rape as a weapon of war in DRC had this sentence in the preparatory text: "The Christian Bible is one of the factors favoring violent behaviour toward women." A Christian NGO distributed this booklet to all Christian members during the consultation in an attempt to remove this offensive sentence from the final communiqué, and it was successful.

In fact, many people of goodwill interested in these issues do not have the basic theological knowledge and cannot effectively confront critics of the Christian faith. This booklet has given them the basic theological perspectives on the encouraging testimony of the Church's respect for human dignity preached by Jesus, including the dignity of victims of rape.

Other booklets have also been published in parallel with the scientific publications of the consecutive workshops: *To dare to defend her in her inviolability, Volume II. God's people in diakonia of the protection of widows*[10] and *Women have the dignity of human beings.*"[11] In addition to these publications, the collection's blog, "Bible and women in Africa," contains all the collection's research.

My ten years with the collection have been exciting but equally challenging; they have been demanding and problematic in terms of theoretical efficiency. I had to be part of a minority; a few biblical scholars have understood the stakes and have collaborated with the collection. The majority of my colleagues suspect these activities to be "feminist" in nature and so do not recognise or value their importance.

The fundamental issue is: can theology serve African societies if male and female theologians are not sufficient in number and in diversity of skills to support it? I answer in the negative; I do not believe the isolated, individual actions I have taken at the collection can impact global society; they affect only a few isolated groups. These activities of the collection are contributions to the thinking on the African continent and have sometimes led to new behaviours in very restricted environments, but they will not shake up African societies. My experience at the collection, however, allows me to ask how theology can best serve Christian communities.

4. Theology at the Service of African Societies

How can theology be at the service of African societies? The answer is not obvious. Is religion society's opium? Are certain current African religious practices factors of social destruction? Some religious beliefs push Christians to hunt for children and the elderly under the pretext that they are possessed by Satan. Religious fundamentalism can cause and perpetrate violence to persons and the social infrastructure.

Fortunately, there are not just negative aspects to religion; contemporary Africa also experiences Christianity as a force for individual and social progress in the areas of education, health, the environment, peace, and justice in the name of religious convictions. What role can Christian theology play in this? We would do well to remember that Christian theology is a diligent search for the understanding of faith. Its concrete practice consists of providing the means and the time to understand the Christian faith in its internal consistency, in its original contribution in the context of the religions of the world, and in its service to Christian communities in the world.

From this point of view, theologians are technicians called by their training to render services to the people of God and to their communities. From my experience at the collection, one must fulfill two minimum conditions for this service to be possible.

First, theology cannot be trapped in academia; to serve society properly, it must prevent society from slipping into bad interpretations of faith. Have not many African Christians, in good faith, destroyed their families and environment because they had learned from some materials in religious thinking that it was God's will? Are they not today in the hands of charlatans who dangerously manipulate biblical texts or Christianity's history to distort religion? Competent theologians can render great service to societies in search of peace and development. In the West, some countries have understood and have integrated theologians at the level of government or ethics commissions.

To serve African societies, male and female theologians must not confine themselves to proving their professional competence. Christian theology does not limit itself to understanding its internal coherence; it articulates faith to all human experience. This is because a distinctive feature of the Christian faith is the concept of the God who wants to walk with humans in their daily lives. To effectively serve African societies, theology will help Christians understand their faith, to adapt to new situations, and discover solutions to their difficulties.

Impoverished Africans are exposed to a barrage of advertising and media coverage of persons (of goodwill and charlatans alike) who offer them biblical solutions all made to suit situations they have no control over. For example, tithing is actually suggested as a way to overcome poverty. The majority of people do not have time to reflect deeply; African theologians are part of the intellectual elite of the continent who must be immersed in their societies but take a critical stance in order to identify theological issues that can help transform society. The quality of commitment of the Christian communities for better African societies depends in part on the success of unbiased dialogue between God and Africans, and theologians can contribute to the effective realisation of this process.

We must not be naive about the ascetical character of this kind of theological approach; doing theology in Africa is not easy or always pleasant. In my ten years at the collection I have discovered the critical importance of a genuine asceticism because it must often work in difficult conditions materially (problems of electricity and other such material concerns) and financially. Does this mean it is impossible? The love of a woman's womb for African societies that has marked my ten years says no! We need volunteers who accept the asceticism of daring to practice a theology at the service of Christian communities and African societies in harsh conditions.

Conclusion

Can theology serve societies? Yes. But African theology can fall into the temptation of offering ready-made answers to unimportant questions in African societies. Theologians must overcome the spontaneous reflexes to be judges and thermometers of Christian communities' orthodoxy and orthopraxis. They must have a competent presence in the actual lives of members of African societies in an interdisciplinary approach that respects other sciences. Otherwise, they will miss a very important dimension: the living faith of the human communities walking with Christ.

What voices are excluded from the practice of African theology? The voices coming deeply from the daily experiences of Christian communities. African theologians must theologise in full recognition of the existential questions of African peoples.

My work with the simple women of our parishes had raised only a corner of the veil; there is so much to hear from men and women in our Christian communities that will allow us to produce a theology really at the service of society!

When some voices are excluded, it prevents the church from being in friendly conversation with the world, being a handmaid to the world, and bringing gospel light to it, as *Gaudium et Spes* requires. African theologians must become servants to Africa and the whole world, humbly sharing their expertise in dialogue with other theoretical and existential expertise.

Translated from the French by
Kpanie Addy, SJ, and Andrew Setsoafia, SJ

Endnotes

1 These are the original words of Cardinal Malula: *"Sans cesser de braquer ses antennes sur les grands courants de la théologie contemporaine, le travail du théologien aura un caractère particulier, celui d'être lié à la vie de l'Église en Afrique, mieux encore, à la vie même du peuple africain d'aujourd'hui. Ce peuple, en général, a déjà la foi en Jésus-Christ; il vit de cette foi et s'efforce de l'exprimer spontanément à travers sa propre sensibilité religieuse africaine. Le théologien sera attentif à tout cela. A l'exemple de son Église, sa théologie partira de la vie de son peuple et sera une réponse évangélique aux interrogations, aux problèmes posés par notre histoire, notre culture, notre mentalité, nos traditions*

telles que vécues aujourd'hui par le peuple africain. Le théologien africain doit évidemment être prudent sans cesser d'être courageux." Published by Léon de Saint Moulin, ed., *Œuvres complètes du Cardinal Malula.* Volume 2 (Kinshasa: Facultés Catholiques de Kinshasa, 1997), 86. On the same subject, one can also read in Volume 3, 143, and Volume 6, 93–94.

2   All the contents of publications of the Collection and workshops activities are available at collbifea.blogspot.com.

3   Original references in French: Josée Ngalula et Jean Ikanga, *Ces femmes qui peuplent la Bible. Anthologie de références et thématiques sur les 250 femmes de la Bible* (Kinshasa: Editions Mont Sinaï, 2005).

4   Original references in French: André Kabasele Mukenge, *Le viol de Tamar, la fille de David (2 Samuel 13). Un récit biblique miroir de notre société* (Kinshasa: Editions Mont Sinaï, 2006).

5   Original references in French: Valentin Ntumba Kapambu, *Femmes guéries et arrachées à la mort par Jésus. De l'exégèse à l'actualisation de quelques récits de guérison* (Kinshasa: Editions Mont Sinaï, 2006).

6   Original references in French: Paul-Marie Buetubela Balembo, *L'apôtre Paul et la femme. Propos pauliniens sur la christianisation des rapports sociaux entre hommes et femmes* (Kinshasa: Editions Mont Sinaï, 2009).

7   Original references in French: Josée Ngalula, (dir), *Oser la défendre dans son inviolabilité. Actes de l'Atelier "Religion et violences faites aux femmes."* (Kinshasa: Editions Mont Sinaï, 2006).

8   Original references in French: Josée Ngalula, (dir), *Le corps féminin, lieu singulier de rencontre entre Evangile et coutumes africaines. Volume I. Rites de purification des veuves. Des traditions africaines à la liturgie chrétienne. Actes de l'Atelier théologique sur les rites de purification des veuves* (Kinshasa: Editions Mont Sinaï, 2007).

9   Original references in French: Josée Ngalula, *Dieu dénonce et condamne les violences faites à la femme* (Kinshasa: Editions Mont Sinaï, 2005).

10   Original references in French: Larethea and Association Femmes et droits humains (Afedh), *Oser la défendre dans son inviolabilité. Volume II. Le peuple de Dieu en diaconie protectrice des veuves* (Kinshasa: Editions Mont Sinaï, 2007).

11   Original references in French: Jeannette Munda Badibanga, Bakaji Mbantu, *Les femmes ont la dignité humaine* (Kinshasa: Editions Mont Sinaï, 2007, 2008).

Bishops as Theologians: Listening, Discerning, and Dialogue

Bishop Kevin Dowling

I would like to begin with some insight from Richard Rohr that I consider thought-provoking:

> Those at the edge of any system and those excluded from any system, ironically and invariably hold the secret for the conversion and wholeness of that very group. They always hold the feared, rejected, and denied parts of the group's soul. You see, therefore, why the Church was meant to be that group that constantly went to the edges, to the "least of the brothers and sisters," and even to the enemy. Jesus was not just a theological genius, but he was also a psychological and sociological genius. *When any Church defines itself by exclusion, it is always wrong.* It is avoiding its only vocation, which is to be the Christ.
>
> Only as the People of God receive the stranger, the sinner, and the immigrant, those who don't play our game our way, do we discover not only the hidden, feared, and hated parts of our own souls, but the fullness of Jesus himself. We need them for our own conversion.
>
> The Church is always converted when the outcasts are re-invited back into the temple. You see this in Jesus' commonly sending marginalised people that he has healed, back into the village, back to their family, or back to the temple to "show themselves to the priests." It is not just for their re-inclusion and acceptance, but actually for the group itself to be renewed.[1]

I found myself reflecting long and deeply about a number of possible interpretations of the role of bishops as theologians. Is the bishop's primary role as a teacher or as a theologian to simply articulate for his people the teachings of the magisterium? And in any difficult situation in terms of faith and morals, is he simply called to consult the professional theologians if, like me, he is not a professional theologian? Must he discern with professional theologians to find what teaching he should give so it can be an authentic interpretation of the magisterium? Or is the bishop called to do what I would term as "theologising" in the context of his people's situations, actual challenges, and even sufferings? Is he called to "do" theology at the coalface, on the front lines, as his experience of his people and situation unfolds?

As a religious, priest, and bishop, I have always taken my inspiration in my calling and ministry from the founder of my religious community, St Alphonsus Liguori, the patron saint of moral theologians. His conversion in his calling and mission came about through a chance encounter as a priest with poor shepherds in an area south of Naples; they were poor people who were completely marginalised in society and the Church. In a very real way, he was evangelised by the poor in their context, and that reality shaped his theology as a moral theologian in spite of the influence of Jansenism; the pastoral context provided the locus for his theology. I will never forget the comment of one of Alphonsus's great followers, Bernard Häring, at the launch of one of his books in Rome: "I have learned all my theology from the poor of the world."

This mirrors the call and challenge of Pope Francis that Church leaders should work with the sheep and smell like them. Pope Francis is calling the Church and its leadership "to go to those 'at the periphery' and 'at the margins,' especially the poor – as he himself did as bishop and even as cardinal. He compares such an evangelical church to a church that is 'self-referential,' which becomes, in his word, 'sick.' He has even said that it is better to go to the margins and make mistakes than become self-absorbed."[2] But unless we bishops actually leave our offices and chanceries and go into the "mess" of life as it really is and experience it personally, firsthand, we will perhaps risk perpetuating a model of Church that focuses inwardly on our "churchy" concerns, which will put us at a further risk of becoming ever more self-referential. And then our theology and our role as bishop-theologians will similarly risk being out of touch with the reality of people's lives and concerns, and consequently our word and teaching may become meaningless and irrelevant for the poor and suffering.

But what about the relationship between professional theologians and the institutional church, specifically, its bishops? A strong focus in the Church in the past years has been on the so-called "new evangelisation." At the conclusion of the recent conference of the Catholic Theological Society of America on the theme of conversion, the outgoing president, Susan Ross, said,

> I think it is fair to say that one basic truth emerging from the new evangelisation is that both the world and the Church are continually in need of conversion.... How can theologians, in cooperation with the institutional Church, engage in the new evangelisation through imagination, humour, commitment, discernment, and hospitality?[3]

The answer, she believes, lies in dialogue with the institutional Church; she was referring to the context of Church in the United States. The question could be asked of theologians in Africa, what is the calling and mission of the theologian in Africa, whether the professional theologian or bishop-theologian? How can the theologian explain and apply with ever greater clarity the teachings of the magisterium to our Church situation in Africa without a sensitivity to or a feel for the cultural and socioeconomic contexts in Africa? Should the call and mission of an African theologian per se be to push the boundaries, as it were, in our discernment as Church in Africa of the revelation of God? Such discernment needs to be interpreted and reinterpreted in the ever-changing reality of our African society, with its own African worldview and all its needs, including the need to care for God's earth on which we as Africans depend for survival.

Many years ago, I sat in a steaming hot, zinc and wood shack amid hundreds of other shacks in a so-called informal settlement next to one of the shafts of platinum mines in the diocese where I minister as bishop. In front of me sat a seriously ill young mother; next to her lay a dying baby. They were both afflicted with AIDS and the infections that go with the disease. They were among the many thousands of such people who have become central to my life as a bishop since 1992, when I first encountered the horror of AIDS in my diocese. Perspiration poured down her face, but this could not hide the tears streaming down her cheeks or the utter hopelessness in her eyes. She said, "Father, I have no hope. There is no hope for me." Her shoulders slumped as she stared at her dying baby. As she spoke to me, all I could do was hold her in my arms and quietly repeat that my community carers would love her and look after her every day, and if she passed on, they would also care for her baby.

However, this was before the advent of antiretroviral drugs. There was indeed no hope for her. She died a horrible death, as did her baby. The community carers on my AIDS team found her one day on the ground in her shack. She was dead, covered in vomit and excrement.

I went through that experience scores of times over the years as I walked around the shacks with my community carers and nurses, trying also to keep up the spirits of those carers so they could indeed love and care for those little ones of God, whose lives I believed and still believe were and are infinitely precious to our God.

And that is precisely the point: if their lives were and are infinitely precious to God, what was – indeed, what is – my role and calling as bishop and theologian? That woman was dying not because she had had any choice about being infected with HIV; she had been subjected to unspeakable brutality and injustice. She, like hundreds of thousands of rural women in South Africa and countries north of South Africa, had been forced to leave her rural home because of extreme poverty, no work, and nothing on which to survive. She had ended up in this shack settlement next to a mine in the vain hope she could somehow find a job and survive. She found quickly she was in an even worse poverty trap. There were no jobs for anyone like her. Her only way to survive for even just a day was to sell herself for sex with men who had money, the miners, who themselves had left their homes and wives far away for employment at the mine.

I quickly termed her only possibility of putting some bread on the table as "survival sex." She would get paid for sex – all she had – to come up with enough for twenty-four hours, and then she would have to do that again and again and again. What utter, despicable, systemic injustice and degradation. The inevitable results were HIV infection, TB, pneumonia, cancer, other infections, pregnancy, birth of an HIV-positive baby – utter misery, and finally death.

What does it mean to do theology in such a situation, to be a theologian, even a bishop-theologian, in the face of such horror? What does it mean to be pro-life in such conditions? How do I as bishop-theologian listen to God speak to me through these "signs of the times" and interpret what God's will and Word means in such degradation? Is the teaching of the magisterium sufficient for me to respond to that situation, or does it perhaps appear to be irrelevant to that situation in terms of being a message of hope to the suffering and poor of our continent? If so, what am I called to as a bishop-theologian?

Our reality in Africa points to the need to positively revive and ground a reflection on the meaning of "collegiality" and of "subsidiarity" as core principles of Catholic social teaching. Subsidiarity in the sociopolitical arena calls for an understanding, namely, that what can be done at the "lower level" of society should not be subsumed, still less done, for the "lower level" by those at the "higher level" of governance in society. The purpose of this should be to ensure the common good of all by promoting a social compact in which everyone in society participates in a spirit of solidarity and collaboration to ensure that all citizens, especially the poorest and most vulnerable, experience growth in their human dignity as human beings made in God's image. In this sense, ensuring that subsidiarity actually works is the way to transform citizens into becoming and being active agents of transformation in their own communities by using their insights and experience to develop policies and practices that will make a real difference in their quality of life.

If we as Church are going to challenge political leadership in our countries to promote the common good on the basis of the values and principles of subsidiarity, this calls for a similar commitment on Church leadership at all levels to ensure the common good of the Church community through promoting subsidiarity as the basis for a living collegiality.

In the first place, the bishop as shepherd and theologian is called to discern with all the people of God in the diocese what the Spirit is saying to that local Church with all its particular characteristics, possibilities, needs, and challenges. And I stress the word "discern." To discern in the Spirit does not simply involve discussion about a particular issue, for example, and then making a decision. Rather, it requires a prayerful spirit of listening to what the Spirit is saying through each person's faith, listening to people's personal experiences in life's realities of the presence and call of Jesus to self-sacrifice and service in view of the common good. It requires an honest acceptance of the human failings present in all of us, including our prejudices, likes, and dislikes (especially with regard to others and their opinions). It requires an openness to admitting, as part of sharing and listening, that our attitudes and perhaps first opinions or thoughts about an issue require a change.

I believe the bishop as shepherd and theologian in the local Church must take the lead in this by creating a spirit and atmosphere of respect for the other, listening not only to words but also to the spirit and experience behind the words, and above all, "feeling" in the people of God that he, the shepherd, deeply values each person and wants the same spirit to be shared by all.

In spite of the inevitable ups and downs due to our human limitations, with good will, this approach could create the conditions for a real discernment in the Spirit and allow the bishop to affirm the *sensus fidelium* and truly speak those faith-filled words at the closure of the discernment, "It seems good to the Spirit and to all of us" at this moment in time that we begin this journey, that we embark on this pastoral plan, that we respond to this need in this way, and so on, but that we remain always open to new insights and inspiration in the faith community.

If this can be done at the local level with sincerity, and in spite of setbacks and human failures, it needs to be taken to the next level, where the bishops' conference discerns as a college of bishops through reflecting in the same way with local theologians and a national leadership of priests, religious, and lay faithful. The next level, the regional conferences of bishops and the synod of bishops, can follow the same model of discerning with theologians and other key advisors so the synod truly discerns and decides what the "Spirit seems to be saying to us and to the worldwide Church" at this time. The role of the various dicasteries in Rome should take on a different spirit, as it were, to confirm the faith and fidelity of the discernment process of the college of bishops gathered with the bishop of Rome and to offer the regional conferences and local conferences of bishops all the practical support the dicasteries can give to implementing the pastoral vision discerned in faith by the college of bishops united with the bishop of Rome.

That "spirit" of respect and valuing what can be discerned and done at the level of the local Church, i.e., subsidiarity, is crucial for the future of African theology and the call and ministry of the African theologian per se and the African bishop as theologian. We in Africa have a very particular sociocultural context impacted by economic policies and decisions taken at global levels and by powerful political entities in Africa and elsewhere.

What is the Spirit saying to the African Church? What is the Spirit inviting and calling the African Church to be and do on our continent and as our particular gift to the worldwide Church? That is the question African theologians and African bishops must grapple with, and we should be trusted and given the space to continue this journey of faith and discernment together as a community that "does" theology in our unique context, which is different from other sociocultural contexts, e.g., in Europe, the Americas, and Asia-Oceania.

The task of a theologian is not simply to articulate and reinterpret church teaching as it has come down to us over the centuries or to dictate the way the deposit of faith is to be understood by God's people through ever deeper theological reflection and research as if God's revelation is complete for all time.

God is continuing to reveal God's Word and will in the unfolding circumstances of every moment and age. And so, if we are open and discerning people, God will continue to challenge our theological reflection on the critical issues that affect the quality of life of humankind, the planet, and its resources in Africa and elsewhere.

That is how I view the call and mission of the bishop as theologian. My primary role in relation to the people of God among whom I live and minister in the diocese is not only and not simply to hand on the faith, to empower and instruct my catechists in handing on the faith to children and adults, and faithfully to articulate the teachings of the magisterium.

My primary role is to discern what God seems to be saying in all the situations in which God seems absent and in which Church maybe *is* absent in terms of its presence and ministry.

The Church may be absent in terms of a presence that gives hope where there is only despair and where people cannot make any sense out of life; a presence of healing when there is only hurt and pain and a sense of loss; a presence that allows us to open the door for God to speak and be present to the little ones of the world in a way that enables them to begin again and take the next step through us and because of us as a Church community.

The bishop-theologian or teacher needs to respond to the actual lived reality in the spirit and practice of listening deeply, discerning what the Spirit seems to be saying to the Churches, and engaging in a dialogical process with his people to promote and build a *sensus fidelium* that will allow God's Word and the mission of Jesus to be incarnated anew in the unfolding reality of people's lives and especially the most vulnerable members of our communities and societies.

The topic of bishops as theologians posits the following questions, among others: How do pastoral experience, pastoral sensitivity, and pastoral reflection impact the Church's living theological tradition? Is it possible for pastoral reality to reform or shape Church teaching so this can be understood and experienced as relevant and valid for our particular time? Should not pastoral ministry be a most powerful and necessary "source" of theology shaped by our African context with its widespread poverty, disease, wars, millions of refugees, and the struggle many go through to live minimally decent lives? Should a bishop's particular pastoral perspective with his people be a key factor in this dynamic?

In that sense, a bishop is or should be a theologian par excellence and constantly invite professional theologians to respond and commit to renewed partnership with all bishops and pastoral workers, because together we seek to discern God's Word and the meaning of faith and evangelisation in the reality in which we live and minister.

Endnotes

1   Richard Rohr, adapted from *Radical Grace: Daily Meditations*, 28, day 2.

2   *National Catholic Reporter*, July 2, 2013.

3   *National Catholic Reporter*, June 10, 2013.

Bishops as Theologians:
Overcoming the Challenge of Academic Poverty

Rodrigo Mejía Saldarriaga

Introduction

hapter 5 of the recently revised *Directory for Bishops*[1] deals in detail with the *munus docendi*, the responsibility of the bishop as a teacher of faith in the people of God.[2] This dimension of the mission of a bishop implies that to teach, the bishop has to have a deep knowledge of the Christian message in the Bible and in the theological tradition of the Church. Does it also imply the bishop should be a professional theologian himself?

Theological knowledge has different levels, from simple catechism to a doctoral degree. In the consultation questionnaire about a candidate who is to be proposed to become a bishop, this theological dimension is verified not only regarding the orthodoxy of the candidate but also whether he has published any writing on biblical or theological disciplines. Though holding a high academic degree is a very positive point in the curriculum vitae of the candidate, a doctoral or a master's degree is not one of the fundamental requirements for his appointment as a bishop.

All the Catholic bishops have to do inevitably with theology in their pastoral ministry occurs through homilies, messages, collective or diocesan pastoral letters, and so on. But even in this aspect, these documents are not always produced by the bishop himself. He may have his own theologian consultant, a priest who is professionally qualified and who can prepare the draft of a document to be corrected and approved by the bishop. This is also the case of bishops convening in a synod of bishops or in an ecumenical council in which collaboration between a bishop and a theologian is clear.

The main focus of our reflection here is not whether the bishop has to possess a sound theological knowledge or whether he has the right to consult a professional theologian, a scriptural scholar, or a canon law specialist; that is taken for granted. The focus of our reflection could be formulated in the following practical questions regarding not the bishops of the world but addressed to our bishops in the countries of Africa and Madagascar: What role should theological research and theological scholarship play in the teaching function of our bishops? In the early Church, the bishops were at the same time the great theologians to the extent that their writings are consulted today as coming from the fathers of the Church. African bishops St Augustine of Hippona and St Cyril of Alexandria are two good examples of this, among others. Is this a matter belonging only to the past, or can we expect that a bishop also in our times to engage in theological scholarship? Is it possible and desirable that we may have in our particular Churches in Africa bishops who are at the same time prolific writers and sound theologians?

In the case of a positive response to this question, what methodological approach and sources are or should be used for this theological production? In the case of a negative response, what should be the dialogue and collaboration between the bishop and the professor of theology at the academic level?

Let us take these two main questions separately for the sake of clarity.

The Bishop as Theologian

I would like to take my personal experience as a starting point for this reflection; the reason is not that my experience should be normative but that it helps me reflect on the challenges the question involves.

Before becoming a bishop, I was a professor of theology for several years in Kinshasa and in Nairobi.[3] I mention that I was a professor of theology, not a theologian; I published some books during those years,[4] but I do not pretend to count myself among the great theological researchers in Africa. However, I was in daily contact with the world of the academy at the university level. The libraries were rich and close at hand, and my teaching responsibilities obliged me to keep myself updated on the subjects of my teaching, mostly pastoral and fundamental theology.

The first change came when I was appointed secretary general of the Archdiocese of Addis Ababa in 1998. The administrative nature of my work and its heavy volume cut me from the academic world to the point that I could not accept the request made to me of teaching at the Franciscan Institute of Philosophy and Theology in Addis Ababa. However, this "parenthesis" lasted only three years, after which I was appointed director of a Spiritual Centre in the small town of Debrezeit, not far from Addis Ababa. During that time, the reflex of the former professor of theology in me reappeared to some extent, and I had the opportunity of being involved in the drafting process of some pastoral letters of the bishops' conference of Ethiopia as well as being responsible for a column in the monthly Catholic newspaper.[5] Small things, but still in the line of theological production.

But the most radical difficulty came when I was surprisingly appointed the bishop responsible for Soddo-Hosanna, the then-biggest apostolic vicariate of Ethiopia in the southern part of the country. At that moment, the shift was complete; a theologian interested in reflecting on the economy of salvation became a pastor and an administrator concerned more with the salvation of the economy in one of the poorest and most-distant regions of the country.

In those circumstances, without access to any library and with a considerable volume of work and challenges of a different nature, my theological sources were practically limited to the Vatican documents on the Internet. I had neither the time nor the facilities to do any theological research. I could barely find the time to read recent books and articles on theology as bedtime reading so as not to completely lose my contact with the world of the academy. Since my situation is not much different from the situation of my colleague bishops in the country, I revised my criticism about the lack of theological reading of the bishops, and I felt the need as well as the challenges of the ongoing formation of bishops, with which I had been an active collaborator in the past.[6]

I think my experience is not unique, and we could make a survey of those bishops of Africa who were and still are good theologians but apparently became silent after episcopal consecration. This calls for a deeper analysis of the structures that are causing this situation. Our bishops teach; it is their duty, but they hardly can continue learning, though this should be their right.

Collaboration with Theologians

To remedy the previously described situation, bishops' conferences usually entrust the composition of their pastoral letters to priest theologians, usually, professors in a university or in a major seminary. They are considered "consultant theologians" of the bishops. Even if there is a good theologian among the bishops, the preference is to call for such theologian consultants so the final document may not appear the opinion enforced by one of the bishops on the others.

The case of a personal theologian consultant for an individual bishop may also happen (though not so often), especially in dioceses in which the clergy are living in the same "academic poverty" as the bishop.

However, the recourse to a theologian brings also a negative effect: the bishops can completely decline the duty of reflecting theologically because there is a "professional" doing so for them and presenting them drafts that in most cases are discussed in just superficial detail before being approved. It happens quite often that pastoral letters at the national level are not appropriated by the individual bishops but are quickly archived and are rarely implemented because the bishops do not consider those letters their own production and property. This also is a point that deserves deeper analysis.

Collaboration between bishops and theologians is absolutely necessary to create a unified body of doctrine and to avoid two different kinds of magisterium: the official magisterium of the bishops and the so-called *magisterium theologorum*.

The role and the work of the theologian should be recognised and respected, but sometimes, the theologian feels looked upon as a potentially dangerous creature who has to be kept away from the hierarchy. Such was my experience during the first African Synod in 1994 as a theologian consultant appointed by the AMECEA bishops who attended the synod in Rome. I was working for them, but it took all their influence and insistence so I would be admitted to enter into the synod aula at least for one morning to gain some experience of the event with which I was actively collaborating from outside.

Conclusion

I proposed a reflection during the Seminar of Rectors and Deans of Studies of AMECEA countries in 1995 concerning the establishment of an association of theologians, at that time circumscribed to the AMECEA countries but today to be conceived on the continental level of Africa. I quote what I wrote at that time in the introduction to the proceedings of that seminar.

I dream of an association of theologians that would not be restricted to professional theologians teaching in major seminaries and universities but that would also welcome all those men and women who are doing theology at a more popular and pastoral level such as teachers, preachers, and writers; an association in which there would be a forum for common research and discussion on all the major areas proposed by the synod of bishops for Africa; an association in which our often dispersed and sometimes opposed efforts could find a common ground for sharing; an association in which the purpose is not necessarily to think in the same way but to be able to express one's views in a climate of freedom, trust, and fraternity.

If we are convinced that not only the new methodology in teaching theology but also the new evangelisation has to proceed from human life to theology, the creation of this association ... is a real necessity.[7]

I am convinced that the Theological Colloquium on Church, Religion and Society in Africa which occasioned the writing of this chapter represents that beginning of the realisation of my dream.

Endnotes

1   *Apostolorum Successores* (24 January 2004).

2   Cf. *Apostolorum Successores*, nos. 118–41.

3   At the major seminary Jean XXIII in Kinshasa from 1973 to 1976, and at The Catholic University of Eastern Africa (CUEA) and Hekima College in Nairobi from 1985 to 1994. I am proud to have been one of the "founding fathers" of these institutions.

4   Some of my books were *Seeking and Finding God in All Things* (Nairobi: St Paul Publications–Africa, 1986); *The Church in the Neighbourhood* (Nairobi: St Paul Publications–Africa, 1992); *The Conscience of Society*, (editor), Hekima College Collection, no. 4 (Nairobi: Paulines Publications–Africa, 1995), and several other books in collaboration with other authors.

5   These articles were later on published together in a book form with the title *We Are the Church* (Nairobi: Paulines Publications–Africa, 2009).

6   We have to acknowledge here the great importance of the ongoing formation sessions organised by AMECEA for bishops such as the one in May 2001 compiled in the book edited by Patrick Ryan, *New Strategies for New Evangelisation in Africa* (Nairobi: Paulines Publications–Africa, 2002). The Catholic University of Eastern Africa organised an interesting seminar for all the rectors and deans of the major seminaries and theological colleges of AMECEA countries, held July 3–7, 1995. Unfortunately, no bishop was invited to this important event.

7   See *From Life to Theology, Proceeding of the Second Seminar of CUEA Staff, Rectors and Deans of the Major Seminaries and Theological Colleges of AMECEA countries* (July 3–7, 1995) (Nairobi: Paulines Publications–Africa, 1996), 8–9.

The Promise of a New Generation of African Theologians: Reimagining African Theology with Fidelity and Creativity

Bienvenu Mayemba

Introduction

My chapter has three parts. The first, my starting point, speaks of the impact of postcolonial consciousness that shapes the world context in which African theologians are called to live and theologise. The second presents fidelity and creativity as two qualities that have characterised our elder theologians and that should characterise today's new generation of African theologians. The third consists of a sketch or outline for a course on (contemporary) African Christian theology. My conclusion shares some of my wishes and dreams concerning African theologians and the articulation of African theological discourse in today's Africa.

I. Postcolonial Consciousness: The World Context in which Today's African Theologians are Called to Live and Theologise

African theologians are doing African theology today in a cultural, intellectual, and political context marked by a major trend that provides us a new rationality and new paradigms of thought and praxis. This trend is postcolonialism or postcolonial theory.[1] Here are its major figures: Aimé Césaire, Frantz Fanon, Patrice Lumumba, Kwame Krumah, Steve Biko, Ahmadou Kourouma, Mabika Kalanda, Chinua Achebe, Wole Soyinka, Marcien Towa, Jean-Marc Ela, Fabien Eboussi-Boulaga, Ngugi wa Thiong'o, Valentin Yves Mudimbe, Achille Mbembe, Kwame Anthony Appiah, Kwame Gyekye, Cornel West, Dwight Hopkins, Marimba Ani, Emmanuel Chukwudi Eze, and Shaw Copeland, and many non-African scholars such as Edward Saïd, Gayatri Chakravorty Spivak, Homi Bhaba,

Ania Loomba, Leela Ghandhi, Robert Young, George Balandier, and Adam Hochschild.

Postcolonialism or postcolonial theory is a constitutive pattern of postmodernity; it refers not only "to intellectual culture, a set of premises in guiding various intellectual disciplines and interpretive theories" but also "to the forms of life which influence and are the effects of intellectual thought."[2]

Speaking of postmodernity, it is appropriate to acknowledge the different theories about the relationship between modernity and postmodernity.[3] Some postmodernists claim that postmodernity constitutes a break with modernity as it negates the foundations of its paradigms of thought,[4] while others say postmodernity is a radicalisation of modernity.[5] Some criticise postmodernity's pretentions and contradictions.[6] Others again affirm that postmodernity is not a rejection of modernity, but rather, that it critically reconsiders the legacy of modernity and provides new perspectives and thought patterns capable of changing the world community.[7]

In this perspective – which I share – postmodernity is understood not just as a break with or a simple radicalisation of modernity but also as continuity in discontinuity. In fact, postmodernity constitutes both a reaction and a response to modernity, especially to its classical, rationalist thought. It integrates the project of modern rationality but challenges it, reevaluates it, and reinterprets it in a new way. "The postmodernist reflexive activity reveals new facets of the modernisation consciousness showing that its conceptual basis should be reconsidered anew in the perspective offered by the contemporary [world]."[8]

As a postmodern phenomenon, postcolonial theory has promoted a contemporary consciousness that, in the light of Roger Haight's postmodern christological book, *Jesus Symbol of God*,[9] can be conceptualised and framed in five dimensions. The first dimension is a "radical historical consciousness" that is "convertible with the relativity of the ideas and values one takes for granted" and that values historicity and new interpretations in light of contemporary models or paradigms of thought.[10]

The second dimension is a "critical social (and political) awareness"[11] nourished by a great awareness of "the social understanding of human existence," showing that "individualism does not correspond to the social construction of the human,"[12] and that the struggle for mutual responsibility, freedom, and social justice are part of our human imperative call to stand and to "to exercise corporate responsibility in the creation of just social structures."[13]

The third dimension of postcolonial theory involves a "pluralist consciousness," that is,

> a sense of the difference of others, of the pluralism of societies, cultures and religions, and of the relativity that this entails. One can no longer claim western culture as the center, the higher point of view.... The world is pluralistic and polycentric in its horizons and interpretations.[14]

The fourth dimension is a "cosmic consciousness"[15] that challenges our classical perception of the cosmos, relativises the centrality of humanity in the universe, and provides a new perspective on the unity of the human race and human solidarity. "We constitute a common humanity on this planet, indeed, a community, despite all the differences in religion and culture." We need to promote the importance of our common humanity, "a human community in a common habitat, and a shared process of nature of which all are a part, and the same time respects human differences in this postmodern world."[16] This dimension also includes a growing environmental awareness.

The fifth dimension is an epistemological consciousness grounded in the conviction that there is a plurality of rationalities and epistemologies and that Western rationality and morality are not normative and paradigmatic and should be decentralised and relativised.[17] No civilisation has the right to establish itself as a universal reference, and any form of epistemological ethnocentrism should be challenged, and its foundations have to be deconstructed.

This quintuple consciousness is associated with a great sense of reflexiveness or critical attitude grounded in modern rationality, refusing to take things for granted, and rejecting totalising paradigms, universalisation of particularities, and absolutisation of historical norms. Indeed, as Haight admits, "Generally speaking, postmodernity's historical and pluralistic consciousness have taken the teeth out of the totalising pretensions of systems of thought."[18]

In fact, this attitude against any type of imperialism or "dogmatism" has led to new theoretical movements such as deconstructionism and, especially, postcolonial theory, whose consciousness has radicalised its challenge and deconstruction not only of Western epistemological ethnocentrism – to use Valentin Yves Mudimbe's concept[19] – but also of any form of colonialist, imperialist, and repressive ideology, what Emmanuel Lévinas calls "totality,"[20] what Jonathan Sacks names "Plato's Ghost,"[21] and what Jean-Marc Ela calls "anti-brotherhood culture."[22]

II. *Voici le temps des héritiers*: Fidelity and Creativity. An Imperative Call to African Theologians Today

African theology has to be articulated in the spirit of dialogue with this quintuple postcolonial consciousness. It should follow "the imperative of Vatican II's *Gaudium et Spes* to address the contemporary world, to make faith intelligible in terms that it can understand."[23] It should be grounded on the conviction that "Christianity in the twentieth-first century must confront new problems and issues that will generate genuinely new understandings and behaviour patterns in and by the Churches."[24] African traditional society should thus not be our only source of inspiration. Many of today's young Africans are urban and city dwellers or citadins. They have never been in their native villages or in the savage jungle that we see on television. They have never wrestled with a South African lion or a Zambian tiger, like Tarzan or a Masai warrior as we see it in Western cartoons. They have never seen or touched a Nigerian monkey, a Tanzanian giraffe, a Namibian zebra, an Ivorian elephant, or a Togolese snake. They do not ride on Egyptian donkeys, Ethiopian camels, or Rwandese horses. They do not run around naked, bare-chested, or covered only with palm branches to protect themselves against Sudanese flies or Kenyan bees. They use the Internet, cell phone, and I-phones, I-pods and I-pads. They use Facebook, Skype, Twitter, and Google; they utilise Yahoo Messenger to chat, and they rely on various websites to watch movies and sports. They wear beautiful African clothes, or brand-name Western ties and suits, or stylish miniskirts or baggy trousers. They travel by plane, car, motorbike, taxi, bus, or woro-woro, gbaka, or matatus.

They play Ugandan drums and Senegalese balafons but also piano, organ, and violin. They play Belgian saxophones but also Congolese likembes or South African vuvuzelas. They dance Congolese ndombolo and Ivorian coupé-décallé but also choreographies from Michael Jackson, Beyoncé, Chris Brown, and Rihanna. They listen to Alpha Blondy, Yvon Chaka Chaka, and Youssou Ndour as well as Mozart, Beethoven, and Handel.

They watch American and South African TV shows, Chinese and Nigerian movies, Ivorian comedy shows, and Congolese choreographies. They pay attention to Robert Mugabe, Oprah, Kim Kardashian, and Barack and Michelle Obama as well as Pope Francis, the Dalai Lama, and Bishop Desmond Tutu.

They hear about Silvio Berlusconi, Boko Haram, Al Qaeda, and M23's rape of women in DRC, but they also hear about Wangari Maathai, Nelson Mandela, UN Human Rights Watch, and the Peace Corps. They do not know many of their own African sports figures but know much about U.S. basketball players such as Kobe Bryant and Latin American football players such as Lionel Messi.

Many young Africans live in the cities, away from villages. They have not gone through initiation rites, and they do not master their ethnic languages, beliefs, customs, or traditions. They do not grasp the depth and meaningfulness of concepts or Christological models such as proto-ancestor, ancestor, master of initiation, tribal chief, muthamaki, muzimu mukulu, witchdoctor, or traditional healer.

Older and younger African theologians should recognise the value of these concepts or models and acknowledge their limits for today's Africa and the new generation of Africans. We need to draw inspiration and wisdom from our elder brothers' and sisters' insights, but we also have to be sensitive to our younger brothers' and sisters' experiences to be relevant, useful, and transformational; this sensitivity requires creativity, imagination, and innovation in our theological investigations.

Yes, it is the heir's time, *le temps des héritiers*. In fact, one of the titles of Jean-Marc Ela's books is *Voici le temps des Héritiers* (1981),[25] with which this Catholic priest, theologian, and sociologist from Cameroon opened doors to a new wave of African theologians and to new ways of articulating African theological discourses. He took into account new realities, new experiences, new audiences, and new signs of the times.

Heritage is not only about the past, or the *zamani,* to use John Mbiti's word.[26] Heritage implies the notion of *lóbí,* Lingala for "yesterday" and "tomorrow," depending on the verb. *Tokoya lobi* means "We will come tomorrow," while *Toyaki lobi* means "We came yesterday." Between yesterday and tomorrow is *lelô,* "today."

In Kikongo, *mazono* means "yesterday," *gunu* means "today," and *mbasi* means "tomorrow." A heritage tells us about the past, supports us in the present, and prepares us for the future; it involves the memory of the past and the memory of the future. Heritage also involves a promise and tells us we should not move forward without looking back. Since our African memory is future-oriented despite the Kenyan Anglican theologian and philosopher John Mbiti's phenomenological interpretation of African concept of time,[27] we look back to the past, to the myth of our ancestors for the sake of the future and future generations.

Such a double "regard" or "view" of the past and the future requires fidelity to the past, to our "dangerous" memories (J. B. Metz) and our pathetic and heroic memories. It also involves creativity to make new paths into the future with hope and optimism. This creativity is what Jean-Marc Ela calls the "ethics of transgression" for the sake of "epistemological rupture." Such creativity led him to articulate theologically his pastoral experience with the Kirdi people of Tokombéré village in northern Cameroun and turn it into a theological paradigm. He extrapolated from it a theology of revelation that takes seriously God's self-communication in history and a theology of salvation as liberation in the name of God's kingdom of peace and justice.[28]

This work of creativity and fidelity appears in the writings of many of our elder brothers and sisters in theological research and teaching. I feel proud when I read the godmother of African feminist theology, Mercy Amba Oduyoye, dealing either with hermeneutics as in her *Daughters of Anowa*[29] or with narrative as in her *A Coming Home to Myself: The Childless Woman in the West Africa Space,*[30] or with apologetics as in her *Hearing and Knowing,*[31] or in her *Beads and Brands,*[32] or in her *Critique of John Mbiti's view on love and marriage in Africa.*[33] I feel the same pride as a young African theologian when I reflect on Engelbert Mveng's notion of "anthropological poverty" and his anthropological interpretation of the pharaonic myth of Osiris and Isis.[34] I feel proud of Jean-Marc Ela's concept of "ethics of transgression" and of Bénézet Bujo's effort to lift us beyond universal claim of Western morality and to provide us with the foundation of an African ethics. I feel proud of our other elders' christological models: François Kabasélé and Charles Nyamiti's christology of "Christ as our Ancestor,"[35] Anselme Sanon's "Jesus Christ as Master of Initiation,"[36] Cécé Kolié's "Jesus as healer,"[37] and Bénézet Bujo's "Jesus Christ as Proto-ancestor."[38]

I am proud of Vincent Mulago's concept of "vital participation" or "vital communion,"[39] John Mbiti's eschatological reflections from an African perspective,[40] Eboussi Boulaga's African hermeneutics of Christian revelation,[41] Kä Mana's deconstruction of African mythical imaginary,[42] Desmond Tutu's *ubuntu* theological model,[43] Meinrad Hegba's quest for a fundamental African theology that includes paranormal phenomena, non-Cartesian rationality,[44] healing by witchcraft, and deliverance from evil spirits and demonic possession.

I am proud of Orobator's theological reappropriation of Chinua Achebe's *Things Fall Apart,*[45] Messi-Metogo's hermeneutics of religious indifference and agnosticism in Africa,[46] Philomena Mwaura's phenomenological approach to new religious movements,[47] Josée Ngalula's impressive edition of African theological bibliographies,[48] Teresa Okure's[49] and Paulin Poucouta's recapture of the biblical message from other eyes,[50] especially from the African perspective, and Nathanaël Soédé and Sebastien Muyengo's integration of African perspectives in the bioethics debate.[51] And, of course, I am proud of myself and my efforts to read African theologians and require my students to read them and engage in theological dialogue with them.[52]

All these African theological initiatives should make us proud and motivate us to be imaginative, creative, and innovative as we are faithful to our Church communities and committed to our faith.

Fidelity and creativity are two qualities the new generation of African theologians should live up to as we assume the past and the theological contributions of our elders and as we embrace the present and articulate our own theological productions. Combining fidelity and creativity is what the French Christian philosopher Gabriel Marcel calls "creative fidelity" when speaking of the phenomenology of the encounter or of the relationship with the other.[53] Creative fidelity is a concept that was theologically taken up by American Catholic theologian Francis Sullivan in his reflection on how to weight and interpret documents of the Catholic Church's magisterium.[54] A commitment to creative fidelity is a requirement for all African theologians; it is a process that should include elaborating new sketches for an African fundamental theology course, rethinking current African theological models, teaching African theologians and theology in our schools and centers, and reaffirming and reconsidering Africa as a theological paradigm.

III. Outline for a Course on African Christian Theology

In the early sixties, Karl Rahner published an essay of a sketch/outline for a course on dogmatic theology. It was not really followed up by other professor of dogmatics, but he stuck to it.[55] A couple of years later, he published another sketch/outline for a course on the theology of the Trinity, and again, it was not followed up, especially since he was accused of promoting modalist Trinitarian doctrine[56] just like Karl Barth.[57] In the late seventies, Claude Geffré published a sketch for a course on theology of revelation. It has never really been followed up, but he stuck to it while teaching at Institut Catholique de Paris.

In a similar vein, I have developed a sketch for a course on African Christian theology. If it not accepted and applied, like Rahner and Geffré, it might generate some personal disappointment, but I remain convinced of its value and pertinence.[58]

The following outline is modeled on the curriculum of Jesuit Institute of Theology (ITCJ) in Abidjan, where one of the courses I teach is "African Theology: Christian Perspectives." My colleagues and I share the conviction that African theology is not just about inculturation or "Christ as our ancestor."

Part 1: Major Characteristics of African Traditional Religious and Philosophical Thought

This part focuses on the precolonial African worldview that through its customs, beliefs, and traditions influences our behaviors, shapes our personality, and provides a cultural and religious ground to our identity. Depending on the teacher's expertise, it may include major concepts of pharaonic religion, such as the principle of Maât, the myth of Osiris, or the religious wisdom from the ancient Egyptian Book of the Dead.

One of the objectives of this part is to teach our students to view African philosophy and religions positively and to introduce them to their major characteristics.

Part 2: Revisiting African Pathetic Memories: Slave Trade, Colonisation, Apartheid, Monopartism, and Dictatorship

This part consists in a hermeneutics of slavery, colonisation, apartheid, monopartyism, and dictatorship. It reflects on their consequences, especially on how Westerners, through their ethnocentrism, "invented," "constructed," and "defined" the Africa continent and African peoples, on how Westerners and Africans perceived each other, on how Africans perceive themselves, and on how these Africans' pathetic and painful memories and experiences have had an impact on contemporary Africa and Africans.

Part 3: Reappropriating African Heroic Memories and Reclaiming African Subjectivity: Negritude, Black Consciousness Movement, and the African Struggle for Independence and for Democracy

This part deals with major movements, such as the Négritude that challenged the "colonial situation," denounced depersonalisation of blacks, promoted black personality and identity, and fought for democracy, political pluralism, and social justice in Africa.

Part 4: The Emergence of African Theological Consciousness and Discourse

This part reflects on the emergence of African theological consciousness and discourse through a variety of publications, with a particular focus on Placide Tempels's *Bantu Philosophy* (1948), *Des Prêtres noirs s'interroge* (1956), the 1960 theological debate between the then-student Tharcisse Tshibangu and his dean, Msgr Alfred Vanneste, at the Catholic Faculty of Theology of the University of Lovanium (now University of Kinshasa), and some of the publications by Alioune Diop's *Présence Africaine* editions, such as *Personnalité Africaine et Catholicisme* (1963). [59]

Part 5: Vatican Council II and the Promotion of Cultural and Theological Pluralist Consciousness

This part integrates African theological discourse in the context and tradition of Vatican II and shows the impact of the council on the development of African theology. Particular attention is given to its sensitivity to cultural and religious pluralism and to Paul VI's contribution to the promotion of pluralism through his letters such as *Evangelium nuntiandi* and *Africae terrarum* and his other speeches on African Christianity during his apostolic travel to Africa and encounter with African bishops.[60]

Part 6: Major African Christian Theological Models

This part presents and interprets a classification of contemporary theological models in five paradigms: inculturation, liberation, reconstruction, ethical-political, and epistemological-hermeneutical.

My Wish and Dreams as an African Postmodern and Postcolonial Theologian

African theology is not just about reflecting on God and finding ways to inculturate the Christian message. It is about who we are as Africans in our relationship with ourselves, with God, with other beings, and with the world. It is about who we are in assuming our past, present, and future; reappropriating our stories, memories, and narratives; and embracing our fears, dreams, failures, triumphs, consolations, and desolation. African theology is about whom the "God of Jesus Christ"[61] is for us Africans, how we interpret his revelation and self-communication to us, how we represent his presence in our midst, and how we present ourselves before him as subjects who hear and practice his message of salvation and liberation. Hence, African theology should engage in dialogue with other human sciences, especially with history, anthropology, sociology, psychology, literature, philosophy, and postcolonial theory.

Does African theology seem relevant or make sense to every African? No, unfortunately! In January 2013, I spoke with two major seminarians from Anyama, in Abidjan, Côte d'Ivoire. When I told them I taught African theology, they seemed shocked. "You teach African theology? Why do you have to speak of African theology? It makes no sense! A course on inculturation is understandable, but on African theology? What would you teach? Do you have materials?"

At another occasion, I spoke with students of philosophy from the University Felix Houphoüet-Boigny in Cocody, Abidjan, Côte d'Ivoire.

We were discussing their thesis projects. It was shocking and painful to hear an African student telling me he would not write his thesis on an African philosopher because his fellow students would make fun of him and would think he was not bright enough! That's what happens when we don't teach our students how to appreciate our own thinkers, philosophers, and theologians.

European and American theologians are known because teachers speak of them and study them. Our theologians are not very well known in African universities or major seminaries because they are not spoken of; indeed, many of them are known more in the West than in their own countries! We need African theology professors who are happy and confident to speak of African theologians with joy, competence, and pride.

My wish is that African theological schools and centres would promote African theology and African theologians. We should teach our students not only European or American theologians but also African theologians. Our students should be able to quote Jean-Marc Ela and Mercy Amba Oduyoye as well as Henry de Lubac and Karl Rahner. They should be able to speak of Charles Nyamiti and Engelbert Mveng as well as Edward Schillebeeckx and Yves Congar. They should be proud to work on Laurenti Magesa, Vincent Mulago, and Teresa Okure as well as Jon Sobrino and Hans Küng.

To paraphrase Orobator's title, we need African theological schools brewed in African pots.[62] African theological schools and centres should keep moving forward in establishing themselves as truly African and truly theological. Being a parrot is dishonorable and prideless; being a monad is ugly and dangerous. A parrot repeats without critical mind and consciousness, and a monad is a threat to postmodern and postcolonial pluralist consciousness.

I am happy and proud to be an African postmodern and postcolonial theologian.

Endnotes

1   As an ongoing trend of thought and praxis, "postcolonialism" is different from "post-colonialism," which is a particular historical period, a moment in African

history that refers to post-independence Africa, to Africa after the "Sun of independence" (Ahmadou Kourouma, *Les soleils des independences* [Paris: Seuil, 1970]).

2   Roger Haight, *Jesus Symbol of God* (Maryknoll, N.Y.: Orbis, 1999), 24.

3   Paul Lakeland presents three perception of postmodernity; cf. Paul Lakeland, *Postmodernity: Christian Identity in a Fragmented Age* (Minneapolis: Fortress Press, 1997), 16–18; Roger Haight, *Jesus Symbol of God,* 331.

4   Cf. G. Vattimo, *The End of Modernity: Nihilism and Hermeneutics in Postmodern Culture* (Oxford: Polity Press, 1991), 80.

5   Cf. A. Giddens, *The Consequence of Modernity* (Cambridge: Polity Press, 1995), 45, 52–53.

6   S. Weiss and K. Wesley, "Postmodernism and its critics"; www.as.ua.edu/ant/ Faculty/murphy/436/pomo.htm; P. M. Rosenau, *Post-Modernism and the Social Sciences: Insights, Inroads and Intrusions* (Princeton, N.J.: Princeton University Press, 1992); R. D'Andrade, "Moral Models in Anthropology," in *Current Anthropology* 5, no. 36: 399–407.

7   Jean-François Lyotard, *The Postmodern Explained* (Minneapolis: University of Minneapolis Press, 1993), 80; David Harvey, *The Condition of Postmodernity: An Inquiry into the Origins of Cultural Change* (Malden-Oxford: Blackwell Publishers, 1991); B. Goubman, "Postmodernity as the Climax of Modernity: Horizons of the Cultural Future," in *The Paideia;* www.bu.edu/wcp/Papers/Cult/ CultGoub.htm.

8   Ibid.

9   Haight, *Jesus Symbol of God.* See also Roger Haight, "The American Jesuit Theologian," in *Jesuit Postmodern. Scholarship, Vocation, and Identity in the 21st Century,* ed. Francis X. Clooney (Lanham-Oxford: Lexington Books, 2006); Roger Haight, *An Alternative Vision. An Interpretation of Liberation Theology* (New York: Paulist Press, 1985).

10   Haight, *Jesus Symbol of God,* 331–32.

11   Ibid., 332.

12   Ibid., 24.

13   Ibid., 332–33.

14   Ibid., 333.

15   Ibid.

16   Ibid., 334.

17   Cf., for example, Valentin Y. Mudimbe, *The Invention of Africa: Gnosis, Philosophy, and the Order of Knowledge* (London-Bloomington/Indianapolis: James Currey-Indiana University Press, 1988); Bénézet Bujo, *Foundations of an African Ethics. Beyond the Universal Claims of Western Morality*, Trans. B. McNeil (New York: Crossroad, 2001).

18 Haight, *Jesus Symbol of God,* xiii.

19 Mudimbe, *The Invention of Africa.*

20 Understood from the perspective of Emmanuel Lévinas's ethical metaphysics, "totality" is the violent imperialism of the self, reducing everything to unity in a process of totalisation that denies to others their radical identity or otherness. Cf. E. Lévinas, *Totalité et Infini: Essai sur l'extériorité,* 4ᵉ ed. (Martinus Nijhoff, La Haye, 1984), 9; *Autrement qu'être ou au-delà de l'essence* (Paris: Fata Morgana, 1974), 181–82; "Totalité et Totalisation." *Encyclopedia Universalis,* tome 22 (1992): 191–94. This violent self can be seen either as individual or as institution, so we can also define totality as an attitude from individuals or institutions that set themselves as a universal reference, imposing their views or ways on others without any sense of dialogue and mutuality. Such individuals or institutions are characterised by a radical intolerance, a highhanded insistence on uniformity, and a universalistic claim of their paradigms.

21 Cf. Jonathan Sacks, "The Dignity of Difference: Exorcising Plato's Ghost," in Jonathan Sacks, *The Dignity of Difference: How to Avoid the Clash of Civilisations* (London–New York: Continuum), 48–49.

22 Jean-Marc Ela, *Le cri de l'homme africain: Questions aux chrétiens et aux églises d'Afrique* (Paris: L'Harmattan, 1980).

23 Haight, *Jesus Symbol of God,* xii.

24 Ibid.

25 Jean-Marc Ela and René Luneau, *Voici le temps des Héritiers. Eglises d'Afrique et voies nouvelles* (Paris, Karthala, 1981).

26 See chapter 3 of his *African Religions and Philosophy,* 2nd ed., (Oxford-Portsmouth, N.H.: Heinemann, 1989).

27 John Mbiti, *African Religions and Philosophy,* 2nd ed. (Oxford-Portsmouth, N.H.: Heinemann, 1989), especially chapter 3.

28 Jean-Marc Ela, *African Cry* (Eugene, Ore.: Wipf and Stock); *My Faith as an African* (Eugene, Ore.: Wipf and Stock, 2009); *Repenser la théologie africaine. Le Dieu qui libère* (Paris, Karthala, 2003).

29 Cf. Mercy Amba Oduyoye, *Daughters of Anowa: African Women and Patriarchy* (Maryknoll, N.Y.: Orbis, 1995).

30 Cf. Mercy Amba Oduyoye, "A Coming Home to Myself: The Childless Woman in the West Africa Space," in *Liberating Eschatology: Essay in Honor of Letty M. Russell,* ed. Serene Jones and Margaret A. Farley (Louisville, Ky.: Westminster John Knox Press, 1999), 105–22.

31 Mercy Amba Oduyoye, *Hearing and Knowing: Theological Reflections on Christianity in Africa* (Maryknoll, N.Y.: Orbis, 1985).

32 Mercy Amba Oduyoye, *Beads and Strands: Reflections of an African Woman on Christianity in Africa* (Maryknoll, N.Y.: Orbis, 2004).

33   Mercy Amba Oduyoye, "A critique of John Mbiti's view on love and marriage in Africa," in *Religious Plurality in Africa: Essays in Honour of John S. Mbiti*, ed. Jacob K. Olupona (New York–Berlin: Mouton de Gruyter, 1993), 341–65.

34   Engelbert Mveng, "Impoverishment and Liberation: A Theological Approach for Africa and the Third World," in *Paths of African Theology*, ed. Rosino Gibellini (Maryknoll, N.Y.: Orbis, 1994), 154–65; "Third World Theology – What Theology? What Third World? Evaluation by an African Delegate," in *Irruption of the Third World: Challenge to Theology*, ed. Virginia Fabella and Sergio Torres (Maryknoll, N.Y.: Orbis, 1983), 217–21.

35   Charles Nyamiti, *Christ as Our Ancestor: Christology from an African Perspective* (Gweru, Harare: Mambo Press, 1984); Augustin Ntima Nkanza, "Charles Nyamiti et la christologie du Frère Ancêtre," in Augustin Ntima Nkanza, *Non. Je ne mourrai pas, je vivrai. Méditation sur le cheminement christologique en Afrique* (Kinshasa: Editions Loyola, 1996); François Kabasele, "Le Christ comme Ancêtre et Aîné," in *Chemins de la christologie africaine*, dir. François Kabasele (Paris: Desclée, 2001), 131–44.

36   Anselme Sanon, "Jesus, Master of Initiation," in *Faces of Jesus in Africa*, ed. Robert J. Schreiter (Maryknoll, N.Y.: Orbis, 1991), 85–102.

37   Cécé Kolié, "Jesus as healer," in *Jesus in African Christianity: Experimentation and Diversity in African Christology*, ed. Jesse N. K. Mugambi and Laurenti Magesa (Nairobi: Acton Publishers, 1998); "Jesus As Healer," in *Faces of Jesus in Africa*, ed. Robert J. Schreiter (Maryknoll, N.Y.: Orbis, 1991), 128–50.

38   Bénézet Bujo, *African Theology in its Social Context* (Eugene, Ore.: Wipf and Stock, 2006).

39   Vincent Mulago, "Vital Participation: The Cohesive Principle of the Bantu Community," in *Biblical Revelation and African Beliefs*, ed. Kwesi A. Dickson and Paul Ellingworth (Maryknoll, N.Y.: Orbis, 1969), 137–58.

40   John Mbiti, *New Testament Eschatology in the African Background: A Study of the Encounter between New Testament Theology and African Traditional Concepts* (Oxford: Oxford University Press, 1971); John Mbiti, "Eschatology," in *Biblical Revelation and African Beliefs*, ed. Kwesi A. Dickson and Paul Ellingworth (Maryknoll, N.Y.: Orbis, 1969), 162–63.

41   Fabien Eboussi-Boulaga, *Christianisme sans fétiche: Révélation et domination* (Paris: Présencce Africaine, 1981).

42   Kä Mana, *L'Afrique va-t-elle mourir: Bousculer l'imaginaire africain. Essai d'éthique politique* (Paris: Cerf, 1991).

43   Michael Battle, *Ubuntu: I in You and You in Me* (New York: Seabury Books, 2009); *Reconciliation: The Ubuntu Theology of Desmond Tutu* (Cleveland: The Pilgrim Press, 1997).

44   Meinrad Hebga, *Sorcellerie et prière de délivrance : réflexion sur une expérience* (Présence africaine: INADES, 1982); *La rationalité d'un discours africain sur les phénomènes paranormaux* (Paris: L'Harmattan, 1998).

45   Agbonkhianmeghe E. Orobator, *Theology Brewed in an African Pot* (Paulines Publications Africa, 2008).

46   Eloi Messi Metogo, *Dieu peut-il mourir en Afrique? Essai sur l'indifférence religieuse et l'incroyance en Afrique noire* (Paris: Karthala, 1997).

47   Philomena Mwaura, "Concept of Basic Human Rights in African Independent Pentecostal Church of Africa and Jesus is Alive Ministries," *Journal of World Christianity* 5, no. 1 (2012): 9–42.

48   Josée Ngalula, *Production théologique africaine (1956–2010)* (Kinshasa: Éditions Mont Sinaï, 2011), 390.

49   Cf. Teresa Okure, *The Johannine Approach to Mission: a Contextual Study of John 4:1–42,* (Tübingen: J.C.B. Mohr, 1988); Teresa Okure, "Women in the Bible," in *With Passion and Compassion: Third World Women Doing Theology,* ed. Virginia Fabella and Mercy Amba Oduyoye (Maryknoll, N.Y.: 1988), 47–59; "Feminist Interpretations in Africa," in *Searching the Scriptures,* Vol. 1, ed. Elizabeth Schüssler-Fiorenza (New York: Crossroad, 1994), 76–85; "The Mother of Jesus in the New Testament: Implications for Women in Mission," *Journal of Inculturation Theology* 3, no. 2 (1995): 196–210.

50   Paulin Poucouta, *Quand la parole de Dieu visite l'Afrique. Lecture plurielle de la Bible (*Paris: Karthala, 2011), 250; *Lettres aux Eglises d'Afrique. Apocalypse 1–3,* 1ère éd. (Paris-Yaoundé: Karthala-PUCAC, 1997), 288, *Lectures africaines de la bible* (Yaoundé: Presses de l'UCAC, 2002), 122; *La Bible en terres africaines. Quelle est la fécondité de la parole de Dieu?* (Paris: Editions de l'Atelier-Ed. Ouvrières, 1999), 144; "Engelbert Mveng: une lecture africaine de la Bible," *Nouvelle Revue Théologique* 120, no. 1 (janv.-mars 1998): 32–45.

51   Nathanaël Soédé, *Sens et enjeux de l'éthique. Inculturation de l'éthique chrétienne. Approche Théologique Africaine* (Paris: L'Harmattan, 2007), 287; Msgr Sébastien Muyengo, *La Bioéthique en Afrique: Pourquoi, Pour qui, Comment?* (Kinshasa: Editions Universitaires Européennes, 2012), 120.

52   Cf.: Bienvenu Mayemba, in "*Telema,* 25 ans de promotion d'une pensée théologique africaine," in *Telema* 100, no. 4 (October-December 1999): 3–14; "La Foi: *Metanoia,* Passion pour Dieu et Redécouverte des Valeurs Religieuses Africaines. Quelques Réflexions à partir de *Africae Munus,*" in *Hekima Review,* no. 47 (December 2012): 48–57; "L'impact du mythe de l'occident et du désenchantement en Afrique sur les migrations des Africains," in *Congo-Afrique,* no. 451 (janvier 2011): 53–63; "Pharaon, Josué ou le Bon Samaritain. Quel salut pour une Afrique en péril?," in *Telema* 110–111, nos. 2–3 (April-September 2002): 51–65; "Par-delà nos différences: la transgression de l'Egotisme identitaire, un impératif socio-politique," in *Raison Ardente,* no. 49 (June 1997): 118–27; "L'espérance africaine par-delà la désespérance. Un écho au livre du P. Ntima," in *Raison Ardente,* no. 47 (December 1996): 65–74; "Le drame de la trahison de la raison. Oser se révolter contre la Mère," in *Raison Ardente,* no. 48 (March 1997): 115–32; "Against Women's Depersonalisation and Striving for Gender Fairness in a World of Biases and Prejudices: Postcolonial Feminist

Perspectives from Africa," in *Akwaba* (December 2010): 55–62; "The tragedy of Societies without Dialogue. Violence, Autocracy, and Terror…," in *Promotio Iustitiae*, no. 78 (2/2003): 1–6; "Plus fort que la mort… Les Evêques congolais face à la guerre en RDC," in *Telema* 109, no. 1 (January-March 2002): 56–72; "La terreur de l'arbitraire. Le drame d'une société sans sens du dialogue," in *Congo-Afrique* 360 (December 2001): 595–606; "De l'Evasion à l'Engagement. Vivre le christianisme dans la lucidité," in *Hekima Review*, no. 25 (May 2001): 49-59.

53 Gabriel Marcel, *Creative Fidelity* (New York: Noonday Press, 1964).

54 Francis Sullivan, *Creative Fidelity: Weighing and Interpreting Documents of the Magisterium* (New York/Mahwah, N.J.: Paulist Press, 1996).

55 Cf. Karl Rahner, "Essai d'une esquisse de dogmatique," in Karl Rahner, *Écrits Théologiques*, Vol. IV: *Axes théologiques pour demain* (Paris: DDB-Mame, 1970), 7–50.

56 Cf. Karl Rahner, *Dieu Trinité. Fondement transcendant de l'histoire du salut*, 2è éd. (Paris, Cerf, 1999), 77–135.

57 Karl Barth, *Dogmatique*, vol. 1: *La doctrine de la Parole Dieu. Prolégomènes à la Dogmatique*, t.1, 2ème partie (Genève: Labor et Fides, 1953), 51–83. Also see the preceding paragraph (§ 8) on "Dieu dans sa révélation," 1–50.

58 Cf. Claude Geffré, "Esquisse d'une théologie de la révélation," in *La Révélation*, Collectif (Bruxelles: Facultés Universitaires Saint-Louis, 1977), 171–205.

59 Placide Tempels, *Bantu Philosophy* (1948), translated by Rev. Colin King (Paris: Présence Africaine, 1959); *Des prêtres noirs s'interrogent*, collectif (Paris: Présence Africaine-Cerf, 1956); Tharcisse Tshibangu and Alfred Vanneste, "Débat sur la théologie Africaine," in *Revue du Clergé Africain* 15, no. 4 (1960): 333–53; Cf. Meinrad Hebga, ed., *Personnalité Africaine et Catholicisme*. Collectif (Paris: Présence Africaine, 1963).

60 Paul VI, *Africae Terrarum*, in *Documentation Catholique*, no. 1505 (1967), col. 1937–1956; cf. also *Acta Apostolicae Sedis* (29 Octobre 1967): 1076–77; "Allocution au Symposium des Conférences Episcopales d'Afrique et du Madagascar (SCEAM) à Kampala." *Documentation Catholique*, no. 1546 (1969), 763–65; cf. also *Acta Apostolica Sedis*, no. 61 (1969); *Evangelii Nuntiandi. Sur l'évangélisation dans le monde moderne* (8 décembre 1975), www.vatican.va/holy_father/paul_vi/apost_exhortations/documents/hf_p-vi_exh_19751208_evangelii-nuntiandi_fr.html.

61 Walter Kasper, *The God of Jesus Christ* (New York, Continuum, 2012), 448.

62 Cf. Orobator, *Theology Brewed in an African Pot*.

African Theologians in Diaspora: Drawing on the Theology of Inclusive Religious Pluralism to Construct an African, Value-Oriented Interreligious Dialogue

Marinus C. Iwuchukwu

A growing number of African-born theologians or theologians of African ancestry live and work in the Western and Middle Eastern worlds. This chapter will explore the potential contributions this group of scholars in diaspora can bring to the field of interreligious dialogue that is driven by an inclusive pluralistic worldview in the current postmodern social order. It will briefly examine how postmodernism promotes inclusive religious pluralism towards effective interreligious dialogue and how African theologians whose critical and constructive approach to theology devoid of the extremes of Western, Middle Eastern, and African cultural worldviews significantly influence interreligious discussion. It will also juxtapose the philosophy of "intellectual de-alienation" of Franz Fanon (the renowned pan-Africanist and postcolonial thinker) with the "inclusive religious pluralism" theology of Jacques Dupuis.[1] This intellectual hybrid seeks to claim its theological authenticity as a contemporary theology that is constructively free of Western and Middle Eastern domination and is uniquely or progressively African without being anachronistic.

This chapter will highlight the inclusive religious pluralism that African theologians in diaspora should exemplify. Such inclusive religious pluralism should be contingent on how African theologians in diaspora juggle the pressures of Western or Middle Eastern cultural influences and the nostalgia for an exclusively African cultural influence. From the perspective of the discipline of interreligious dialogue, such an inclusive, religious, and pluralistic worldview is a balanced theological approach, given the exclusive and polarising dominance in Western and Middle Eastern societies by Western and Middle Eastern value-oriented Christianity and Islam respectively.

As is the case with Western cultural influence on African Christians, Arab cultural influence on African Muslims is not only unmistakably prevalent but also imperial and exclusive. Therefore, African Muslims in diaspora in the Middle East and other Arab culturally influenced societies wrestle with some challenges identical to those their Christian counterparts grapple with, and some of them have responded to the imperial influence or dominance of the Arab culture in ways similar to those some African Christians have responded to Western imperial influence.

As scholars, some of whom are primarily raised in multidimensional cultures and worldviews, African theologians in diaspora, for the most part, have the privilege of being steeped in Western or Middle Eastern culture but from the vantage point of cross-cultural influence. Their highly Western – or Middle Eastern – influenced education grants them sufficient familiarity with the thought process and intellectual as well as cultural paradigm shifts of the West or the Middle East. However, some of them, being born and raised in societies and cultures that reflect a strong African worldview, have gained the advantage of being able to weigh and balance the Western or Middle Eastern cultural influences and their African-rooted values and ethos.

There are certainly individual differences in the way diaspora theologians respond to life and living and what impact they bring to bear on their host societies or newly adopted homes. Their influence on the landscape of theology, whether in Europe, North America, or the Middle East, is determined by how each scholar has chosen or has been forced to respond and adjust to the influences of non-African cultures on them.

The Different Groups of Diaspora Theologians

Three distinct groups of diaspora theologians are identifiable on the basis of how each has responded to Western, Middle Eastern, and African cultural influences or values. The first group consists of those who tend to impress on society that they are truly and impeccably Africans. They are the so-called promoters of orthodox African cultural values. This group's members insist that there is a certain or exclusive way of being truly African and therefore are not willing to negotiate their identity or allow the mitigation of what they consider authentic African cultural values with foreign cultural influences. For this group, what is authentically African must reflect the values, philosophy, and practices associated with

Africans before they were confronted by foreign cultures, religions, and sociopolitical norms.

The second group comprises the opposite extreme of the first, namely, those who assume and conclude that either the Western or Middle Eastern cultural dominance should be normative in today's African societies. Andrew E. Barnes refers to this group as "denationalised Africans."[2] In their minds, what is generally considered authentic African cultural values and ways of life are obsolete, primitive, or even barbaric. Therefore, for such a group of Africans, the European or Arab cultural values and ways of life are superior and most appropriate for contemporary African society. This group constitutes a major focus of Frantz Fanon's celebrated work, *Black Skin and White Masks*.[3]

The third group consists of African scholars who appreciate that every culture, way of life, and worldview needs to be dynamic and evolutionary; they straddle the fine line of blending the best of their African cultural values and philosophies with the best of foreign cultures and philosophies that have impacted their lives. You may wish to call this group the people of "the middle way."

This chapter focuses on exploring and recommending this third group of African scholars. This group is recommended because people in this group are more accepting of the reality of postmodernism as well as the pragmatic appreciation of inclusive religious pluralism.

Reflecting the thoughts of Frantz Fanon, Tsenay Serequeberhan references the need for a thorough, critical reevaluation of an authentic or progressive African worldview. According to him, "The non-European peoples have to 'exert [*s'efforcer*] themselves' in order to originate 'values, methods, and a style' grounded in their own lived historicity."[4] The key phrase here is "lived historicity." His suggestion is that neither those who have embraced Westernised or Middle Eastern lifestyles and worldviews hook, line, and sinker nor those who insist on living or holding onto anachronistic African lifestyles or worldviews are what is required of Africans in the twenty-first century. Rather, it requires a balance of life and a worldview that recognise the social, political, structural, and human developmental changes that the average African society has undergone.

Admonishing this evolutionary development and changes among Africans and other developing societies, Fanon writes, "The Third World ought not to be content to define itself in relation to values that precede it.

The underdeveloped countries, on the contrary, have to exert themselves to bring to the light of day their own proper values, methods, and a style specific to themselves."[5]

Fanon strongly advocates a thorough overhaul of the approach taken by Africans and others in the Third World. The approach he recommends requires a comprehensive appreciation of what it entails to be an African today, which rejects both a static cultural mentality and an overbearing leaning toward a Westernised cultural ethos.

Postmodernism, Dialogue, and Pluralism

Postmodernism as a social ethos legitimates all three groups of African theologians in diaspora. However, postmodernism dethrones the former so-called superior mentality or superior cultural concept or even the previously accepted dominance of cultural bullies by appropriately dignifying and legitimising every cultural worldview and authentic human philosophy. This new world order has given voice and legitimacy to previously oppressed and marginalised peoples and cultures. More important, postmodernism justifies and legitimises the application of multiple or diverse approaches to resolving social, religious, cultural, and political conflicts or problems. Grounded on this understanding, pluralist theologians are able to infuse their theological worldview into the landscape of the theology of religions as well as the empirical struggles of interreligious dialogue.

Interreligious dialogue by definition is a theological enterprise that engenders and advocates diversity, plurality, and common ground; it flourishes best in an atmosphere of pluralism since this philosophy or theology respects and dignifies the other.

Inclusive Pluralism and Typical African Social and Life Philosophies

Inclusive religious pluralism, as the phrase suggests, is the disposition to hold other religions in esteem and open one's world for the others in a meaningful, fulfilling way. The others are appreciated and treated as positive extensions of self while honouring and dignifying the autonomy of others. Alan Race writes from a Christian theological perspective, "Inclusivism avoids confrontation, but seeks to discern ways by which the non-Christian faiths may be integrated creatively into Christian theological reflection."[6]

The desire to avoid confrontation should be paramount in the quest for effective dialogue between Christians and Muslims globally. But in addition it should avoid confrontation in a way that finds and appreciates the beauty in each faith, a necessity to eliminating some of the root causes of conflicts emanating from religious differences.

With Vatican II, the Catholic Church fully embraced inclusivism as its new theological model. This new theological model more inclusively underscores the universal salvific impact of Christ but with the assumption that the Church remains the pinnacle for all humanity and that all are ultimately oriented towards becoming Christians. This new theological model rejects the old mantra *extra ecclesia nulla salus*. The hermeneutics of this new theological model suggests that all human beings can be saved in Christ even if they exist outside the Church.

Jacques Dupuis took the new inclusive Catholic soteriology to a new logical height, namely, inclusive pluralism. Although the Catholic Church rejected through Vatican II documents its previous exclusivist stance and embraced inclusivism, its manifest, expressed understanding of religious pluralism is more of a de facto reality than a de jure fact of divine relationship with all humanity. But Dupuis, by adopting and advocating the theology of inclusive religion's pluralism, strongly affirms that religious pluralism is not just a *de facto* reality but more important, a *de jure* fact of the divine-human relationship, thus affirming that it is God who willed the existence of multiple religions in human society. He defended the theology of inclusive religious pluralism from the Christian perspective of Trinity and Christology.[7]

At the heart of Dupuis's concept of inclusive pluralism is the theological assumption that the man Jesus unquestionably belongs to the order of signs and symbols, but in him who has been constituted "Lord and Christ" (Acts 2:36), God's saving action reaches out to people in various ways, knowingly to some and unknowingly to others.[8]

To paraphrase his theology of inclusive pluralism in simple terms, Dupuis is saying that if Christ is God, the second person of the Trinity, Christ is part of the religious life and experience of any and all who believe in the one God.[9]

William R. Burrows's interpretation of Dupuis's inclusive pluralism runs along the same line of thought as above. According to Burrows, "In Dupuis' construal of God's relation to the world, wherever there is authentic value and truth, there the *Logos to Theou* ("the Word of God") is present."[10] Therefore, Dupuis's preference for the theology of "inclusive pluralism" or "pluralistic inclusivism" stems from the fact that the phrase holds together the universal constitutive character of the Christ event in the order of salvation and the saving significance of the religious traditions in a plurality of principle of the religious traditions in the one manifold plan of God for humankind.[11]

Explicating the inclusive religious pluralism hermeneutics of Hebrew 1:1 text, Dupuis writes: "At every step God has taken the initiative in the encounter between God and human beings. This is why it seems that it can and must be said that the world's religious traditions are 'ways' or 'routes' of salvation for their followers.[12]

The inclusive pluralism worldview is fundamentally an operative paradigm in the theories and practices of sociology and other human sciences. It also forms the bedrock of constitutions of modern states. Historically, the pre-Islamic and pre-Christian cultural and religious worldviews of African societies were hinged on an inclusive religious pluralism paradigm.[13] Therefore, until the coming of Islam and Christianity, Africans observed normative respect and appreciation of others' religions and cultures.[14] In the African ethos, the others' religious identity is always respected and validly recognised. Moreover, an inclusive religious pluralism reflects a worldview in which the approach to pluralism is advocated on the grounds of people's common human origin and destiny.

The normative inclusive religious pluralism consistent with African pre-Islamic and pre-Christian societies is derived from the heterogeneity of religion in Africa as well as the African worldview and accommodation of religious plurality.[15] This phenomenon of inclusive religious pluralism is illustratively described by Jan G. Platvoet: "Traditional believers are known to have eagerly adopted, and adapted, the religious practices, ideas, and at times institutions, brought in from far and near by traders, hunters, pilgrims, and visitors, or members who had travelled, or those who had married into their society.[16]

Platvoet persuasively argues, using historical data and anthropological findings, that African society is home to advanced as well as basic forms of religion among human beings and has continued to accommodate the major religions of the world. But even before the advent of other world religions into Africa, African peoples had a diversity of religious practices and beliefs, which explains the insistence by scholars on the nomenclature "African traditional religions" rather than "African traditional religion."[17] The conviction about the former is why Newell Booth strongly asserts, "There is no such thing as 'African religion' but only 'African religions.'"[18] However, due to the seamless blending of the different expressions of beliefs and religious practices among Africans into a healthy society and the absence of the kind of exclusivism prevalent in Christianity and Islam, Africans south of the Sahara were often regarded as adherents of the same religion by colonialists and foreign missionaries.

It is imperative for a comprehensive rearticulation of the African inclusive religious pluralistic stance to appreciate that African traditional religions, in accord with the African philosophy of life, normatively operate under the philosophical assumption often referred to in religious studies as the "functionalistic approach" to religion.[19] This approach to religion deemphasises the metaphysical in favor of the empirical realities of everyday life. Therefore, for Africans, religion is meant to facilitate their daily life experiences and ensure that they successfully proceed from one day to the other. This approach assures that peace, security of life and property, and presenting the best model of human relationship with one's neighbors are primary concerns rather than obsessive desires for a paradise or heaven when daily life experiences are in shambles and disaster.

Paradoxically, although Christians and Muslims lay significant emphasis on the life hereafter, both religions have a strong empirical focus, which reminds their adherents that paradise or heaven is reserved for women and men who have successfully managed their earthly daily lives based on justice, peace, love, compassion, and forgiveness.

Conclusion

Because the African worldview and cultural engagement are pluralistic, an African diaspora scholar who has an orthodox African or so-called pristine African approach to life (if he or she does not manifestly demonstrate hate or complete rejection of the apparent presence and influence of foreign cultural values) invariably accommodates and demonstrates pluralism. It is very convenient and easy for such an individual to latch onto interreligious dialogue with an inclusive, pluralistic perspective.

However, the African diaspora scholar who is able to healthily negotiate and adopt a blend of Western, Middle Eastern, and African cultural
ethos is better equipped for the task of effective interreligious dialogue
that operates on the presupposition of inclusive pluralism. Conversely,
those who have jettisoned African cultural values as obsolete, primitive, or
barbaric while exclusively embracing Western or Middle Eastern cultural
values and ethos as both superior and normative will have serious problem
engaging in interreligious dialogue guided by inclusive pluralism.

Appealing to the intellectual and theological inspirations of Fanon and
Dupuis respectively, it is appropriate that African theologians in diaspora
reflect in their works both a critical assessment of themselves in the context
of contemporary social theological reality as well as the inclusive religious
pluralistic theology of Dupuis toward the crucial need for successful and
progressive interreligious dialogue. Therefore, it does not suffice toward
establishing a progressive African worldview to continue to replicate a
Western designed and rubber-stamp idea of inculturation. A progressive
African approach will advocate for a thoroughly incarnational theology
(initiated and designed by progressive-minded Africans) as the foundation
for all theological and religious adaptation of Christianity or Islam in
Africa. It will be a theology that reflects the intellectual dealienisation
of Africans advocated by Fanon and the inclusive religious pluralism
theology proposed by Dupuis (which this chapter identifies as necessary
for effective interreligious dialogue in most religiously pluralistic societies
in Africa).

The fact that twenty-first century Africans defend the practices of
polygamy or polygyny or the ranking of people into categories of freeborn
and non-freeborn is nothing to be proud of. Christians or Muslims who
insist their religion is the only authentic religion or mainline Christian
churches that subject entire people to a system of ecclesial, hierarchical
governance while preaching democracy for society have nothing to
celebrate. The vexing male chauvinism that prevails in many mainline
Christian denominations and Islam leaves you wondering if in the twenty-
first century, the leadership of these religions are still convinced that God
distributes charisms based on gender or that the Holy Spirit prefers males
as ministers for God's people.

The primary focus of this chapter is to urge African diaspora theologians as well as African-oriented theologians to "hold the past, present, and

future together."[20] These words of John S. Pobee critically but clearly state his argument that it is unrealistic to think or expect an African society of today will be the same as the African society of a century ago. According to him, "The communication and scientific revolution of our day means that even the most 'primitive' African has advanced from his pristine stage to something else."[21]

More appropriately, Pobee succinctly articulates the core message of this work thus.

> While we affirm a certain Africanness, we wish also to warn against treating African man as a museum piece or an anthropological curio. He has not been static; he has grown in stature, mentality, culture, and in other ways. But above all, he shares with the rest of the mankind some human traits. In the ebb and flow of cultures, he has borrowed from other groups. Consequently, some of the things that may be paraded as African theology may yet speak to others belonging to other racial groups. We see African theology as one more fragment in the world mosaic of cultures and theologies.[22]

To hold the past, present, and future in harmony successfully, as recommended in this work, we need to adopt theological principles and approaches that will promote a Christianity or Islam that is truly incarnated into the African world, or to borrow the metaphor of Agbonkhianmeghe Orobator about authentic African Christianity, "brewed in an African pot."[23] When both religions are pragmatically African in texture and flavor, interreligious dialogue between African Christians and Muslims, which has been an uphill task in certain parts of Africa, will be more productive. Such progressive and successful dialogue will be possible when African Muslims and Christians embrace an inclusive religious, pluralistic worldview because such a worldview resonates strongly with the African religious pluralistic world and understanding or appreciation of religion in society.

Endnotes

1   See Jacques Dupuis, *Christianity and the Religions: From Confrontation to Dialogue* (Maryknoll, N.Y.: Orbis, 2001), and Frantz Fanon, *Black Skin, White Masks*, transl. Richard Philcox (New York: Grove Press, 2008).

2   Andrew E. Barnes, "'The Great Prohibition': The Expansion of Christianity in Colonial Northern Nigeria," in *History Compass* 8, no. 6 (2010): 441. What Barnes means by "denationalised" Africans is Christianised Africans from

southern Nigeria who have abandoned their African traditional way of life to adopt Western lifestyles due to the influence of Christianity.

3   Frantz Fanon, *Black Skin, White Masks*. Fanon explains that these two are the dominant worldviews of Africans or colonised people across the globe. He urges an active and progressive development of a third group that consists of people who constructively and critically reevaluate life for themselves in the context of where they live and the influences around them with the intent of evolving a new but vibrant way of being Africans.

4   Tsenay Serequeberhan, "Theory and the Actuality of Existence: Fanon and Cabral," in *A Companion to African Philosophy*, ed., Kwasi Wiredu (Malden, Mass.: Blackwell, 2004), 226.

5   Frantz Fanon, *Les Damnés de la terre* (Paris: François Maspero, 1974), 56.

6   Race, *Christians and Religious Pluralism* (London: SCM Press, Ltd., 1983), 38.

7   Ibid., 52–54 and 87–97.

8   Ibid., 88.

9   Dupuis crystallises his theology of inclusive pluralism in *Christianity and the Religions: From Confrontation to Dialogue* (Maryknoll, N.Y.: Orbis, 2001).

10   William Burrows, *Jacques Dupuis Faces the Inquisition* (Eugene, Ore.: Pickwick, 2012), 20.

11   Dupuis, *Christianity and the Religions*, 95.

12   Ibid., 254.

13   Except in the cases of northern Nigeria and the Sudan in sub-Saharan African, Islam in most parts of the region was quite accommodating of religious differences insofar as such traditional religions did not obstruct the practice and development of Islam.

14   Historically, Islam in sub-Saharan Africa was more tolerant of the normative religious pluralism in African societies. Lamin Sanneh affirms this fact: "In most places ... Muslims embraced local versions of pluralism and tolerance rather than committing themselves and others to inflexible compliance with the religious code." See Lamin Sanneh, *Piety and Power: Muslims and Christians in West Africa* (Maryknoll, N.Y.: Orbis, 1996), 2.

15   For an attestation to the religiosity of Africans and the pervasive presence of God in their collective worldviews, see John S. Pobee, *Toward an African Theology* (Nashville, Tenn.: Abingdon, 1979), 26.

16   Jan Platvoet, "The Religions of Africa in their Historical Order," in *The Study of Religions in Africa Past, Present and Prospects*, ed., Jan Platvoet, James Cox, and Jacob Olupona (Cambridge, UK: Roots and Branches, 1996), 52. Many other scholars also make the argument that the African inclusive pluralistic worldview is the reason many world religions have found themselves comfortable in their adopted homes in Africa – a phenomenon that has led some scholars such as Platvoet to describe the religious landscape in Africa as "Africa's rainbow of religions." See Platvoet, "The Religions of Africa in Their Historical Order," 46–102, or other scholars such as Jacob Olupona, who concedes to the authenticity

of nomenclatures such as "African Independent Churches," "African Pentecostal," and "African Islam" in his article "Thinking Globally about African Religion." See Olupona, "Thinking Globally about African Religion" in *Global Religions*, ed., Mark Juergensmeyer (Oxford, UK, and New York: Oxford University Press, 2006), 527–35. Using the illustration of Ifa divination among his native Yoruba religious culture and theology, Olupona underscores the inclusive pluralistic paradigm in the African religious worldview. See Olupona, "Religious Pluralism in Africa: Insights from Ifa Divination Poetry," in *Ethics that Matter: African, Caribbean, and African American Sources*, ed., Marcia Y. Riggs and James Samuel Logan (Minneapolis, Minn.: Fortress Press, 2012), 51–58.

17 Platvoet, "The Religions of Africa in their Historical Order," 52 ff. Laurenti Magesa argues, however, that the essence and fundamental beliefs among Africans are identical, albeit with different rituals and practices. He is therefore of the opinion that the religion of Africans should be considered in the same vein as Christianity or Islam, both of which encompass a certain level of diversity. See Magesa, *African Religion: The Moral Traditions of Abundant Life* (Maryknoll, N.Y.: Orbis, 1997), 15–18.

18 Newell S. Booth, "An Approach to African Religion," in *African Religions: A Symposium*, ed., Newell S. Booth (New York: NOK, 1977), 3.

19 Martien E. Brinkman, *Non-Western Jesus: Jesus as Bodhisattva, Avatara, Guru, Prophet, Ancestor, or Healer?* (London: Equinox, 2009), 210 ff. Brinkman, while affirming the "functionalist approach" to religion of African traditional religions, argues that even though African traditional religions significantly emphasise an immanent God, they do not deny the transcendence of God. He makes the case that African traditional religions hold both views in harmony as composite understanding of God and life. Therefore, African traditional religions do not deny the existence of life after life but require a balance of focus on both the life now and the life hereafter. Uzukwu confirms this fundamental philosophy and religious view of life. See Elochukwu E. Uzukwu, "Missiology Today: The African Situation," in *Religion and African Culture: Inculturation – A Nigerian Perspective,* ed. Elochukwu E. Uzukwu (Enugu, Nigeria: SNAAP Press, 1988), 151-152.

20 Pobee, *Toward an African Theology,* 18.

21 Ibid. Pobee also argues for a pragmatic religious pluralism and calls for people to recognise and respect the multiple or pluralistic theologies of Africans. Therefore, he affirms the existence of "African theologies" rather than an African theology. He feels strongly about the *a priori* religious pluralism of African society because, based on his theological assumption, pluralism in society, especially in African society, is "part of the divine economy." See Pobee, *Toward an African Theology,* 19.

22 Pobee, *Toward an African Theology*, 19.

23 Agbonkhianmeghe E. Orobator, *Theology brewed in an African Pot: An introduction to Christian Doctrine from an African Perspective* (Nairobi, Kenya: Paulines Publications Africa, 2008).

Teaching African Theology in the Diaspora: The Promises and Challenges of a Western Academia

Lilian Dube

Introduction

In fall 2014, I will take on new responsibilities and challenges as chair of the Theology and Religious Studies department (THRS) at the University of San Francisco, which I joined in 2006. After a twenty-four-year career of university teaching, I cannot help wondering, what if my journey had not meandered into the diaspora and I was not teaching African theology on these shores?

This could not be a better time to reflect on a vocation rooted in the Teachers in Rural Africa (TIRA) campaign to educate black children emerging from years of seclusion during the Rhodesian minority rule that ended in 1980. With the limited education of a graduate student, I received in-service training to bring basic formal education and literacy to an enthusiastic postindependent generation of children and adults in rural Zimbabwe. These formative years of my career in underdeveloped rural African tribal trust lands were very humbling and certainly relevant to my African theology classes in Lone Mountain 253, ED 110 or any of the fancy "smart classrooms" at the University of San Francisco (USF) particularly because of the social justice focus of Jesuit education.

After years of training and a decade of teaching African theology at the University of Zimbabwe and another decade of international teaching at prestigious universities such as Birmingham University in UK, Northwest University in Chicago, Lee University in Cleveland, Harvard as a guest lecturer, and now USF, my core values have not changed. It has been gratifying to embrace a vision for education that humanises academic excellence, and I uphold a culture of service and bring diversity to the classroom.

Upon arrival at USF, I was determined to pursue excellence in teaching guided by the Jesuit Catholic vision, mission, and core values of the University of San Francisco that I embrace as an African Catholic. The details of my teaching accomplishments acknowledged in letters, student evaluations, and the SUMMA[1] are indeed my evidence of commitment to excellence in teaching African theology in the diaspora regardless of some formidable challenges. To clearly demonstrate the challenges and progress I have made since coming to USF, where I have stayed the longest as an African theologian in the diaspora, I draw attention to my enormous efforts on a journey marked by institutional core requirements and the cultural uniqueness of USF as a Jesuit university on the West Coast of the United States of America.

Professional Development (Retraining)

I arrived at USF in 2006 determined to excel in teaching African theology, my strongest area as evidenced by pre-USF evaluations and letters from my former chair, dean, and president. I had earned my professional teacher qualification, a graduate certificate in education (Grad.C.E.), at the University of Zimbabwe in 1993 and had invested many years at "teaching" universities where lecturing to large numbers counted the most. However, I soon realised there were necessary adjustments needed to meet USF's standards and American students' needs.

In terms of technological training, teaching skills, pedagogical approach, and cultural orientation, there was no perfect match with my pre-USF experience. Initially, this was very frustrating, but as an international scholar, I quickly focused on excellence and discovered that USF was well prepared for such transitions, and the faculty were clearly very hospitable to newer faculty.

I seized every opportunity to learn through informal interaction with distinguished USF teachers in the school and the THRS department. I welcomed peer assessment from my colleagues teaching Catholic social thought and liberation theology, and I enjoyed observing the cross-disciplinary teaching of a senior Afro-American scholar I admired.

I also benefitted greatly from skills training opportunities at teaching-related workshops organised by the university. Additionally, I invited my then-associate dean to observe me while I taught, and I loaned my African feminist theology class to my then-dean. In my absence and unannounced, she walked in and had a "conversational assessment" (chat) with my students about their learning experience and of me as a teacher. Consenting to this "conversational assessment" was one of the boldest steps I have taken to achieve teaching excellence. It privileged the dean with a rare glimpse into student perceptions of my teaching of African feminist theology and professional standing that outweighs the SUMMA assessment by far.

Service-Learning Training

My postgraduate professional teacher's training, graduate certificate in education (Grad.C.E.) at the University of Zimbabwe, though thorough, was not carved out of the passion for community engagement through service-learning pedagogy. Instead, learning was a grave, competitive business, and so was teaching. This did not seem to be the culture at USF, so I registered for a semester-long service-learning seminar with the Leo McCarthy Center for Public and Common Good's Office of Service-Learning.

The service-learning seminar brought me into dialogue with faculty across the board and the nonprofit community partners of USF. Thus, early in my term at USF, I deepened my relationship with USF colleagues and the local Bay Area community.

At the end of ten weeks, I developed a service-learning syllabus that has completely reshaped my understanding of teaching of African theology as a humanising social activity evidenced in the global service-learning program, USF in Zambia INTD331-01, that I later developed and implemented.

Technical Training

Upon hire, my teaching world revolved around books and chalkboard – the basics. I had used neither *Blackboard* nor a *smart classroom* already popular at USF. My starting point was obviously behind some of my colleagues in that regard, hence the surprised remark to my inquiry about *Blackboard*, "Blackboard is the online web page for courses. It is fairly standard in many parts of the world." Obviously not in my African world, but I attended lectures on classroom technology and was soon comfortable in both Level 1 and Level 2 smart classrooms.

I keenly attended *Blackboard workshops* offered by USF on how I could use *Grade Center* and all its features for online assessment. The delivery of my lectures was perfected by PowerPoint workshops on the *Academic Impressions webinar.* I even trained to use *Wimba for Teaching and Learning* (an online meeting room/web conference) to enhance teaching and prepare for emergency teaching outside the physical space and was amased by a "class out of the classroom." There has not been an end to catching up with technology that helps me deliver my African theology classes as different versions keep popping up.

Online Training

My efforts to become a better college instructor were further supported by my then-dean Jennifer Turpin, who paid for an online summer program for teaching effectiveness in 2008. *Online Seminar: 15 Survival Strategies for New College Instructors* provided me with skills to improve my instructional success such as setting clear instructions for my students, integrating technology into my classwork, and using classroom teams, among other strategies. It was a very fascinating way to spend a summer preparing for teaching effectiveness with my ego in the backseat. With a track record of teaching African theology at the university level dating to September 1994, I was anything but a new college instructor, yet here I was, an absolute beginner!

Administrative Support

As an international scholar, I worked very hard through cultural and institutional variances presented by USF's theology core curriculum. I welcomed with appreciation all the support and effort of administrators and colleagues who believed in me. A comprehensive list is stored in my memory, but I will mention a few individuals who positively influenced and pushed my teaching to unprecedented levels. First, my deans' hands-on guidance concerning syllabus assessment, classroom visits, and evaluation ensured I was not lost in the dust and debris of cultural variances that tend to diminish the teaching portfolio of those who dare cross borders as international scholars of African theology.

In addition, the dean's office offered *strategies on Linking Teaching to Learning: Using Classroom Assessment,* which influenced my newly offered classes on African theology. *The New Faculty Workshops* brought newly hired faculty together, around a table, to discuss the most formidable challenges they encountered in the classroom. The more we shared from the breadth of our pre-USF experiences, the more I realised the complex contours of teaching African theology in the diaspora. These workshops addressed a plethora of teacher-student issues from interaction, grading, and professors' emotional investment to teaching expectations, evaluations, and more. I learned a lot from these workshops and have become a better teacher, though it certainly felt like "retraining" for the teaching vocation.

Collegial Support

A colleague in the THRS department who had recently earned distinguished teaching credentials at the university offered me a peer-evaluation opportunity and later teamed up with me on a semester-long teaching of a course we developed together. *Team-teaching Reading from the Margins: Diverse Biblical Interpretations* was a great experience for pedagogical dialogue on overlapping hermeneutical lenses and the theological passion we shared from a diverse spectrum. The interpretation of Exodus 1–24 for African Theology against his exegetical analysis for Gay, Green and Black created a fun feast for the students and us one summer semester.

Additionally, university-wide, colleagues offered a variety of presentations and conversations on teaching excellence that helped me perfect my teaching of African theology in the diaspora. These included *Conversation with Master Teachers,* which covered ways to engage learners, principles of good teaching practice, and different ways of knowing; the New Faculty Advising Workshop, to enhance student-advising skills, which helped to create rapport with my students. Finally, the educational benefits of diverse learning environments and diversifying the curriculum stressed in the *New Faculty Lunch: Diversity* earlier in my career at USF emphasised the value of what I brought to the USF classroom and boosted my teacher confidence and my desire to achieve excellence.

Service in Distinguished Teachers' Committee

Since coming to USF, I have served on many outstanding committees and have quite an impressive "service" binder. However, I served on one committee for selfish reasons regarding my teaching in this new terrain. I jumped at the opportunity to serve on the *Distinguished Teachers' Committee* when I was elected to fill in the gap left by a faculty member who became ill. As I read through the numerous dossiers of aspiring distinguished teachers, I gained insight into what really constituted a distinguished teacher in the diaspora. Although I have not yet received the distinguished teaching award, the review process helped me focus on excellence in my teaching.

Media Training

An invitation from *The Lane Center for Catholic Studies and Social Thought* landed me in media training on topics that covered a wide range of issues such as the importance of doing media interviews; the difference between TV, radio, and print interviews; and the specific qualities of Catholic media dos and don'ts of media interviews.

This lecture and workshop equipped me with rare skills that prepared me for online teaching and media presentations. Just how this would impact my teaching of African theology was obscure until I was awarded the prestigious *Jesuit Foundation Pedagogy Grant* to shoot a movie in Africa for my *USF in Zambia Today Service-Learning* program focused on religion and HIV/AIDS.

Besides this major film project, I also participated in Loyola University New Orleans's extension program in Benin City, Nigeria, which consists primarily of lay catechists.

In 2010, during the American Academy of Religion (AAR) Annual Meeting in Atlanta, the director of the Loyola Institute for Ministry interviewed me on a wide range of issues from my research and teaching that define Catholicism in Africa, the implications for feminist theologies, and HIV/AIDS and African traditional religions for theological reflection in Africa. My big contribution was to give attention to context in critical theological reflection in the Catholic tradition in Africa. This media program created an opportunity for service to my community of accountability and as well chipped away lingering guilt for "abandoning" the African cause, an issue often raised by African scholars who stayed put.

All these efforts have resulted in a steady and consistent progress as I accomplished my goals to excel internationally in a profession I love, a process that left me more excited than exhausted. In addition to the extensive diaspora in-service training articulated above, the core curriculum capped the multilayered challenges of teaching of African theology in the diaspora.

Challenges of Teaching African Theology in the Diaspora

Core Curriculum

THRS has few majors, so the majority of our courses simply service the core curriculum. Students do not embrace the core, and tenure-track faculty loathe the imbalance between work-input and student response reflected in their evaluations. The students' expectations are usually not congruent with course objectives, their motivation is often low, and their reasons for taking core classes are usually simply to fulfill graduation requirements. It takes a caring teacher to understand this somber attitude and the caliber of students who quickly fill classes on day one.

When you teach core classes, you continuously develop strategies to reach the special needs of students in your classes who have never flipped through a religious text. This is what makes core classes more exciting but extensively challenging. How do you teach African theology without diluting it and reducing its content beyond comprehension?

My first class since 2006 has been with a student assessment quiz to help me pitch my lectures more appropriately. Thus, Quiz 1 is my opportunity to ask, before I start teaching, what students know about theology and what they bring to class from their different majors and get an idea of what they understand about theology and its varied branches, including African theology and what they could do with African theology, particularly in real life. Consistently, their response carries the general message about fulfilling a core, having minimal to no background in the subject, and being convinced that they would not need the class in their careers as doctors, businesspeople, teachers, and so on.

Twice a semester we revisit Quiz 1, and the students edit it according to their progress chart. It fascinates me to observe the giant steps students articulate on their impressive African theological journey. Any teacher would get great satisfaction from the student growth that they chart for themselves and reflections on how they have outgrown their biases and misconceptions about African theology and its real-life applications in their context.

Quiz 1 is the best student learning assessment I reward with five points on a chart with pseudonyms for anonymity and therefore accuracy in evaluation. While this may not be relevant to those teaching majors and minors in which students are fairly well motivated, this assessment model I developed could indeed help professors struggling with students' reluctance or even disdain for the core. This is complemented with other standardised student evaluations such as the SUMMA, which do not consider the challenges most African theologians are subject to, particularly those on tenure track.

Teaching in the Context of the Jesuit Mission of Social Justice

As faculty in the THRS department at USF, I have committed to the core needs of my department first. I have taught diverse students who have taken my courses to meet their core requirement even as I taught from my passions, and they walked out with more than they had signed up for! I have developed new courses that have proved popular with students whose horizons were often pushed beyond their limits through the "cultural diversity" designation on all my courses. In the department, I have also taught across a broad spectrum to meet the needs of THRS major and minors, the MA program in theology, and the St Ignatius Institute's Catholic Social Thought minor. I have also developed, designed, and introduced new African theology courses for the THRS department that have included a team-taught course. The topics included globalisation and poverty; gender and sexuality; health and HIV/AIDS; art, music, and dance; new religious movements, and diaspora theology. In this regard, all the courses I developed and introduced to the curriculum reflect a commitment to African theology and social justice. As I explored these topics, the "moral traditions of abundant life" espoused by Laurenti Magesa[2] became more pivotal.

Literary works of African theologians and scholars of religion, gender, and sexuality in Africa and the diaspora have dominated the required and recommended texts for my courses over the years.[3] USF's bookstore has, therefore, sold scores of these texts to my students every semester, and copies of these texts did not gather dust on library shelves while I taught. This has given me an opportunity to keep up with the dynamics in African theology that inform my own research and has broadened the scope of African theological knowledge for diaspora scholars.

For a good number of my students, theology becomes their first academic African experience. It therefore matters how even the most sordid issues are presented to an audience that has experienced Africa only through prejudiced media. My selection of texts addresses this problem and presents African-brewed solutions. In this regard, the best texts have been those that discuss a progression *From Crisis to Kairos.*[4]

Core Courses Developed

Theology in HIV/AIDS Contexts THRS306-01(CD)

This course discusses the role of religion in the context of HIV/AIDS. It presents the challenges of HIV/AIDS to contemporary African theology in particular and Christian theology in general. The course redefines what it means to be the Church in a world in which AIDS ravages the lives and dignity of millions. Thus, the course introduces theology of HIV/AIDS as a theology of passion, compassion, hope, and life.

Feminist Theology from the Third World(s) THR305-01(CD)

This course is designed to introduce feminist theology from Africa, Asia, and Latin America in the context of Third World liberation theologies. It derives the basis of feminist reading and reinterpretation of Christian Scriptures from the economic, political, cultural, and artistic contexts of the Third World. While acknowledging the feminist contextual discontinuities, this course restates global continuities and connections that support women's struggles for liberation. Hence, its emphasis on cultural diversity is aimed at understanding how the "other" forms a model for collective action.

African Theology and Cosmologies THRS270-01(CD)

This course is an introduction to African Christian theology. It offers a brief history of Christianity in Africa in the context of traditional African cosmologies. It explores the interaction of African traditional religions and cultures with Christianity. The early African Christian story unfolds through the critical narrative genre of selected novels that explore religious conflicts and resolutions. The course also discusses the appropriation of the gospel into African sociopolitical and economic contexts that characterise the contemporary African Church.

Reading from the Margins THRS275-01 (CD; in collaboration with a colleague)

Hermeneutics is as much a craft as a science. Maintaining a critical interpretive balance between personal subjectivity and the potential rigidity of the scientific method, this course is designed to introduce students to the basic methods of historical-critical interpretation of the Bible while emphasising in particular those hermeneutical lenses that are often marginalised by more-dominant social and ecclesial renderings. While examining various samplings of biblical texts from Jewish and Christian Scriptures, the course is woven together by a particular focus on Exodus 1–24 because of its central importance for Jews and Christians alike. After establishing the exegetical groundwork for modern historical-critical interpretation of the Bible, the course examines the Exodus event (Exodus 1–24) with a "hermeneutic of suspicion." In particular, we examine postcolonial, indigenous, and African-American interpretations, feminist and womanist readings, and "green" interpretations as well as readings from the LGBT community and those living with HIV/AIDS. In this course, students develop a greater appreciation for the multitude of legitimate meanings a biblical text might possess as well as an appreciation for their own biases, which when acknowledged become contributions rather than liabilities to a community's understanding of the Scriptures.

The Christian Village (THRS 100-01; CD)

The Christian Village explores the central concepts of Christian theology. Using the lens of teaching, whether as a future parent, a teacher, or as a member of the "village" that it takes to raise a "child," I take up the following topics: human existence, God, Jesus Christ, and the Church's nature and mission.

Religion, Sexuality, and AIDS in Africa (new course)

The course offers an analysis of religion, sexuality, and AIDS in Africa through a social justice lens. It explores the intersection of religion and sexuality in sub-Saharan Africa, where HIV has the highest prevalence in the world. The course discusses sexuality in a region in which three quarters of all the women live with HIV according to the UNAIDS, 2010 Report,[5] and men who have sex with men (MSM) are four times more likely to be HIV-positive than the general population.[6] An analysis of the gender and sexuality in sub-Saharan Africa demonstrates that where AIDS prevails, inequalities tend to increase and justice becomes more difficult to achieve.[7] The course offers students an opportunity to develop ethical ways to stop AIDS by addressing religion and sexual injustices.

Graduate Course

My experience of teaching theology in graduate schools at Northwest University, Birmingham University (UK), and the University of Zimbabwe prepared me well for teaching in the Graduate School of Theology at USF (though short-lived, as the program abruptly ended a few years ago). It is not surprising that the best SUMMA evaluations came from my first graduate class at USF in fall 2006.

Religions in Dialogue (CD)

This seminar explores the plurality of religions from within the vantage point of the Christian faith. The course addresses contemporary dilemmas created by the multireligious global reality and provides the basis for understanding and respecting various worldviews essential for better-informed global citizens. It explores the world's diverse religions (including African indigenous religions) and attempts to foster dialogue to understand and respect various worldviews and to create eco-human wellbeing. Thus, using the dialogical and comparative methods, the interaction between selected religions is analysed.

This course draws from Hans Kung's observation that "there can be no peace among nations without peace among the religions. There can be no peace among the religions without dialogue between the religions. There can be no dialogue between the religions without research into theological foundations."[8]

Service-Learning Program

Service-learning programs are different from other approaches to experiential education by their intention to benefit the provider and the recipient of the service equally as well as to ensure equal focus on both the service being provided and the learning that is occurring.[9]

USF in Zambia Today (INTD 331-01)

The program creates integrated learning and service opportunities in communities battling HIV and AIDS, opportunities for interaction and reflection, for personal and interpersonal development, for serving and learning, and for praxis-based learning processes. The program offers an understanding of HIV and AIDS that transcends biomedical and epidemiological research by introducing socioeconomic factors, gender, cultural, war, migration, and political factors to the complex study of HIV and AIDS in Zambia and sub-Saharan Africa. The program encourages students to interpret their experience of contemporary Zambia though interaction with and service to communities infected and affected by HIV and AIDS. What does the Catholic Church say about economic, social, and cultural dilemmas that confound Zambians?

My recent effort to humanise education by channeling teaching through avenues that equip students with skills, knowledge, and unique experiences needed to be men and women for others in a global context is USF in Zambia (INTD 331-01). I find it exciting to take African theology beyond the classroom walls into communities that inform the theology. This service-learning study-abroad program is the most comprehensive, life-changing teaching project that I have developed and implemented in my teaching career. It was also remarkable that the College Curriculum Committee unanimously approved it. This program enhances USF's prestigious standing as a beacon of service learning in the world. Incidentally, USF was among five institutions of higher education in the country to win the 2010 Senator Paul Simon Award for Comprehensive Internationalisation. This signals the important role African theology plays in bridging the gaps between worlds. The program engages local and global communities in a way that captures the core values of Jesuit education and helps students become men and women for others. An extract from a student's summer 2011 says it all.

> After going around with Chris and other members of the organisation in both day and night outreach, it is clear they all work hard to build a relationship with the kids. They do not see the kids as poor street children who have no hope; they see them as individuals who all have different personalities and stories, and with every kid, the workers have hope that they can be saved from life on the streets.
>
> I had never been exposed to anything like this in my life, and while we had read articles and had lectures to prepare us, nothing can prepare you for coming face to face with a five-year-old who is homeless, living on the streets, starving, and high on jet fuel.... I want to thank everyone at Friends of the Street Children for doing the most amazing work and really inspiring me to better my life and the lives of others.[10]

Educating leaders who are fashioning a more humane world through African theology in the diaspora heals the painful struggle of transition and retraining. The program allows cross-cultural bridges and nurtures my diaspora dreams.

Diaspora Dreams[11]
Multiple borders crossing
Firm orders embracing,
I feel hot tears flowing,
Last respects paying
Painful joy mingling

The brave wisely ruling,
Elders only advising
I dream our nation bonding,
Children streets shunning
A, E, I, O, U, learning

Bouncy bachelors whistling
Prayer cells finding
I hear laughter markets filling,
Happy women negotiating
Organics fairly selling

Praying churches groaning
Divine powers unlocking
I see cathedral locks unbolting,
Bishops never revenging
Social Justice doing

Conclusion

Doing African theology in the diaspora requires being in a new net of relationships and participating in students' intellectual and spiritual journeys since theology is done in a context, not from the clouds.[12] Some rapport and familiarity with local contexts is an absolute imperative for African theological inroads in the diaspora. It is absolutely its own journey that needs to be carefully mapped out. Thus, the impact of local perspectives in shaping African theology in the diaspora cannot be understated even with a clear understanding that "theologies that simply conform to the local rules are not doing justice to the local context."[13]

The challenge is to remain loyal to African theology while creating space for adaptation to new contexts and dynamic classrooms anxiety. On this journey, pressure weighs more heavily for "home-trained" theologians, those trained and recruited from Africa. The situation is made worse by a core curriculum, unsupportive systems, and biased peers and reviewers. This creates a daunting experience of extensive anxiety particularly for pre-tenure African theologians who migrate in early to mid-career with pressure to prove themselves in the face of demotion and deportation.

My realities have evolved from a timid, newcomer African theologian teaching core classes to nontheology majors while striving for tenure to an integrated African scholar taking new leadership service as the chair-elect of the THRS department at the University of San Francisco and also serving as a member of the St. Ignatius Parish council. With this privilege more is expected in terms of African authenticity and inclusive collaborations across all "isms." This new self-location influences my response to questions raised by fellow African theologians at the Theological Colloquium on Church, Religion and Society in Africa (TCCRSA) in Nairobi in August 2013. Their questions ranged from my experiences of overt racism and exoticism, demands of religious pluralism that threaten my own religious identity and sovereignty, concerns about accountability to our fathers and mothers in our diaspora voices, and our engagement with a plethora of the struggles of other diasporas besides the African diaspora.

My response addresses interfaith and intercultural experiences and responsibilities of Africans in the diaspora. It points towards blending and working with the local goalkeepers of justice without compromising the core identity of being an African and a theologian. This happens in a process in which the insider-outsider binaries are dissolved by conscious efforts from the African immigrants and the welcoming parishes, a process that both parties have to desire and work towards.

As clearly demonstrated in this chapter, newcomers have numerous formidable limitations, survival priorities, and empowerment precedence as they wait to exhale or engage other diasporas. The receiving community has home advantage and therefore an upper hand in determining the pace of progress. Supportive and welcoming parishes fare well in fostering religious and sociocultural interactions necessary for meaningful transitions for both communities. This takes care of overt racism, exoticism, and multiple phobias of the other.

Endnotes

1   This is a teaching assessment evaluation mechanism used by students at the end of the course that has a strong bearing on tenure and promotion assessment in most American universities, including the University of San Francisco.

2   Laurenti Magesa, *African Religion: The Moral Traditions of Abundant Life* (Maryknoll, N.Y.: Orbis, 1997).

3   Includes but is not limited to Musa Dube, *HIV/ AIDS and the Curriculum: Methods of Integrating HIV/AIDS in Theological Programmes* (Geneva: WCC Publications, 2003); Waris Dirie, *Desert Flower: The Extraordinary Journey of a Nomad* (San Francisco: Harper, 1992) Ogbu Kalu, ed., *African Christianity: An African Story* (Trenton, N.J.: Africa World Press, 2007); Magesa, *African Religion*; Michael J. Kelly, *HIV and AIDS: A Social Justice Perspective* (Nairobi: Paulines Publications, 2010); Michael J. Kelly, *Education: For an Africa without AIDS* (Nairobi: Paulines Publications, 2008); Kwesi Dickson, *Theology in Africa* (Maryknoll, N.Y.: Orbis, 1984); Mercy Amba, Oduyoye, *Daughters of Anowa: African Women and Patriarchy* (Maryknoll, N.Y.: Orbis, 1998); Mercy Amba Oduyoye and Musimbi Kanyoro, eds., *The Will To Arise: Women, Tradition, and the Church in Africa* (Maryknoll, N.Y.: Orbis, 1992); Jacob K. Olupona, *City of 201 Gods: Ilé-Ifè in Time, Space, and the Imagination* (Berkeley: University of

9 Andrew Furco, "Service-Learning: A Balanced Approach to Experiential Education," *Expanding Boundaries: Service and Learning.* Washington, DC: Corporation for National Service 2–6, (1996): 12.

10 Statement by a student from *USF in Zambia Today Program,* August 2011.

11 Lilian Dube, July 30, 2013.

12 Clemens Sedak, *Doing Local Theology: A Guide for Artisans of a New Humanity* (Maryknoll, N.Y.: Orbis, 2002), 16.

13 Ibid, 17.

PART THREE

THEOLOGICAL REIMAGINATION
OF THE NATURE AND MISSION
OF CHRISTIANITY AND CHURCH
IN AFRICA

Religion in Africa: A Curse or A Blessing?: On Daring to Reinvent Christianity in Africa

Emmanuel Katongole

Introduction

The invitation extended to me was to offer a general assessment of the success/failure of religion in Africa under the title, "Religion in Africa: A Curse or a Blessing?" For reasons I hope will become obvious, I have subtitled my essay "On Daring to Reinvent Christianity in Africa."

When I think about religion, more specifically about Christianity in Africa, three observations come to mind: the starting point, the critical direction, and the constructive orientation for African theological exploration in our time. My chapter will focus on these three sites of theological engagement to highlight three distinct but interrelated tasks for the African theologian. Rather than engage an abstract discussion about "religion" in Africa, I focus my comments on Christianity and the Christian churches to make my discussion concrete.

A more critical reason why I try to avoid the notion of "religion" while taking on the task of reinventing Christianity in Africa involves a determined effort to break loose of the ideological as well as the conceptual limitations of "religion," whose effect is to police the social and political dynamism of Christianity by confining it in an essentially spiritual mold.

1. Of Coffins and Churches: The Starting Point of Theological Reflection in Africa

Theological reflection on Africa in our time needs to begin with a disturbing observation, namely, that churches and coffins are perhaps the two most prevalent images associated with Africa today.[1] That Africa is a continent of churches requires no elaborate argument. In the twentieth century, the Catholic population in sub-Saharan Africa exploded from 1.9 million to 130 million, an astonishing growth rate of 6708 percent. A similar shift is underway in other Christian denominations. If the growth confirms the observation that Africans are notoriously religious,[2] it reflects the growing global confidence of African Christianity as the centre of gravity of world Christianity inexorably shifts to the global south.[3]

That Africa is also a continent of coffins is pretty obvious. In fact, in many parts of Africa, we have reached a place where, as Toloki, one of the principal characters of Zakes Mda's memorable novel *Ways of Dying,* notes, "Death lives with us every day. Indeed, our ways of dying have become our ways of living. Or should I say our ways of living are our ways of dying?"[4]

Theological reflection on Africa must begin not only by noting this irony but also by investigating the relationship between these two faces of Africa: a massively Christian Africa on the one hand and a socially distressed continent on the other.[5] What is the connection between the reality of coffins and the growth of Christianity on the African continent? Is Africa distressed because it is Christian, or it is so in spite of being Christian? Is Africa's Christianity merely a form of desperation? Is religion in Africa a blessing or curse? What difference does Christianity make in Africa? Can Christianity be a positive resource for social transformation in Africa? Why has it not been so?

No issue presses these questions more urgently than the ongoing cycles of violence, especially as these take on (as they often do in Africa) an ethnic or tribal expression. The memory of Rwanda 1994, of the post-election violence in Kenya 2007, of the ongoing civil war in the Congo, to name but a few, leave one wondering whether being Christian makes any difference when it comes to politics and tribal identity. Is the blood of tribalism thicker than the waters of baptism?

Similar questions are evoked by widespread corruption, mismanagement in public office, and massive abuse of human rights in overwhelmingly Christian countries. Does Christianity make any difference when it comes to issues of economics and public accountability?

The point of pressing these questions is not to give way to despair but to ground theological reflection on Africa in the discipline of lament. Just as the gospel of Matthew begins the proclamation of the good news by invoking the memory of a woman, Rachel, who weeps for her children and refuses to be consoled (Matthew 2:18 Holman Christian Standard Bible), any reflection of religion and society in Africa must begin by naming and mourning the slaughter of Africa's children (through violence, war, corruption, dictatorship, poverty, and so on), a slaughter in which Christianity is often complicit. That is why grounding theological reflection on Africa in lament is a way of resisting consolation.

Consolation takes many forms. A ready form of consolation when it comes to reflection on Christianity in Africa in our time has to do with focusing only on the good Christianity has done or can do in Africa. A related form of consolation takes the form of an uncritical celebration of Christianity's success in Africa. Commentators look at the numerical growth of Christianity in Africa, its lively expression, the rise in the number of priestly and religious vocations, the visibility of a few African churchmen on the global scene,[6] and the devotional and liturgical dynamism of Christianity in Africa as a confirmation of Africa's hour of faith. Africa is not only the new centre of gravity of the Christian faith, commentators note; African Christianity also holds the key to the global future of Christianity.

Africa's dynamic and apparently more traditional and orthodox expressions of faith are often held up as a refreshing antidote to the fledging, anemic forms of Western Christianity steeped in an increasingly secular and materialistic world. As Pope Benedict put it so succinctly, African Christianity can serve as "the spiritual lung" of humanity.[7]

Such descriptions of African Christianity are of course very encouraging, but they can be mesmerising and even consoling, especially when they are abstracted from the social, economic, and political realities in which Africans live. A celebration of Africa's spiritual dynamism, which however fails to see the distressing social, political, and economic realities of Africa as matters for spiritual concern, is a form of consolation.

Grounding theological reflection on Africa in the irony of coffins and churches is a way of probing the connections between Christianity on the one hand and the social, political, economic, and cultural dynamics of African society on the other. The more closely and honestly one probes these connections, the more one is faced with the realisation that Christianity in Africa has not always been experienced as "good news." On the contrary, quite often, Christianity's performance in Africa's social history has been ambivalent[8] and in some cases even outright negative.[9] But this observation need not lead one to despair. On the contrary, it is only by acknowledging the ambivalent performance of Christianity that one is able to grasp the full potential of Christianity for the renewal and social transformation of Africa. That is why it is by holding together the irony of churches and coffins that one is able to avoid the other – correlative (to the naïve optimism) form of consolation when it comes to thinking about religion and society in Africa.

This consolation takes the form of despair about Christianity's potential for social transformation. This despair underlies many social, economic, and political analyses that diagnose African society and offer recommendations for a transformed African society with little or no attention to Africa's Christian dynamism.[10] Often offering pre-packaged proposals for economic reforms, political adjustments, technical expertise, and ethical guidelines, the recommendations either assume that religion has very little to offer in terms of positive contribution or simply dismiss religion as a source of violence.[11]

No doubt many of these recommendations simply reflect a Western, modernist, secularist bias, but they perpetuate a misleading impression that religion in general and Christianity in particular operate in their own ephemeral spheres, separated from the concrete, lived realities of economic and political logic.

At any rate, the first moment of theological exploration in Africa has to do with illumining the contradictions in African society and probing the connections between the reality of churches and coffins. Grounding theological reflection in this lament and ambivalence is a way of acknowledging the historical shortcomings and limitations of Christianity in Africa and opening up fresh ways of thinking about and thus seeing the immense social and political possibilities of Christianity in Africa.

2. Beyond Religion: The Critical Direction of Theological Engagement

What the foregoing discussion points to is the need to learn to think about the nature, role, and social significance of Christianity in Africa different from what we are accustomed to under modernity. As I note in *The Sacrifice of Africa*, the discussion of the relation between religion and society follows a rather predictable pattern.[12] Within this discussion, Christianity is assumed under the more generic notion of "religion," and its social significance is depicted under three dominant paradigms.

In its *spiritual* paradigm, Christianity is understood to primarily be about the salvation of souls and the formation of one's inner, spiritual identity. Christian efforts under this paradigm focus on the life of sacraments, on being born again, on piety, and on efforts to be good, moral persons. Activities to this end include masses, evangelisation efforts, crusades, and overnight vigils. No doubt these activities are very public, but the key issue is that their goal is understood as essentially *spiritual:* the inner, personal wellbeing or salvation of the individual.

In Christianity's *pastoral* paradigm, its social contribution is understood in terms of efforts to help the poor, the outcast, and the needy through programs fostered by hospitals, schools, and social services that take care of those abandoned or abused by the systems. This is doubtless a very public and much needed role, but Christianity's social role is understood in terms of compassionate, humanitarian responses to needs that are made available and urgent by the more determinative processes in the political and economic spheres.

Under the *political* paradigm, Christianity's social role is viewed in relation to the way the Church tries to influence political developments through advocacy and recommendations, e.g. pastoral letters urging peace, reconciliation, and political reforms.

Under these three paradigms, Christianity indeed plays a very public, visible role in society that moreover seems to suggest the Church is a powerful social force in Africa. However, the more closely one examines the roles Christianity is assigned, one realises these are roles that allow the Church to play a public social role without however any expectation or option to change the fundamental visions and imaginations that drive African society.

The case of Rwanda makes this obvious. Years of evangelisation and Christianity's high public profile in Rwanda – most notably, its close ties to political power and its expansive catechetical, educational, and social programs – were not able to fundamentally change the way Rwandans viewed themselves. During the 1994 genocide, Rwandan Christians readily killed fellow Christians in the name of Hutu and Tutsi, which make it obvious that even though publicly visible and impressive in its outward expression, Rwandan Christianity remained socially shy or "weak"[13] when it came to issues such as "identity." It simply reflected, fit neatly in, and did the dirty work of policing and enforcing the political imagination of Rwanda constructed around the myth of Hutu and Tutsi as age-old enemies.

In this case, as in many others, Rwanda serves not as an exception but as a metaphor for much of postcolonial African society.

Another way to put the observation is that under the three paradigms, Christianity is allowed to operate (the much touted "freedom of religion") and to contribute to society (or the status quo) but cannot reimagine the fundamental visions that drive and shape modern Africa. If this allows Christianity to play a visible and public role in African society, that visibility comes at a cost – the cost of surrendering the possibility of peeking behind, questioning, and thus possibly interrupting the basic visions and imaginations that shape modern Africa.

As I note in *The Sacrifice of Africa*, the realities of poverty, tribalism, and violence in Africa are wired, so to say, in the imaginative landscape of Africa's modernity.[14] Time and space do not allow for a full discussion of the process and history through which these visions came to be set in the architectural foundations of modern Africa; suffice it to say that the same foundational narratives that help underwrite the notions of poverty, tribalism, and violence in the imagination of modern Africa help frame Christianity as merely a "religion" whose competence lies only in the private, personal, and spiritual dimensions of life and thus limits its capacity to question let alone re-frame the dominant visions and imaginations that drive modern Africa.[15]

And yet, it is now obvious that a new future for Africa will require the uninstalling of these expectations and the rewiring of Africa with fresh imaginations and expectations of what Africa is and can be. For as Achille Mbembe notes, "The challenge is to create another picture of ourselves in the world."[16]

But it is this task of creating another picture, another imagination – what I call the reimagination of Africa – that Christianity has tended to shy away from and cannot engage as long as Christianity is content to operate under a neat sphere of religion that is detached from the concrete life experiences of Africans in their villages, cities, and slums and from the social, political, and economic processes that make Africa a continent of coffins.

What does this concretely mean? Can the Church in Africa fundamentally change the direction of African society? Can Christianity interrupt the ongoing realities of poverty, tribalism, violence, and corruption in Africa? Can Christianity change the way we view ourselves and the direction of African society? What would this take? And what would this reimagined Africa look like?

Whatever else might be deduced from the discussion so far, I am not simply calling for Christian churches to be more actively involved in the economic and political fields in Africa. In a way, this is already the case; the foregoing discussion confirms that Christian churches have been busy offering "relevant" recommendations for the reconstruction of economics and politics in Africa, but these recommendations are in basic visions of modern Africa that are never questioned or engaged. What the foregoing discussion helps to make clear is the need for Christianity to step back from this predictable activism and look at the underlying visions that drive African society to engage in the quieter but more-fundamental task of reimagining and reconstituting itself.[17]

What the foregoing discussion has also made clear is that this task of reimagination is one Christianity cannot engage in as long as it is content to operate in the standard spiritual, pastoral, and political paradigms whose effect is to confine Christianity in a neat "religious" mode. So confined, Christianity is never able to tap deeply into its own social vision. And yet, it is only by living more fully in its own social vision that the Church will become an interesting social experiment and the gospel a force for social transformation in Africa.[18]

That is what makes the second moment of theological exploration – the critical task of learning to think differently about Christianity in Africa – so necessary. To the extent that this task involves thinking more deeply about Christianity's essential social nature, it involves nothing short of daring to reinvent the Church and Christianity itself. To get a sense of how this might actually look like in Africa, we need to turn to the positive or constructive direction of theological engagement.

3. Daring to Reinvent Christianity: The Constructive Direction of Theological Engagement

In his 1980 signature book, *African Cry,* the late Cameroonian theologian Jean Marc Éla, quoting a native missioner, noted, "In the churches of Africa the time has come to re-invent Christianity, so as to live with our African soul."[19] Éla arrived at this conclusion through his work with rural communities of northwestern Cameroon. It is this pastoral experience that brought Éla face to face with what he called "the shock of the Gospel" in Africa – the practice of Christian faith that "wafts above the everyday."[20]

In Cameroon, Éla noted, Christianity had become merely a "system of beliefs" with no impact on social, economic, political, or cultural realities of life; it was just another layer of moralising strictures in the lives of millions who lacked even the bare necessities, including drinking water, food, and shelter.

But if Éla's pastoral experience with the rural, marginalised communities brought him face to face with the shock of the gospel, it also strengthened his conviction in Christianity's potential as a way of life, indeed, in the midst of so many death-dealing neo-colonial structures, the "experience of another society, another humanity, another style of living together."[21]

It is this potential for Christianity to become the experience of a different world right here as it is provisionally and experimentally worked out in an ongoing fashion in the "shade-tree theologies"[22] in African villages and townships that unleashes and explodes Christianity's social vision in Africa.

The kind of shade-tree theology Éla envisioned is what is going on in the work of Bishop Paride Taban in South Sudan.[23] In 2005, Taban retired as the Catholic bishop of Torit and moved to the remote village of Kuron of South Sudan's Eastern Equatorial Province, where he founded a village settlement, the Holy Spirit Peace Village. This was Taban's response to Sudan's history of civil war, poverty, and tribalism, realities that defined the history of Sudan and Taban's ministry as priest and bishop.

A number of noteworthy elements about the Holy Trinity Peace Village confirm it as a revolutionary experiment of a new future in South Sudan. First, in the Peace Village, people from different tribes and different religions – Moslems, Christians, and Traditionalists – seek and commit to live together in harmony and raise crops and animals, learning new farming methods. The village also has a school that offers formal education for girls and boys and runs programs to promote adult literacy. The clinic runs a number of healthcare programs and training in sanitation and other basic healthcare skills. In all this, Taban envisions and describes the village as an "oasis" of peace, harmonious relationship, and food security.

Second, Taban also describes the Peace Village as an "an ambitious experiment" in nation building in that it displays the kind of new future he hopes to see everywhere in the Sudan. Thus, even though Kuron is a small village in the remote region of Eastern Equatoria in South Sudan, it is goal is to end tribalism, war, and famine. These realities, Taban notes, are real and everywhere in the Sudan and need to be eradicated. But Taban also knows that it cannot be done all at once; it can be done only in a small way. Holy Trinity Peace village is thus a demonstration of a future beyond war, violence, and tribalism. It is a kind of first installment of that future, a small flame he has ignited that he hopes will ignite other flames and ferment a revolution. (The logo for the peace village is a small flame underneath an African pot; more below). In this respect, it is telling that the government of South Sudan is sending some of its leaders to Kuron to learn how such peace villages can be planted throughout South Sudan.

However, by far the most provocative aspect of the peace village is its name: Holy Trinity Peace Village. Taban has reworked the traditional doctrine of Christian life in a way that shows that Trinity is not simply a set of beliefs but also a social vision. He is, in this case, involved in reinventing the Christian faith Éla talks about, and in so doing, he is reinventing African society; reimagining a new South Sudan in a way that unwires the patterns of violence, tribalism, and poverty of Sudan's neocolonial history and rewiring Sudan with a new social vision whose inspiration and framework draws from traditional Christian doctrine.

I believe there are many "small ways" such as Holy Trinity Peace Village in which Christians in various parts of Africa are reinventing Africa and African society as a whole beyond tribalism, violence, corruption, and poverty. Our role as theologians (and this constitutes the third dimension of theological exploration) is to point to these stories, to tell them in ways that reveal their freshness, and to display them as illuminations of what the Church is and can be in Africa and as evidence of Christianity's potential for the reconstitution of Africa.

Conclusion

So is religion in Africa a blessing or curse? Whereas there is no simple, clear-cut answer to the question, the point of my reflection has been to suggest that Christianity can generate new visions, a new social imagination, for Africa. However, for this to happen, Christianity itself needs to be reinvented. As a midwife and agent of this reinvention of both Christianity and of African society, African theologians are faced with three distinct but closely interrelated tasks. First, they must ground their reflections on Christianity and society in a discipline of lament through which they note and probe the contradictions of a massively Christian but a socially distressed continent.

Second, they must not be satisfied by simply offering relevant contributions and ready-made solutions but must constantly question and push beyond the standard formulations that confine Christianity to a neat supernatural realm.

Third, they must point to and tell stories that reveal Christianity's full potential in Africa; these stories will confirm that not only is Christianity capable of offering a new future for African society but also that such a fresh reimagination of society is already underway.

Endnotes

1   For a more elaborate statement of this observation, see my, *The Sacrifice of Africa. A Political Theology for Africa* (Grand Rapids, Mich.: Eerdmans, 2011), 29–32.

2   John S. Mbiti, *African Religions and Philosophy* (London: Heinemann, 1969), 1.

3   For a more elaborate discussion of the shift and its significance for global Christianity, see Philip Jenkins, *The Next Christendom: The Coming of Global Christianity* (New York: Oxford University Press, 2002); Philip Jenkins, *The New Faces of Christianity: Believing the Bible in the Global South* (New York: Oxford 2006); Andrew Walls, *The Cross Cultural Process in Christian History* (New York: Orbis, 2002). See also my reflection on how to live in this moment of world Christianity, "Mission and the Ephesian Moment of World Christianity: Pilgrimages of Pain and Hope and the Economics of Eating Together,"*Mission Studies* 29 (2012): 183–200.

4   Zakes Mda, *Ways of Dying* (Oxford, 1995), 98.

5   I am grateful to Professor Tinyiko Maluleke, who first drew my attention to this irony as the inevitable starting point for Christian social reflection in Africa. See Tinyiko Maluleke, "Christianity in a Distressed Africa: A Time to Own and Own Up." *Missionalia* 26:3 (November 1998), 324–40.

6   Archbishop John Ssentamu of York; Pastor Matthew Ashimolowo of the The Kingsway International Christian Church, in Walthamstow, and closer at home, high-ranking prelates such as Cardinals Arinze, Turkson and others, which always raises interesting if unproductive discussions about the possibility of an African pope. On ways I think these discussions are unproductive and even distracting, see my "Prospects of *Ecclesia in Africa* in the 21st Century," *Logos: A Journal for Catholic Thought and Culture* 4, no. 1 (2001): 179–96.

7   Pope Benedict, *Apostolic Exhortation, Africae Munus, The Church in Africa in Service to Reconciliation, Justice and Peace* (no. 13). For my extended reflection

on *Africae Munus,* see my "Africae Munus: The Church in Africa in Service to Reconciliation, Justice and Peace, in *Mission as Ministry of Reconciliation*, ed. Robert Schreiter and Knud Jorgensed (Oxford: Regnum Books, 2013): 66–78.

8   Coming from a different angle, Scott Appleby, a historian of religion, offers an extended argument for the ambivalence of religious traditions. He writes, "Religious traditions, symbols and are internally plural, which means they be equally a resource for peace or fuel for violence and war. Religious militancy is not the problem. Violent religious militancy is, extremism is." R. Scott Appleby, *The Ambivalence of the Sacred: Religion, Violence, and Reconciliation* (New York: Rowan & Littlefield, 2000), 13.

9   Whether with apartheid in South Africa; genocide in Rwanda; tribal violence in Kenya, Uganda, Ivory Coast, Sierra Leone, and elsewhere, there are numerous instances where Christian churches, rather than providing an alternative to racism or tribalism, simply radiated and even intensified those divisions. For some of these instances in the genocide in Rwanda, see my *Mirror to the Church: Resurrecting Faith After Genocide in Rwanda* (Grand Rapids, Mich.: Zondervan, 2008).

10   After studying the public role of Christian churches in select African countries, Paul Gifford includes in his otherwise impressive treatment a note of despair. African sociopolitical systems, he notes, "certainly needed radical restructuring, and it is not self-evident that … churches will contribute much in the direction." See Paul Gifford, *African Christianity, Its Public Role* (Bloomington: Indiana University Press, 1998), 348.

11   For the cultural suspicion of religion as a source of violence, see Scott Appleby, *The Ambivalence of the Sacred,* 7.

12   Emmanuel Katongole, *The Sacrifice of Africa*, 33–50.

13   On the distinction between "strong" and "weak" religion, Appleby writes, "A religion is strong, first of all, if its institutions are well developed and secure and its adherents 'literate' in doctrinal and moral teachings and practiced in its devotional, ritual, and spiritual traditions … A weak religion is one in which the people retain meaningful contact only with vestiges of the broader religious worldview and network of meanings and resources, in which they are isolated from one another and from educators and spiritual moral exemplars, and in which ethnic, nationalist, secular-liberal, and other worldviews and ideologies have a free rein to shape the meaning of those vestiges." *The Ambivalence of the Sacred*, 77. Commenting on Yugoslavia and on the failure of Christian leaders to stem the spate of ethnic violence, Appleby describes factors that contributed to make Christianity a "weak" religion. In general, "inadequate or nonexistent programs of religious education, politically unprepared religious leaders and the lack of viable ecumenical and interreligious structures conspired to limit the religious potential for peacemaking" (75). More specifically, "religious leadership led too little and followed too much. Preoccupied with the state, religious leaders did not attend sufficiently to the task of sharpening the attitudes and behaviors of their 'natural constituencies.' By and large the faithful, the potential base of

the independent political power of the churches, were not mobilised for non-violent forms of religious activism, such as conflict mediation and healing and reconciliation ministries" (74).

14 See Emmanuel Katongole, *A Future for Africa: Critical Essays in Christian Social Imagination* (Scranton: University of Scranton Press, 2005).

15 It would take us too much afield to get a discussion of the modern notion of "religion"; its genesis is in the history of European Enlightenment and the historical and ideological shifts in European society that led to the rise of a "secular" sphere, out of which religious sentiments had to be restricted – a secular sphere in which the disciplines of politics and economics increasingly became the unquestioned authority in determining the frames of reference for modern society. For a more detailed discussion, see my *Beyond Universal Reason: The Relation between Religion and Ethics in the Work of Stanley Hauerwas* (South Bend, Ind.: Notre Dame University Press, 2000): 5–33.

16 Quoted in KäMana, *Christians and the Churches of Africa: Salvation in Christ and Building a New African Society* (Maryknoll, N.Y.: Orbis, 2004): 9.

17 For the distinction between reconstruction and reconstitution that closely parallels my use of the terms here, see John Randolph LeBlanc and Caroline Jones Medine, *Ancient and Modern Religion and Politics: Negotiating Transitive Spaces and Hybrid Identities* (New York: Palgrave Macmillan, 2012), 188–89.

18 For as Scott Appleby notes, "Contrary to the misconceptions popular in some academic and political circles, religious actors play this critical and positive role in world affairs, not when they moderate their religion or marginalised their deeply held, vividly symbolised, and often highly particular beliefs in a higher order of love and justice. Religious actors make a difference when they remain *religious* actors." *The Ambivalence of the Sacred*, 16.

19 Jean Marc Éla, *African Cry*. Translated by Robert R. Barr (Maryknoll, N.Y.: Orbis, 1986), 120. Original French title: *Le cri de l'homme Africain* (Paris: L'Harmattan, 1980).

20 Éla, *African Cry*, 48.

21 Jean Marc Éla, *My Faith as an African*. Translated by John Pairman Brown and Susan Perry (Maryknoll, N.Y.: Orbis, 1995), 84. Originally published as *Ma foid' Africain* (Paris: Editions Karthala, 1985).

22 Shade tree theology is a theology developed not in libraries or office or sanctuaries but by and among brothers and sisters searching shoulder to shoulder with unlettered peasants for the sense of the Word of God in situations in which this Word touches them. See Éla, *African Cry*, vi, 119.

23 For a full discussion of Paride Taban's work, see my *The Sacrifice of Africa* (chapter 7); for a good narrative account of Taban's life and ministry, see Alberto Eisman, *Peace Deserves a Chance: Bishop Paride Taban. A Sudanese Shepherd* (Nairobi: Paulines Publications, 2011).

Church Family of God: Icon of the Triune God, as Listening Church and Africa's Treasure, Reinventing Christianity and the World

Elochukwu Uzukwu

This chapter is an attempt to explore the ecclesiological imagination underlying the recommendations of the first synod of bishops for Africa. The 1994 synod summed up its insight in the captivating and inspiring phrase, "Church Family of God in the image of the Trinitarian Family."

The Church in Africa, from patristic times, has made significant contribution to the advancement of theology in general and ecclesiology and sacramentology in particular. Cyprian and the Church of Carthage, in the third century, advanced in the midst of controversies and persecutions the image of a resilient local Church marked by what some call "autonomism."[1] However, communion and unanimity are crucial to the understanding of the ecclesiology of North Africa. The catholicity of this Church was never in contention. Carthage was a Catholic Church endowed with all it needed to be church. It was recognised as such especially by the sister Church of Rome. Synodality characterised this Catholic Church. The confidence of the North African Church in the synodical process is captured in a canon of the twentieth council of Carthage (fifth century, attested 525 CE) that threatened to separate from communion those who appealed to the Roman church over issues already resolved by the Church of Carthage: "ut nullus ad Romanam ecclesiam audeat appellare" (let no one dare to appeal to the Roman Church).[2]

Augustine of Hippo, in the struggle with Donatism, succeeded in expanding the North African ecclesiological imagination while at the same time demonstrating to the Donatists that he was interpreting Cyprian more accurately than they. In the process, Augustine drew the African church closer to the position of Rome and to Rome as the centre of Catholic communion, more than was the case under Cyprian.

One notes that in the Middle Ages, centralisation gathered momentum and became more and more entrenched. The sense of unity in the Catholic Church was clearly different from the unity argued by Cyprian.[3] Uniform practice was preferred, informed by what Congar called an ideology of unity that functioned within a monotheistic sociopolitical imagination. The political monotheism, pre-Trinitarian or a-Trinitarian, was based on Greek cultural assumptions. It ensured the confession of one God and the acceptance of one Bible, one liturgy, one law, one pope, and one emperor.[4] In practice, this resulted in paternalism, considering people as minors, objects rather than subjects.

In ecclesiological terms, the identity of a true local church disappeared; unity was confused with uniformity. Residential bishops, and even metropolitans, functioned as the vicars of the Roman pope.[5] Congar, quoting von Allmen, captured the drama of the monotheistic ideology that drove ecclesiology: "The urban community of Rome integrated into the small space of its *urbs* [city] the whole Latin world [*orbis*]."[6] Collegiality disappeared. This uniform vision is not consonant with the Christian Trinitarian confession that introduces the Incarnation of the Word and the death and resurrection of Jesus as the template for the Christian understanding of monotheism. Trinitarian confession, in contradistinction to a sociopolitical monotheism, adopts an ecclesiology of the interdependence and communion of churches in imitation of the Trinitarian reciprocity (*perichoresis*).

Today, only ongoing reform in the Church can generate the energy to configure church life in the Trinitarian image.[7] The image of Church family of God, dear to the African synod, embodies this reform. It is unlike the image of the Church dominant from the Council of Trent and through Vatican I, guided by the ecclesiology of Robert Bellarmine, the "hammer of heretics," who understood communion as uniformity in the Catholic Church made visible by the profession of faith, the administration of the sacraments, and the regime of Church leadership subject to the Roman pope.[8]

Church family of God is in harmony with Vatican II that introduced a radical interruption by opening a window for understanding the mystery and mission of the Church, the people of God or the family of God, in terms of Trinitarian reciprocity. The Church that "is in Christ like a sacrament or as a sign and instrument both of a very closely knit union with God and of the unity of the whole human race" originates from the will of "God the Father" and "was constituted ... by the outpouring of the Spirit."

(*Lumen Gentium,* nos. 1 and 2). Communion and collegiality prevails in the ministry of service in this church:

> Bishops, as vicars and ambassadors of Christ, govern the particular churches entrusted to them ... The pastoral office or the habitual and daily care of their sheep is entrusted to them completely; nor are they to be regarded as vicars of the Roman Pontiffs, for they exercise an authority that is proper to them, and are quite correctly called "prelates," heads of the people whom they govern *(Lumen Gentium,* no. 27).

However, since the Church has always operated with a pre-Trinitarian (i.e., monotheistic but non-Christian) ideology of governance, there certainly are going to be obstacles to a sociological realisation of church life rooted in Trinitarian *perichoresis,* as opposed to the more familiar sociopolitical monotheism. This makes opportune the argument for a Trinitarian ecclesiological metaphor, church-family, adopted by the synod of bishops for Africa. Can this metaphor assume a sociopolitical visage? What are its chances and mission in contemporary Africa and the world Church?

My objective in this chapter is not only to comment on the ecclesiological insight of the 1994 synod; it is also to draw lessons from the insight and point to the advantages of this image for renewal or reform in the church, a church of communion informed by a sibling relationship that imitates and displays communion as reciprocal interiority emerging from the life of the Triune God.

I begin by pointing out the rarity of the family idiom in the perception of the Trinity in Catholic theology, especially in Western Trinitarian theological discourse (perhaps the a-Trinitarian focus of Western ecclesiology moved this Church towards excessive centralisation). This leads me to explore the metaphor church-family of God in the image of Trinitarian relationality. In view of the agony that trails ethnic and human relations in Africa and the consequent betrayal of family, I decide to search for the place of gestation of church-family, imitating the Trinity-family, at the margin, i.e., at the critical or kairotic point in the life of Jesus spatially located at the place of the skull, Calvary. Local Churches birthed from the opened side (margin) of Jesus (according to the fathers of the Church) become empowered to embrace the social margin of Africa and the world, e.g., the slums of Kibera in Nairobi and Ajegunle in Lagos. This chapter, therefore, argues that the cornerstone of the Church was laid at the margin, the place of the skull, Calvary!

At Calvary, Jesus was crucified crying out to his Father with the Holy Spirit attesting in the blood and water that gushed forth from his side – painful relational Trinitarian *perichoresis*. The church, founded at the place of the skull, born at the margin, becomes empowered to respond to the challenges of marginalisation in our context and time. The theology of the Letter to the Hebrews will be used as the base for this analysis.

After proposing the insight of the Trinitarian imprint on the church-family, I point to the intimations of this relational ecclesiology in the work of the nineteenth-century Spiritan missionary, Francis Libermann, second founder of the Spiritans (Congregation of the Holy Spirit). Libermann dared to request, for Africa, true local Churches, not "missions"; churches with residential bishops and metropolitans who had full pastoral authority to resolve ecclesiological issues in their territories, as is normal in the communion of churches. Though, by the nature of the dominant post-Tridentine ecclesiology of the time, the request was considered unrealistic and could not be granted. Libermann was advised to ask for vicariates. Nevertheless, the shape of Libermann's local Churches anticipated Vatican II ecclesiology and the church-family of the African synod.

Finally, it is important to acknowledge that the task of developing this ecclesiology of church-family in the image of the Trinitarian family has far-reaching implications for the church of Africa and the world.

1. Trinitarian Family and Church Family of God – Who Inspired the Ecclesial Model of the Synod of Bishops for Africa?

It is ultimately by answering the question, "How is Trinity family?" that one will suggest an answer to the question, "How is church-family in the image of the Trinitarian Family?" This is crucial in view of the ambiguity of family relations in the contemporary African social context.

The declaration of the first bishops' synod for Africa that the church is family in the image of the Trinitarian family is astounding in view of the crisis ravaging the continent in 1994. The Rwandan genocide as quintessential "sacrifice of Africa"[9] exploded April 6, 1994, and continued until mid-July, 1994. The African synod opened April 10, 1994, and ended May 8, 1994. Amidst the fratricide and genocide, amidst the betrayal of family relations, should the synod be projecting the utopic ecclesiology of family? Curiously, the synod fathers never addressed directly the 1994 Rwandan genocide. However, they were not totally insensitive to the shocking happenings in a country where Catholics constituted the majority. The message of the "Synod of the Resurrection," or the "Synod of Hope" made frequent references to "fratricide." In article 2 of the *Message*, one reads,

> At this time when so much fratricidal hate inspired by political interest is tearing our peoples apart ... we want to say a word of hope and encouragement to you, the Family of God in Africa; to you, the Family of God all over the world: Christ our Hope is alive; we shall live![10]

Family is a rich experience not only in Africa but also in Asia and the rest of the world. But is the use of the expression "Church as family in the image of the Trinitarian family" dependent on the African experience? Precedents of the theological use of the family metaphor abound in the Jewish and Christian Scriptures. Family metaphors or images, "father," and at times "mother" are used of God in the Hebrew Scriptures. For example, in Isaiah 63:16, the prophet cries out, "For you are our father, though Abraham does not know us and Israel does not acknowledge us; you, O LORD, are our father; our Redeemer from of old is your name" (See also Is 64:8). God the Father is the beginning or foundation of our discourse on God derived from the complex history of Hebrew faith and Hebrew monotheism. In the Gospels, Jesus is called "Son of God"; Jesus calls God "Father" and refers to himself as "Son" (e.g., Mt 11:27; Jn 14:31).

But the recourse to the family metaphor to describe the Trinity is uncommon in the history of theology. This makes intriguing the adoption of the metaphor church-family in the image of the Trinitarian family by the 1994 synod. In the Eastern Church, Saint Methodius, the Gnostics, and Saint Gregory of Nazianzen (whose orthodoxy was admired both in the East and in the West) used the family imagery to describe the Trinity: Adam-Eve-Seth or Adam-Seth-Eve analogy for Father-Son-Spirit. While in the West, under the influence of Saint Augustine, the metaphor was rejected.[11] Gregory of Nazianzen correlated God-Father and Adam as "un-engendered"; the Son is related to Seth as "engendered"; and, finally, Eve is related to the Holy Spirit as "coming forth from" (*ekporeusis*, i.e., procession).[12] On the contrary, Augustine forcefully underlined the absurdity of correlating "a trinity of the image of <u>God</u> in three <u>persons</u> so far as regards <u>human</u> <u>nature</u>." The Trinity cannot "be discovered as to be completed in the marriage of male and female and in their offspring" (*De Trinitate* XII, 5).

The influence of Augustine put a stop to any theological developments of the Trinitarian family analogy. This stirs one's curiosity as to the historical, sociological, and theological promptings that led to the use of the metaphor by the 1994 synod of bishops for Africa, a synod that took place in the Western Church. The prayer by both the synod fathers and John Paul II (in *Ecclesia in Africa*) to develop an ecclesiological discourse based on the family model is worth repeating:

> It is earnestly to be hoped that theologians in Africa will work out the theology of the Church as Family with all the riches contained in this concept, showing its complementarity with other images of the Church (EIA, no. 63).

Apart from scattered references in Vatican II documents (e.g., *Lumen Gentium* no. 6, the church as the "house of God ... in which dwells his family"), post–Vatican II official Church documents do not appear to consider the "family" imagery vital to the ecclesiology of communion. It becomes interesting to analyse critically how the imperative role of family in African social organisational structures is perhaps engineering an interesting model of the Church that is promising for the renewal of the Church and the world.[13]

I suggest in this chapter that the family metaphor, the sibling relationship of the natural human family functioning in ecclesiology will be so radically transformed by the Trinitarian energy (mystery) that what the church has never lived before in sociopolitical terms is received as grace that restructures relationship in the Church and the world. John Paul II in *Letter to Families* (1994) implied that being created male-female and endowed with power to increase and multiply (Gn 1:26-28) could best be appreciated from Trinitarian life: "In the light of the New Testament it is possible to discern how *the primordial model of the family is to be sought in God himself,* in the Trinitarian mystery of his life. The divine 'We' is the eternal pattern of the human 'we,' especially of that 'we' formed by the man and the woman created in the divine image and likeness."[14] This justifies the dream of the African synod to anchor an inculturated ecclesiology on the metaphor of "the *Church* as *God's Family* as its guiding idea for the evangelisation of Africa." The images highlighted by this metaphor include "care for others, solidarity, warmth in human relationships, acceptance, dialogue and trust." Building up the Church as family enables "avoiding all ethnocentrism and excessive particularism." It encourages "reconciliation and true communion between different ethnic groups, favouring solidarity and the sharing of personnel and resources among the particular Churches, without undue ethnic considerations" (EIA, no. 63).

Anywhere the local Church functions fully in communion and reciprocity, the Trinitarian energy is present. Even under the centralised regime of the post-Tridentine Church, Francis Libermann, founder of the Congregation of the Holy Heart of Mary (devoted to work among black people in Africa and beyond) and the eleventh superior general of the revitalised Congregation of the Holy Spirit, successfully devised a template for ecclesiology that trusts the local initiative, ready through suffering and uncertainty, to birth a church that truly bears the marks of the relational Triune God. I first explore the emergence of this Church from the heart of the Trinity and then note the elements of this Church in the ecclesiology of Libermann, and, finally, I outline the tasks facing the church-family according to the 1994 African synod.

2.   Trinitarian Family and Church-Family Emerging at the Place of the Skull

The Rwandan genocide displayed painfully the collapse of relationship in Africa. The dream ecclesiology of the 1994 synod strove to redefine the self-understanding of the Church as the embodiment of Trinitarian relational life. However, for this novel ecclesia-talk to permeate and renew relationship in agonising Africa, I believe that its takeoff point should be the "ground zero" of the Christian faith, Golgotha.

Golgotha, in the Christian story, dramatises the culmination of abandonment and dereliction that at the same time encapsulates the Christian experience of God (the Paschal mystery). It appears to me, therefore, that Golgotha is indissociable from, nay, is the radical embodiment of, the sense of Trinitarian family that spawned the church-family of God. The Fathers of the Church unanimously contemplated in the pierced side of the crucified the channel from which the en-Spirited church emerged in "blood and water." This signals the fulfillment and the fructification of the new covenant: "Where a will is involved, the death of the one who made it must be established" (Heb 9:16).

The geographical location of Golgotha at the time of Jesus was outside the city walls. The physiological location of the channel through which Jesus' "blood and water" flowed was the side of Jesus. The Letter to the Hebrews states emphatically that people must relocate to the margin to become people of God, family of God, a Church of mimetic self-donation and communion:

For the bodies of those animals whose blood is brought into the sanctuary by the high priest as a sacrifice for sin are burned outside the camp. Therefore Jesus also suffered outside the city gate in order to sanctify the people by his own blood. Let us then go to him outside the camp and bear the abuse he endured (Heb 13:11–13).

Today, the need for the Church to relocate to the margin of our agonising world, a Church that painfully emerged from the side of Jesus, powerfully revalorises the nature and origin of the church. However, to appreciate the power of this reality, one must consider the sense that this Church bears the imprint of Trinitarian sacrificial reciprocity (*perichoresis*) or generosity.

Trinity at Golgotha

The Golgotha event as revelation of Trinitarian interrelationship is very difficult to grasp. Still, one must grapple with Golgotha as the critical test of the self-giving communion within the Triune God, imprinted in the very being of the Church. Our perception of the drama of Jesus' death unraveling in broad daylight is available as mystery in dark and obscure symbols. The crucifixion event – that "utterly vile death" that is "madness" for Greeks and "scandal" for Jews (1Cor 1:23) – is paradoxically the takeoff point for the search of Father-Son-Spirit family (analogically reflected in the Adam-Seth/Abel-Eve) that created the church-family. This has enduring dramatic and saving meaning for Africa, the world, and for all humanity.[15] The vision or insight into this mystery may be blurry; it is like seeing "in a mirror, dimly"; later "we will see face to face" (1Cor 13:12).

Golgotha offers a pre-resurrection vision of Trinitarian interrelationship that dramatises the words of Jesus: "Yet I am not alone because the Father is with me" (Jn 16:32). How does one mark out with clarity the transparency of the Father-Son relationship at Golgotha where the principal signals are abandonment and death? Communion and interrelationship are difficult for us to comprehend in such obscure and dark symbols. However, paradoxically, it was in the opaque experience of godforsakenness[16] at Golgotha that a candle is lit to help us grapple with the complexity of presence and reciprocal interrelationship of the Triune God, an interrelationship that created the church-family.

At Golgotha, Jesus' liminal experience of being betwixt and between "for us" offers a glimpse of the process of Trinitarian reciprocal interiority, a revelation of what makes God, God-Father-Son reciprocal interiority (love) with the Holy Spirit testifying. Jesus' piercing cry in a "loud voice" was "Eloi, Eloi, lema sabachthani?" which means, "My God, my God, why have you forsaken me?" (Mk 15:34; cf. Mt 27:46 – echoing Ps 22:1). The question of God is raised by the one "hanging on a tree." Hanging, not as a pollutant (cf. Dt 21:22-23), but as a vicarious offering: "Christ redeemed us from the curse of the law by becoming a curse for us – for it is written, 'Cursed is everyone who hangs on a tree'" (Gal 3:13).

In addition, the evangelists struggled to make sense of this death and the question of God that it raised; it was the death of the Just One. Some commentators suggest that the actual words uttered by Jesus on the cross may be the cry of the persecuted just in the Hebrew tradition: *Elî' atta'* ("You are my God"). The bystanders and soldiers understandably confused this with a call to Elijah. This hypothesis still echoes Ps 22:1, "My God, my God, why have you forsaken me?" (Though some think that the Hallel Ps 118:28, "You are my God, and I will give thanks to you; you are my God, I will extol you" could be the inspiration or the psalm prayer of Jesus). The suggested *Elî 'atta'*, "You are my God," evoking either Ps 22 or Ps 118, appears to both Brown and Léon-Dufour as the best or the most acceptable understanding of the last words of Jesus. Accepting *Elî 'atta'* suggests that one is not only tracing certain words to Jesus on the cross, but also that the words bear "some similarity to the oldest Gospel tradition."[17] This could be an additional indication of a powerful self-awareness, at Jesus' liminal experience, of the presence of God-Father beside the dying Jesus. God is present to God's Son!

The total outpouring of the only begotten of the Father, on the cross, in the cry of abandonment and death continued in the drama of the piercing of his (right) side and the flowing out of "blood and water." The whole narrative process is an attractive embodiment of the revelation of the Triune God. The emergent Church is a Trinitarian icon precisely because the characteristics of Trinitarian reciprocity revealed at this critical point are imprinted in the life/being of the church; this is particularly relevant for the Church in sacrificed Africa.[18]

The cry of abandonment and the response of the Father in deafening silence remain disconcerting. Perhaps this silence bespeaks of God's (Father's) presence, as in the experience of Elijah at Horeb, where God is revealed in "a sound of sheer silence" (1Kg 19:12-13)![19] The "blood and water" from the Dead-Crucified, according to the fourth gospel, is recognised as the surge of "living water" or the outpouring of the Holy Spirit and the emergence of church-sacrament and church and sacraments.[20] The kenotic, sacrificial outpouring of Jesus dramatises the interrelational reciprocity and Trinitarian availability that describe communion in the Trinity. This reciprocity/availability is imprinted in the being of the Church thanks to God's Spirit, the "living water": "Out of the believer's heart shall flow rivers of living water" (Jn 7:38). It is only at Jesus' glorification through his death wherein he gave his whole life that the Holy Spirit would be poured out.[21]

Church-Family's Being-Mission Deriving from Golgotha

The imperative evocation of the sacrificial in Trinitarian reciprocal interiority (*perichoresis*), as Rumanian theologian Stãniloae stresses,[22] makes Golgotha critical for the understanding of the Triune God "for us." It also makes Golgotha critical for the origin and understanding of the life and mission of the Church, the icon of the Trinity. This Church is necessarily located at the margin. True, it must be admitted that the preresurrection event of Golgotha is accessible as a saving and founding event for Christians only in the resurrection and outpouring of the Holy Spirit. Nonetheless, the power of the place of the skull lies in the fact that without Golgotha, the discourse on the resurrection-outpouring of the Spirit would be pure myth! The myth could justify the failed scheme of Docetism; in other words, the Son of God appeared only to die. The power of the priority of Trinitarian communion or reciprocity at Golgotha (God is radically present at Jesus' experience of suffering-abandonment-death) keeps on the front burner the Church's mission of healing/ reconciling profoundly wounded brothers and sisters and transforming the destructive social ecology that characterises the world in general and Africa in particular.

The mission of Jesus that achieves completion at the point of dereliction, revealing the relational interiority of Father-Son with the Spirit testifying, is then imprinted on the church. The symbol of the new community emerging from the mystical Trinitarian relationship was at hand; "standing near the cross of Jesus were his mother, and his mother's sister, Mary the wife of Clopas, and Mary Magdalene." Finally, "the disciple whom he [Jesus] loved" was standing beside his mother; to him Jesus entrusted his mother (Jn 19:25–27).

When the fourth gospel proclaimed that Jesus "bowed his head and gave up his spirit" (Jn 19:30), the beloved disciple was indeed declaring the outpouring of Jesus' Spirit to seal the emergence of the new community. From the margin, Calvary, every local Church birthed from the heart of Trinitarian relationality is family empowered by the same Spirit of Jesus to witness to the healing/reconciling ministry of Jesus. Each local Church, from New Testament times, in the communion of Churches, is fully endowed, thanks to the Spirit of Jesus, with all that is necessary to bear this witness. It is from this perspective that one appreciates the contribution of Francis Libermann to the birthing of Churches at the margin, local Churches of Africa, founded on the episcopacy to ensure communion as well as to retain autonomy as local Churches of Africa.[23]

3. Missionary Indications of the Idea of the Local Church in Africa – Francis Mary Paul Libermann

I was bemused during an outing to a Spiritan parish at Mbalmayo, Cameroon, when a parish leader remarked that Spiritans created the idea of church-family of God.[24] I explained to the elder that Church as family of God is the brainchild of the first Synod of Bishops for Africa. However, the idea was not totally alien to the original proposal contained in the proposal that Libermann submitted to *Propaganda Fide* in 1846.

Libermann (1802–1852) was the founder of the Congregation of the Holy Heart of Mary (founded in 1842), devoted to mission to the Blacks (*l'œuvre des noirs*), representing at the time the margin of margins. The new congregation channeled its energies to the liberated slaves in Haiti and Reunion and to Africans along the Guinea coast (called the two Guineas). Libermann's congregation later merged with the Congregation of the Holy Spirit (in 1848), with Libermann as the eleventh superior general of the revitalised congregation. Before the merger, Libermann and his group struggled to secure approval for their mission along the Guinea coast of Africa. The Congregation of the Holy Heart of Mary was dominated by a missionary spirituality that could rightly be described by what Koyama called the "crucified mind" as opposed to the "crusading mind."[25] This kenotic spirituality (cf. Phil 2:5-8) was deeply shared by members of the new congregation. For example, Msgr Benoit Truffet, the first apostolic vicar to Dakar, described the mystic empowerment of slaves by Christian evangelisation as enabling them to realise that "they are *children* and *brothers* of a crucified God to whom they should offer, with resignation and confidence, their tears, their hard labour and their prayers."[26] Libermann went further than Truffet, rowing against the tide of the times by upholding the human dignity of Africans. In his *Letter to the Community in Dakar and Gabon – November 19 1847*, he made memorable remarks:

> To close, a final observation, do not listen easily to the stories of those travelers around the coast when they speak to you about the small tribes they had visited, even if they have stayed there for a number of years. Hear what they say to you, but let their words not have any influence on your judgment. Scrutinise things in the spirit of Jesus Christ, free from all impressions, prejudices, but filled and animated by the charity of God and the pure zeal that his spirit gives you. I am sure that you would be able to judge quite differently our poor blacks than those who speak to you about them…. Strip yourself of Europe, its customs and its mentality; make yourselves Black with the Blacks in order to form them as they ought to be, not in the European manner, but leave to them what is their own.[27]

This missionary spirituality informed the account Libermann submitted to the *Propaganda Fide* in 1846, which contained wide-ranging ideas about the education (civilisation) of African peoples, especially the establishment of technical schools. Furthermore, he proposed novel ecclesiological structures at a time when post-Tridentine centralisation was the rule. For example, catechists should dress as clerics and should receive minor orders. In Libermann's view, catechists were closer to the people; they took over the function of the priest who were few in number and who visited irregularly. Their ordination to minor orders and their clerical dress were consonant with the structure and practices of the early Church. Above all, Libermann proposed the formation of priests and the establishment of residential bishops and metropolitans to ensure the independence of the local church that would be self-supporting and self-regulating. Though Libermann was inclined to ultramontanism, there was no doubt in his mind that the flexible structures of the early Church should inform the new Churches of the Guinea coast.[28]

Libermann's daring ideas had no chance of being approved in 1846. Advised or pressurised by the secretary to *Propaganda Fide,* Msgr Brunelli, he withdrew the original proposal and submitted a more acceptable text that requested apostolic vicars. However, the original text that is the subject matter of this discussion, which was discovered in manuscript form at the Vatican archives by Spiritan historian Paul Coulon in 1988, displays revolutionary ecclesiological ideas that captured, in my view, the imprint of Trinitarian relationality. It portrays a hierarchical structure of the Church that captures the views of Ignatius of Antioch, Cyprian of Carthage, and Vatican II. (According to Cyprian, one must know "that the bishop is in the Church").

Libermann requested five residential bishops and two metropolitans along the Guinea coast, from Senegal to the Cape. It is important to note that he was not talking about "indigenous bishops" but rather an "indigenous hierarchy." His theological argument is grounded in the ecclesiology of Msgr Jean Luquet, his former disciple and missionary to India belonging to the Missions Étrangères de Paris. Luquet was commissioned by the synod of Pondicherry, 1844, to present *Clarifications* to the Propaganda on the request of the synod for residential bishops, a request that was radically ahead of the practice of the time. Luquet's *Clarifications* (*Éclaircissements*) were widely diffused. His views influenced the 1845 encyclical of Gregory XVI, *Neminem Profecto*, calling for the establishment and formation of a local clergy. Libermann read, digested, and made the *Éclaircissements* fully his own. He incorporated the ecclesiology into his proposal without acknowledging his sources. The most important element of this ecclesiology concerns the episcopacy. Libermann underlined:

> Having a true clergy is the sign [of the presence] of a church; it is a church with a bishop acting freely and fully by virtue of the grace reserved to the episcopal consecration (p. 8).

> The Episcopacy, an indigenous Episcopacy, is therefore the true foundation of those churches that our Lord reserves to be enduring. One may assemble all sorts of objections against the application of this principle in the present mission countries, but it remains incontestable that the Episcopacy is established as the base of the churches by our saviour Jesus Christ (p. 81).[29]

These lines compare well with Vatican II's teaching on the episcopacy. It separated Libermann from the dominant Jesuit penchant for centralisation that Libermann considered unsuitable for the local Churches of Africa.[30]

The five residential bishoprics that Libermann requested were: (1) Senegambia (covering Western Sahara/Sierra Leone to the Sudan), with residence in Dakar; (2) Sierra Leone and Liberia (covering Cavally river/ Cote d'Ivoire), with residence at Freetown; (3) Cavally to Volta River, Gold Coast and Gulf of Benin, with residence in Kumasi of the Ashanti kingdom; (4) Gulf of Benin to the mouth of the Niger and the Gulf of Biafra, with residence in Dahomey; and (5) east of the Niger to the river Congo, with residence in Gabon.

Libermann was well informed about the geography of the Guinea coast. In the interim, Libermann asked for two bishoprics, i.e., Senegambia/Sierra Leone to the Volta, and Volta to the Congo. But even with these two bishoprics, he requested a metropolitan see in Dakar. The reasoning behind the metropolitan see was to ensure the empowerment of the local Church to take decisions *in loco* freed from extraversion. Furthermore, it assured the independence of the bishop (indigenous hierarchy) *vis-à-vis* religious superiors and the superior general of the missionary congregation. While apostolic vicars could be intimidated, resident bishops would be independent to act with greater freedom. If conflicts arose from abuse of power either by the bishop or the superior, a synod would easily settle the matter.[31]

The insistence of the Church being in the bishop (Cyprian) and on synodality is what this chapter highlights as the local church bearing the imprint of the relational Trinity. Libermann's views, dependent on the ecclesiology of Msgr Luquet, were revolutionary for his times. Under pressure from the secretary to the Propaganda, who saw the hidden hand of Luquet in Libermann's proposal, the request for bishoprics was replaced with the request for apostolic vicars.[32]

Although Vatican II came close to the position of Libermann, it was handicapped by an institutional and juridical ecclesiology. Its stress on the absolute authority of the bishops, on the immediate jurisdictional power of the bishop of Rome in every diocese, on docility and obedience, requiring "religious submission of mind and will" to teachings of Popes (*Lumen Gentium*, no. 25) did not sit well with Trinitarian ecclesiology.[33] Only the Trinitarian energy, accessed in the agonising event of Calvary, informed by divine reciprocal kenosis, can bring its warmth, passion, and ongoing reform to the structures of the Church. Could the recent call of Pope Francis for decentralisation and the juridical empowerment of episcopal conferences strengthen the gains of Vatican II?[34]

Challenge of a Church-Family Model – A New Ecclesial Utopia

The church-family of God in the image of the Trinitarian family is the dream of the 1994 African synod. It proposed a new sociopolitical ecclesial storyline that indicates the way forward in the contemporary world full of disasters. The storyline initiated by the African social experience of family, deeply wounded and ambiguous, is viable thanks to the miracle of Trinitarian relationality. The Trinitarian energy entrusts the Church, the local Churches of Africa, and the world Church with a mission: "The pilgrim Church is missionary by her very nature, since it is from the mission of the Son and the mission of the Holy Spirit that she draws her origin, in accordance with the decree of God the Father" (*Ad Gentes*, no. 2). The dream-mission of the church is to transform relationships across the board and have an impact on the social, economic, and political life in the Church and in the wider world. It is a mission of reconciliation.[35] Unlike the post-Tridentine, pyramidal, top-down ecclesial relationship based on a pre-Trinitarian monotheistic ideology, Trinitarian-informed ecclesial reciprocity takes off from the margin and is attentive to the voices at the grassroots, enabling the pilgrim people of God to live the dynamics of a listening Church.[36]

The claim made in this chapter about the dream vision, Church-family of God, is possible because the church bears the kenotic Trinitarian family imprint. The Church, people of God, family of God, birthed from the Paschal mystery, testifies to the truth of the Paschal mystery. Rooted in the Paschal mystery, there are no illusions about the witness of service by this pilgrim family of God that announces the *eschaton*: "Whoever wants to be first must be last of all and servant of all" (Mark 9:35).

The sacrificial experiences of church-family, the shocking betrayal of family in Rwanda, the Congo, and in many parts of Africa, rather than make the family metaphor irrelevant, look upon the Trinitarian reciprocity for strength and healing. "I have said this to you, so that in me you may have peace. In the world you face persecution. But take courage; I have conquered the world!" (John 16:33). African Catholic Church leaders underscored this need of unflinching confidence in the Lord, in the church-family-servant in imitation of the Triune God. During the meeting of the Symposium of Episcopal Conferences of Africa and Madagascar in Johannesburg, October 31, 1997, the bishops' declaration echoed the 1994 Synod:

> It is to be expected that in the Church as Family of God we are to love and serve one another as brothers and sisters and avoid all forms of hatred, division, discrimination, domination and pride. Bishops, priests and Church leaders should be seen as the servants of the people of God. In such a family, we expect greater sense of solidarity, sharing and caring most especially for the poor and needy. At this assembly we also emphasise the need for sharing

of resources, human and material amongst the local churches both in Africa and in the universal church. We call on the local churches of Africa to send priests and Religious, their own sons and daughters to work in other parts of the universal church.[37]

If the local churches of Africa are converted to live the Trinitarian reciprocity imprinted in the very being of the church, testifying to love and solidarity, preferring synodality to power plays, they will achieve their mission as witnesses to the Trinitarian generosity and energy in the communion of Churches. This is perhaps what Libermann was dreaming about in requesting for independent episcopacies in the Church of Africa. This is perhaps the way toward the realisation of the utopia of the 1994 synod of bishops for Africa that declared:

> The Church-as-Family ... manifests to the world the Spirit, which the Son sent from the Father so that there should be communion among all ... to restore the world to unity, a single human Family in the image of the Trinitarian family. We are the family of God ... The same blood flows in our veins, and it is the blood of Jesus Christ.[38]

The aim of exploring the potential for the renewal of Church and world with the image of "outside the city walls" (Golgotha) arises out of a dream that the streams or wells for humanising our world mediated by a church-family in the image of the Trinitarian Family are located in the margin of our prostrate and agonising world. I draw lessons from the ecclesiological insight of Libermann and the metaphor of church-family proposed by the 1994 African synod.

I think the Church in Africa and the world needs to take a decisive step to harvest the ecclesiological and humanising potential of the margin or abandoned and pierced side of our cities – like the slums of Kibera in Nairobi or Ajegunle in Lagos. Welcoming the world and culture of the poor margins, not as the objects of mission but as subjects providing the resources for accessing truly the being or nature and mission of the Church, no matter how inchoate, mixed, or inarticulate, appears to be the way the listening church-community is being led by the Spirit of that Jesus who on completing his mission "bowed his head and gave up his spirit" (Jn 19: 30). Places like Kibera and Ajegunle that can be replicated all over the continent of Africa enclose African Christians thirsting for the transforming blood and water of the Savior and to become full participants in the Christ, the pledge of a new humanity, mediated by a Church that is icon of the Trinity.

Endnotes

1   See J.P. Brisson, *Autonomisme et Christianisme dans l'Afrique romaine, de Septime Sévère à l'invasion vandale* (Paris: Edition E. de Boccard, 1958). See my monograph: Elochukwu E. Uzukwu, *A listening church: autonomy and communion in African churches* (Maryknoll, N.Y.: Orbis, 1996).

2   See Charles Munier, "Un Canon inédit du XXe Concile de Carthage: 'Ut nullus ad Romanam Ecclesiam audeat appelare'," in *Revue des Sciences Religieuses* 40 (1966).

3   See Cyprian, *De Lapsi and De Ecclesia Catholicae Unitate*, trans. M. Bénevot (Oxford: Clarendon, 1971).

4   Yves Congar, "Le Monthéisme politique et le Dieu Trinité," in *Nouvelle Revue Théologique* 103, no. 1 (1981). Aspects of the history are given in greater detail by Congar in: Yves Congar, *L'Écclésiologie du haut Moyen âge:de Saint Grégoire le Grand à la désunion entre Byzance et Rome* (Paris,: Éditions du Cerf, 1968).

5   Congar, "Le Monthéisme politique et le Dieu Trinité," 13–14, 16–17.

6   See Yves Congar, "Le Pape comme patriarche d'Occident. Approche d'une réalité trop négligée," in *Istina* 28, no. 4 (1983) 380–81. See my detailed discussion in Uzukwu, *A listening church: autonomy and communion in African churches* (Chapter 4).

7   See Yves Congar, *True and False Reform in the Church*, Rev. ed. (Collegeville, Minn.: Liturgical Press, 2011).

8   Many have written on this. See Augustin Ramazani Bishwende, *Pour une Ecclésiologie trinitaire dans la postmodernité et la mondialisation,* vol. 1: De R. Bellarmin à Y. Congar (Paris: L'Harmattan, 2008). And also Bernard P. Prusak, *The Church Unfinished: Ecclesiology through the Centuries* (New York: Paulist Press, 2004).

9   See Emmanuel Katongole, *The sacrifice of Africa: a political theology for Africa* (Grand Rapids, Mich.: W. B. Eerdmans, 2011).

10   Citations of the *Message of the Synod* in this study are taken from Maura Browne, ed. *The African Synod – Documents, Reflections, Perspectives* (New York: Orbis, 1996).

11   See Bertrand de Margerie, *The Christian Trinity in history (Studies in Historical Theology)* (Still River, Mass.: St. Bede's Publications, 1982).Chapter Eight.

12   See Marc Ouellet, *Divine likeness: toward a Trinitarian anthropology of the family*, Ressourcement (Grand Rapids, Mich.: W. B. Eerdmans, 2006): 21–22. Ouellet depends on the study of Lionel Gendron to stress the viability of the family analogy with regard to the Trinity (e.g., L. Gendron, "Le Foyer chrétien: une Eglise véritable?" *Communio* XI, 6 (1986): 65–83.

13   Nothomb's interesting article gives statistics of the family of God imagery in post-Vatican II documents before the 1994 synod. D. Nothomb, "L'Église-famille:

concept-clé du Synode des évêques pour l'Afrique - une réflexion théologique et pastorale," in *Nouvelle Revue Théologique* 117 (1995).

14   John Paul II, *Letter to Families no. 6*, www.vatican.va/holy_father/john_paul_ii/letters/documents/hf_jp-ii_let_02021994_families_en.html [accessed 12/25/2013]; see also Ouellet, *Divine likeness: toward a Trinitarian anthropology of the family*, 20–22.

15   See the interesting essay of Martin Hengel that studied crucifixion from the literature of the ancient world, highlighting its vileness; Docetism wanted to get around the embarrassment by affirming that the Son of God only appeared to die. Martin Hengel, *Crucifixion in the ancient world and the folly of the message of the cross* (London: SCM Press, 1977).

16   See David Emmanuel Goatley, *Were You There? Godforsakenness in Slave Religion* (Maryknoll, N.Y.: Orbis, 1996). African American theology grapples with God's presence in the obscurity of slavery. See Riggins R. Earl, *Dark Symbols, Obscure Signs. God, Self, and Community in the Slave Mind* (Maryknoll, N.Y.: Orbis, 1993).

17   See Raymond E. Brown, *The Death of the Messiah – From Gethsemane to the Grave. A commentary on the Passion Narratives in the Four Gospels.*, ed. David Noel Freedman, vol. 2, The Anchor Bible Reference Library (New York: Doubleday, 1994):1087–88; Xavier Léon-Dufour, *Lecture de l'Évangile selon Jean*, IV vols., vol. IV - L'Heure de la Glorification (chapters 18–21), Parole de Dieu (Paris: Éditions du Seuil, 1996): 152–153.

18   See Katongole, *The sacrifice of Africa*.

19   I analysed this in Elochukwu E. Uzukwu, *God, Spirit, and human Wholeness: appropriating Faith and Culture in West African Style* (Eugene, Ore.: Pickwick Publications, 2012):122–23.

20   I draw from the works of Brown and Léon-Dufour. Léon-Dufour, *Lecture de l'Évangile selon Jean*, IV - L'Heure de la Glorification (chapters 18–21).Brown, *The Death of the Messiah – From Gethsemane to the Grave. A commentary on the Passion Narratives in the Four Gospels.*, 2.

21   See Brown, *The Death of the Messiah – From Gethsemane to the Grave. A commentary on the Passion Narratives in the Four Gospels.*, 2, 1178–82. Léon-Dufour, *Lecture de l'Évangile selon Jean*, IV - L'Heure de la Glorification (chapters 18–21).

22   Dumitru Stăniloae, *Theology and the Church*, trans. Robert Barringer (Crestwood, N.Y.: St. Vladimir's Seminary Press, 1980).

23   For the powerful story of the contribution of Libermann to mission and spirituality, see Paul Coulon and Paule Brasseur, eds., *Libermann (1802–1852): une pensée et une mystique missionnaires*, Histoire (Paris: Editions du Cerf, 1988).

24   This was a visit to St Frederick's Parish, Sunday, July 14, 2013. Mbalmayo is fifty kilometers from Yaoundé, the capital of Cameroon.

25 See Kosuke Koyama, *No Handle on the Cross – An Asian Meditation on the Crucified Mind* (London: SCM, 1976).

26 This text, sent to the annales of the archconfraternity of Our Lady of Victories in Paris, was never published. It is not yet the language of liberation and equality. See Paul Coulon and Paule Brasseure, eds., *Libermann (1802–1852):* 410–11.

27 See Coulon and Brasseur, *Libermann (1802-1852):* 489–546. Note the original text read, "Faites-vous nègres avec les nègres"; I decided to translate "Black" instead of "Negro" preferred by other readers of Libermann. See Christian de Mare, ed. *Anthologie Spiritaine: Textes de Claude-François Poullart des Places ... et de François-Marie-Paul Libermann* (Rome: Congrégation du Saint-Esprit, 2008): 270–76.

28 See Paul Coulon, "Un Mémoire Secret de Libermann a la Propagande en 1846? Enquête et suspense," in *Mémoire Spiritaine* 3, no. 1e Semestre (1996). See also Raymond E. Brown, *The Churches the Apostles Left Behind* (New York: Paulist Press, 1984). I discussed aspects of the ecclesiology of Libermann in Elochukwu E. Uzukwu, "Inculturation and the Spiritan Charism," *Spiritan Horizons*, no. 2 (2007).

29 See Coulon, "Un Mémoire Secret de Libermann a la Propagande en 1846? Enquête et suspense," 41.

30 Libermann discussed the Jesuit's penchant for centralisation that is unsuitable for the local Church in his letter to Mother Javouhey, foundress of the Sisters of Cluny. A. Cabon, ed. *Notes et Documents Relatif à la Vie et à l'Œuvre du Vénérable François-Marie-Paul Libermann*, vol. VII (Paris: 1938), VII, 227.

31 Details of Libermann's position in Coulon, "Un Mémoire Secret de Libermann a la Propagande en 1846? Enquête et suspense," 43–45.

32 Luquet reported in his diary that he had become very unpopular with Msgr Brunelli, secretary to the Propaganda. See Coulon, ibid., 49–50.

33 See the study of Tillard on the thorny question of jurisdiction of the local bishop and the bishop of Rome in the same location, from Vatican I (*Pastor Aeternus*) to Vatican II (*Lumen Gentium*), and the issues it raises for communion of churches and collegiality, J.M.R. Tillard, "The Jurisdiction of the Bishop of Rome," *Theological Studies* 40, no. 1 (1979).

34 See *Evangelii Gaudium* nos. 16 and 32. www.vatican.va/holy_father/francesco/apost_exhortations/documents/papa-francesco_esortazione-ap_20131124_evangelii-gaudium_en.pdf.

35 This was the theme of the second synod of bishops for Africa, 2009.

36 Uzukwu, *A listening Church: Autonomy and Communion in African Churches.*

37 SECAM, Message, Church as Family of God and Hope for Africa, nos. 20–21, Johannesburg, Friday, October 31, 1997.

38 *Message of the Synod*, no. 25.

Reimagining African Theology:
The Promise of a New Generation

Anne Arabome

Introduction

Recently deceased Cameroonian theologian Jean-Marc Ela located the vocation of the African theologian in the realm of concrete commitment rather than at the level of academic discourse. As he put it,

doing theology is no longer an academic exercise, but a spiritual adventure. That is why what is happening today in the villages and slums of Africa prevents theologians from shutting their eyes and drifting off to sleep with the purring of a clear conscience – created by producing the type of discourse that, up until now, has been oriented around demands for indigenisation and acculturation.[1]

In deciding how to approach this topic, I have had to withdraw several times to a place of prayer and retreat, something I minimally did in writing other essays. I have experienced moments of pain, confusion, and distress in trying to "reimagine" the future of theology in Africa. The word *imagination* in itself calls for enormous creativity. Reimagining what has been tirelessly imagined and probably created or being created by others appears even more daunting; it would be sheer hubris to pretend to cover the entire gamut of approaches, issues, and personalities captured under the title "African theology."

From where I stand as a Nigerian African woman, I can speak and theologise only in the way I believe is true to who I am. Part of the stress I had in approaching this topic stemmed from the fact that I didn't quite understand what African theology really means. What is the usefulness of such a theology in the twenty-first century? Who is benefitting from it? Where is it operating? These questions are my own cry as an African woman theologian. In essence, my question is: how relevant is the African theological enterprise to the postcolonial, globalised world of the twenty-first century?

My purpose in this chapter is threefold: First, I will try to identify my ancestors in theology and identify aspects of their methods and focus that have left a significant imprint on African theology.

Second, I will undertake a personal assessment of what leaves me content and inspired or dissatisfied in their contributions, what are the gaps in methods, and what issues and voices have been left out. I will identify particular elements and characteristics of the changing context of theological reflection in Africa: What new issues are emerging in the context of Africa that I as a new scholar think are very critical? Why do I think theology ought take them into account or pay attention to them?

Third, I will examine what I imagine to be the promise of a new generation, namely, relevant and creative ways of doing theology in Africa today.

The anticipated outcome of this analysis is to develop a fresh conception of African theology that speaks to the twenty-first century experience of the African in the wider context of Church and society.

The Journey of a People

My dad and mom, my first ancestors in theology, taught me informally. They cared for nine children and taught us to love and serve each other, although mostly through the teachings of the Church that presented Christ as head of the Church and men, like my father, as head of the family. That was my first encounter with and the beginning of my experience and understanding of Christian patriarchy.

My other ancestors in theology were my grandparents and extended family members, who were a combination of Muslims and practitioners of African traditional religion. They introduced me to an imageless God, the source of life who permeated everything and being. Mine was a multireligious family. They taught me about being a good person, not about a God. What were important were the norms that guided us as a family and a people, protected life, and encouraged us to act as brothers or sisters to our neighbors because they were family. Food and good wishes were exchanged and shared during Muslim and Christian feasts, a confirmation of Ghanaian theologian Mercy Amba Oduyoye's observation that "Africans of all three religions [African-Cosmic, Christianity, and Islam] are united by their extended-family obligations.... One could say that, in Africa, common interests are more important than common religious creeds and theological correctness."[2]

In this context as well, I encountered the feminine face of God in the *Olokun* (goddess of the sea), whose shrine was prominently placed in the center of my maternal grandmother's home in Benin City, Nigeria. At the same time, I learned from the songs and myths and stories that women were to be subject to men. Ironically, the powerlessness and the powerfulness of women were reflected in my tradition. That was why my semiliterate grandmother could be the leader of a political party in Benin City at that time.

Furthermore, I also knew of the God who healed through herbs and traditional medicine through my paternal grandmother, who consulted with the oracle during the week, took eggs and chickens for gifts to the white missionary priest on Saturdays, and went to Mass faithfully on Sundays. Through her, I also learned the songs of call and response and the value of African communities. She was the matriarch; she had more authority than my grandfather did. They wrote none of this down, but who I am today has been partly formed by what they passed on to me orally.

I still hear them in stories and songs. Some of them were very painful, like seeing my mother and the rest of my uncle's wives swearing ritual oaths at the grave of the king, my grandfather, that they would forever be faithful to their husbands, whereas the men had nothing binding them to marital fidelity. The Levirate tradition practiced in my family allowed an uncle to marry the widow of his deceased brother.

Between African traditional religion and Christianity lay a vexing paradox: in the former, women oftentimes seemed very strong, but to be good Christian wives, they had to be totally submissive and subordinate to men.

The second category of my ancestors in theology includes my teachers, pastors, and mentors. Although born and raised in the postcolonial era, I was trained with a colonial mentality. The little rhymes and poems and content of my studies were all Western. In kindergarten, I knew how to recite "London bridge is falling down" even though I had no idea where and what "London" meant. I also learned to read Shakespearian books I memorised well and narrated eloquently though they had no real significance in my existence. Except for a few books such as *Things Fall Apart* and *African Night Entertainment*, most books contained images and messages that were totally foreign to me.

In religion classes, we read about people who knew and followed God, and again, all were white. The Church gave me a white Jesus and God. Not only was this God Western and white, he was also Roman. So I learned to sing all the Latin songs very well.

Here was the beginning of my confusion, doubt, and distress. I had all the answers supplied by the Baltimore Catechism in which I was schooled, but they had no connection to how I thought, prayed, laughed, played, cried, celebrated, mourned, questioned, believed, ate, danced, and acted as an African. The dichotomy between my religiosity and my real actions could best be likened to taking a fish out of water; I was totally disconnected.

In addition to all this in my background, joining religious life in Africa amounted to becoming a white woman. I knew all the St Louis Jesuits' songs and the Euro-American church songs and hymns; I sang and prayed very few of the Nigerian songs and prayers that had formed me. The language and character of my religion were patriarchal; the white male God controlled and owned the world and would punish anyone who deviated from his norms. As one of the American Catholic nuns told me in the novitiate, "All the men and women who have left religious life have gone to hell." She was telling me that there was no salvation outside the Church.

I discovered another group of ancestors through my academic and scholarly pursuits. In encountering Augustine, Aquinas, Tertullian, and the others who are revered as Church fathers, I became more alienated than ever from the Church. Their teachings, from Augustine's original sin that spoke against women, to Aquinas's idea that women are deformed men, and to the history of a Church that has over the centuries disregarded women, put a seal on our lips in regard to women sharing in the priestly ministry of the risen Christ.

In sum, I was a confused and distressed African woman trying to reimagine theology in Africa. The question here for me is, what do all these have to do with the issues of life and death that have plagued Africa and today's globalised world?

African Theology: In the Beginning Was the Beginning

There are various debates about the beginning of African theology, or what I refer to as formalised, academic, half-African theology. Some African theologians date it to the apostolic era, justifying the ancient African roots of Christianity and the fact that most of the Church's teachings and writings were done by African church fathers. Others attribute it to the Second Vatican Council, especially in relation to documents such as *Gaudium et Spes, Nostra Aetate,* and *Ad Gentes.*

On the other hand, others argue that there is a link between the formation and development of African theology and the origin of nation states and the era of independence from the colonial leaders and missionaries. In this sense, the beginning of African theology belongs to the context of the Negritude movement, whereby people began to denounce and renounce colonial oppression by reclaiming and reviving part of their culture and religion that gave dignity and respect to their personhood. It was for them a retrieval of their humanity. The leaders included Leopold Senghor, Aimé Cesaire, and Cheikh Anta Diop. For them, a return to their culture would lead to more freedom.

Another most-recent group argues that African theology began at a January 1966 meeting in Ibadan, Nigeria. According to an eyewitness account credited to John Mbiti,

> It was organised under the auspices of the All Africa Conference of Churches, and we were an ecumenical gathering – Roman Catholics, Anglicans, Methodists and Coptic Church. We came from all regions of our continent except the south, which was still under the unrelenting shackles of apartheid. Official participation were African and male... plus a few guests from Britain, Europe and America with interpreters [English and French]. It was a great significance that we met for the first time on our own soil, with our own hoes, our own seeds and our own agenda.[3]

From Mbiti's account, there was no doubt that the foundation of African theology in Africa was to be formalised and birthed just as its Western predecessors had been formalised and birthed. Noticeably absent from the evolution and development of this enterprise and the imagination of its proponents were African women. The concrete and disturbing proof of this systematic exclusion of African women from historical accounts of the origins and development of African theology is Benezet Bujo's two-volume account of the same.

My task is not to pick a quarrel with a futile debate about the existence or nonexistence of African theology. We can agree that the debate on African theology arose some years before Vatican II. By now, one fact has been established: we no longer need to discuss the principle of the possibility or legitimacy of an African theology because the principle has been established.[4] Today, a venerable cast of African theologians have pioneered, shaped, and defined the contours of theological speculation on the continent. These theologians could be considered as our "ancestors" in the struggle of faith in search of understanding. These African theologians pioneered a more formal theological discourse nestled blissfully in the haven of academia; among their numbers are Elochukwu Uzukwu, Vincent Mulago, Ngindu Mushete, Charles Nyamiti, Jean-Marc Ela, Mercy Amba Oduyoye, Benezet Bujo, Laurenti Magesa, Anne Nasimiyu, and Teresa Okure. I will not give a historical lineup of these theologians but engage a few of them in brief conversations to identify what they have been able to understand and articulate for us.

Charles Nyamiti

Nyamiti's passion and preoccupation was with exploring the relationship between two sets of concepts relating to God: African and Christian. Although Nyamiti concedes the importance of taking seriously elements of African traditional religion – with all its values of hospitality, community, religious devotion, and life – he has no doubt about the inferiority of African traditional religion and the superiority of Christianity.

In Nyamiti's theological framework, in the encounter between both, scholastic metaphysical constructs provide fitting receptacles for molding African ideas into Christian forms or of translating the latter into the former in a process of inculturation, hence his conviction that the God revealed in the Bible is also the God of traditional African religion. Thus, African teachings on God are very close to the Old Testament. However, only if African theology is anchored in scholastic metaphysics can it claim to be validly Christian.

Jean-Marc Ela

Jean-Marc Ela asserts,

We do not know what we believe unless we say it in our own language. Until now, the African churches have spoken a kind of Christian "creole" that includes expressions from translations of the catechism going back to Trent. We must re-hear everything previously spoken about God and God's revelation to people in all times, all languages, and all cultures. If everything were fixed for all time, we would be useless to the world of faith. But this is not so. By accepting the mission to announce the gospel to their peoples, the churches of Africa must take up the gospel once again, and rethink it so they can announce the Good news in a new way.[5]

This is what prompted him to propose a "theology under the tree" to which reference was made above.[6] Thus, for Ela, "to create a poetics of faith, we must rediscover the African soul, or anima, where symbol appeals through metaphor and helps us speak of that God who raises up the meek and feeds the hungry."[7]

Mercy Amba Oduyoye

As John Parrat has observed,

In common with American black theology (and indeed Latin American liberation theology), women's issues were not in the forefront in the early debates
about African theology. One reason for this, no doubt, was the paucity of
theologically trained women, a situation that is now rapidly being rectified.
Feminist theology in Africa has not been as strident as in some parts of the
Western world, and it would probably be right to characterise it (like its sister
movement in Asia) as concerned with women's role in the wholeness of a single
humanity rather than in the feminism as a revolutionary counter-movement.[8]

Yet, if anyone knows the depths and the agony of nonrecognition and exclusion, it is the African woman, as Oduyoye poignantly argues. Oduyoye provides a foundation for theological explorations by African women and a glimpse of the African woman's relationship with God in the context of African culture. Her analysis exposes the cultural and ancient heritages at "the roots of belief systems that continue to dehumanise woman" and distort the face and truth of womanhood in the name of tradition.[9] This situation recalls the experiences of women in Latin America and in North America. Whether Christian or not, the African woman finds herself in a dilemma. While her society saddles her with so-called unchanging ancient cultural mores, at the same time, she struggles to cope "with the social changes of intruding foreign cultures" that have become strongly embedded in the African postcolonial experience.[10]

Postcolonial Africa remains the stomping grounds of entrenched colo-
nial traditions. Nowhere is this more manifest than in the highly patriarchal practices of the mainline Christian churches in Africa which transmits their message in a manner foreign to Africa. The concomitant effect resembles

a reality at variance with African understanding of self and God. Consequently, the African Christian woman is challenged first by a culture that tenaciously holds on to customs and traditions that denigrate women and second by a church that imposes another layer of structural challenges through its traditions and theology in the African context.

For African women theologians such as Mercy Oduyoye, Daisy Nwachukwu, Anne Nasimiyu, Teresa Okure, and Teresia Hinga, the capacity for the Church to hear the "voice of the voiceless" is severely compromised by not addressing the question of the other half of the human community, that is, women whose experience in Africa tellingly illustrates systemic exclusion and marginalisation in Church and society in a male-dominated process of theologising.

> African women theologians have come to realise that as long as men and foreign researchers remain the authorities on culture, rituals, and religion, African women will continue to be spoken of as if they were dead.[11]

My point has been vividly and anecdotally expressed by Oduyoye in the following narrative:

> Once there lived on earth Half and Half, each of them only half a human being. They spent all their time quarreling and fighting, disturbing the rest of the village and trampling upon crops. Every time a fight began cries went up to Ananse Kokroko: *"Fa ne Fa reko o!* They are at it again, Half and Half are fighting."* So one day God came down, brought Half and Half together, and a whole human being appeared.[12]

In light of the foregoing, where does African theology leave me? How does it seem to me? I will make two brief points. First, the pioneers of African theology must be commended for being brave and courageous in the face of all odds to name their own identities and forge theological discourse grounded in the African reality. I am always very fascinated by the writings of Mbiti, Nyamiti, and Bujo. However, what I have yet to understand from their writing is the place and role of women in African Christianity and African theology. There seems to be a romanticisation of the African culture as if inculturation will be perfect for African Christians once we can transport it to our own situation. The problem here I believe is that Christianity and culture are not neutral and that it is a myth to think that Christianity came to liberate women. How could Christianity be liberating them when in fact it reinforces and promotes the very part of the African culture that is most dehumanising to them?

Second, to adopt the position of Ela,

the claim that Africa is "incurably religious" must be demystified. Our societies are no longer sheltered against secularisation, atheism, or religious
indifference. We need only read African literature to realise the attitude of
the new generations toward Christian missions. The disaffection of a large
part of the *intelligentsia* is a serious challenge to the African Church. Faced
with the invasion of sects into university campuses and intellectual circles,
we can no longer entertain comfortable illusions of security. Why should we
orient theological research around rites and beliefs alone, while modernity
causes the masses to be aware of another set of problems?[13]

How Would I Reimagine African Theology?

First, from a methodological perspective, I envision African theology as
a circle – a conversational, dialogical enterprise that includes all voices. In
making this point, I am reminded of a recent dramatic event in the Roman
Catholic Church: On Holy Thursday, Jesuit Argentinian Pope Francis
washed the feet of women – something that had never happened in this
highly patriarchal Church. As the pope explained, "This is a symbol, it
is a sign – washing your feet means I am at your service."[14] The pope in
this instance was reflecting the model of a Church radically different from
what we are used to. I discerned in his action elements of a theological
enterprise at the service of all, including women, rather than one who
serves to reinforce the clerical and doctrinal privileges of the few.

As may be clear to some, in advancing this approach, I am merely
retrieving the methodological approach pioneered by the Circle of Concerned Women theologians. Their idea of a circle is simple: to create "for
many women … a safe place to reflect on and analyse these [pertinent]
issues."[15] By adopting "circle thinking" or a "circle approach" to theological reflection, these women pioneered a new way of doing theology that
they described in the following terms:

The most important learning is that the motivation for Africa women's
commitment to doing theology comes as a result of the inner conversion by
concerned women theologians. It is not motivated by a need to confront;
impress or even wins [sic] the church or other religious institutions. If this
were the case, we would give up because many do not read our works. Our
goal is to make Theology in Africa fly by equipping it with the missing wing.
A bird with one wing does not fly. African Theology without the story of the
faith of the women of Africa is handicapped. The distinct gift that we bring

to the Theology of Africa is to repair the imbalance. The Circle Theology has posed questions to the content of the Theology taught in centers of learning and practiced in religious spaces.[16]

As one of the founding circle members, Oduyoye, further described it, circle theology does not satisfy itself by being a purely "intellectual exercise"; rather, the circle approach focuses resolutely "on the issue at hand," on critical matters in church and society.[17] From this I propose that African theology focus on pertinent and critical issues, not the issues of Greek mythologies and scholastic metaphysics of the past that are totally irrelevant to the African context.

Second, many issues have plagued the continent, and many African theologians are writing on such issues. However, theology ought not to be a matter of only discourse and narrative; the enterprise and its proponents must both be rooted or incarnated in reality. I am convinced that written words have failed us at this point. We as Africans comprehend more in experience rather than in abstract realities as taught by the West through books. This is an area of importance if African theology is to make any impact on the lives of our people. How do we live out the incarnation in concrete experience? We need to pay attention to context.

In this regard, Nigerian theologian Agbonkhianmeghe Orobator makes the important observation that

> as soon as a theologian in Africa begins to pay attention to method and context, he or she is confronted by the unsettling complexities of the African experience. To many outsiders, onlookers, and bystanders, Africa resembles an "ocean of misfortune," but this epithet hardly defines the primary challenge of context.[18]

Zambian economist Dambisa Moyo argues that

> it's time for dramatic innovation in Africa. Africa tends to be viewed under the guise of this, what I call the Four Horsemen of Africans Apocalypse and the four things being war, disease, poverty and corruption. And unfortunately, that has meant ... Africa has been held back and suffers from most serious negative PR problem.[19]

My third point: it is not enough to write about or name the "four horse-men" of Africa; we need to do or be seen doing something about them. Some of us African theologians have done very well in writing about the issues that confront us and have in various ways tried to offer solutions to them, but they have yet to bring credible results or make substantive changes in people's lives.

What I imagine African theology to be is a dialogical, conversational, and inclusive enterprise that deals with concrete matters at hand that face Africa and Africans and that attempts to generate effective solutions. As a new scholar, I imagine a theological enterprise that "does not float above culture and context. Doing theology is not an exercise in conceptual weightlessness. It develops within the particular culture and context of the community."[20] In essence, there is an urgency for an African theology grounded in the true experience of the African people.

African Theological Imagination: One Example

To illustrate this imagination of African theology, I consider Emmanuel Katongole's approach, in particular, his book *The Sacrifice of Africa* as an example. His theological methodology prioritises listening to narratives of the lives of Africans whose personal witness to the gospel inspires change. The gem of Katongole's construction or reconstruction of Christian social ethics in Africa is his ability to encapsulate its narrative in living entities or bodies. In *The Sacrifice of Africa*, theology comes to life in the lives of three remarkable Africans: Paride Taban of South Sudan, Angelina Atyam of northern Uganda, and Maggy Barankitse of Burundi. We find microcosms in their stories of the birthing of a new Africa full of hope and possibilities. I focus on the narratives of the two women.

Angelina Atyam, who lives in northern Uganda, was a woman well-grounded in her life as a wife, mother, and a professional nurse-midwife. Her serene life was shockingly interrupted when her daughter, Charlotte, was abducted from St Mary's Boarding School on October 10, 1996, by the Lord's Resistance Army (LRA).[21] After the kidnapping of her daughter and the fruitless effort to get her back, Angelina found a new vocation, namely, to speak and live for others.

A few months later, she was approached by two LRA members with a deal: if she would just be quiet, she could have her daughter back. She refused the deal. She wanted the release of her daughter, but she also wanted the release of all the children who had been captured and kidnapped during LRA's leader Joseph Kony's reign of terror in northern Uganda. She became a major leader in the fight for all the thousands of children who had been kidnapped.[22]

Angelina found deep within her psyche a hidden fountain that welled up within her, the waters of new life that enabled her to forgive her daughter's captors and to continue demanding the release of the other children. Thus, "a tragic interruption in her own life led Angelina to discover the gift of this new story."[23] This kind of strength, courage, and faith are essential ingredients in the process of imagining a new Africa and a concomitant theological discourse. They contain the power to believe that self-sacrificial and life-giving love can make a difference and that new stories are possible in Africa.

Marguerite "Maggy" Barankitse of Burundi is another woman of remarkable faith and action. Like Angelina, she exemplifies the ability of one woman to change a society. Identified as a Tutsi, Maggy grew up wanting to bridge ethnic rivalries and discrimination. In October 1993, the civil war began. At the bishop's house where she was working, Tutsis tied her up and forced her to watch the slaughter of seventy-two Hutu adults and children. She was left sitting in the midst of these bodies with a choice to make: despair or choose life. For her, there was only one option – life. Soon she was taking in Hutu, Tutsi, and Twa children, calling them "Husitwa," combining all three identities into a new one.[24] She created homes in which these children live together and learn to embrace one another while acquiring life skills.

Maggy embodies an inclusive paradigm founded on new narrative that is Africa's saving grace. Maggy alters the "narrative of the lie" that had lodged itself deep in the psyche of the people, that generates low self-esteem and despair and breeds tribalism and nationalism. Maggy's alternative narrative embraced all children regardless of their ethnicity; it opened a new door of optimism and self-esteem, strong enough to imagine a new narrative for Africa.

The lives of Angelina and Maggy are not quaint stories for tourists' consumption; in their stories, we see the "character" required to contradict and rebuff the "narrative of the lie."

Angelina altered this narrative during a speech to the UN Security Council in 2005: "There are hundreds of Charlottes in my country and beyond.... Every child is my child."[25] The "new future that Angelina dreams and talks about is a future beyond war, which begins with acceptance of God's gift of forgiveness but extends to all aspects of human life and well-being."[26]

Likewise, Maggy stands against the narrative of the lie. She experienced a "newly rediscovered relationship with God [that] liberated her from her fear, but also raised her beyond herself to a new place and a new story, into which she now wished to invite others."[27]

Both Angelina and Maggy are writing new narratives with their lives. The stories embodied in and exemplified by their lives invite the Church in Africa to choose life by opening itself to the gifts within. For the Church and African theology, accepting this "commitment to a new future in Africa"[28] means accepting the talents and abilities women can and do offer on the continent. The gifts that African women bring to Church and society are not exhibited in speculative disquisitions; African women narrate stories of new life and new beginnings here and now.

Thus, the new narrative expressed by Angelina is not built on structures of power and control but on the raw story of her own experience and that of others whose children have been taken away. It is a movement that is rooted in selflessness and loving abandon to God through forgiveness of others. Both Angelina and Maggy challenge the story of the church and its theology in which

> women are being excluded because of their gender instead of being admitted on the merits of their gifts which are vital to the advent of the reign of God. The early Christian community operated in the "Spirit" and welcomed the gifts of the Spirit active in all members of the community. Women and men exercised their pastoral and spiritual gifts accordingly as teachers, preachers, visionaries, prophets, healers, exorcists, and community leaders. Exercising these gifts had little to do with gender.[29]

How long, then, will the church and African society hinder the full participation of women and their gifts to weave a new narrative? When will the stories of women be acknowledged? Is the highly patriarchal church ready to be part of the new future for the world by promoting and allowing the gifts of women, of all the Angelinas and Maggys on the African continent, to flourish?

> There is an urgency in this regard, especially at it relates to African women. As Benedict XIV has said, the Church and society need women to take their full place in the world, so that the human race can live in the world without completely losing its humanity.[30]

In Angelina and Maggy, the Church has exemplars of what it means and takes to be midwives of a new imagination and a new story that unfold in love.

Conclusion

When I survey the vast expanse of theological scholarship in Africa, I am amazed at the colourful, diverse plants that have been grown by so many theologians not as voices of a bygone era but as living descendants of the faith in quest of understanding. Yet, as a new scholar who stands on the shoulders of theses living descendants, theology opens a vast horizon for further dialogue and conversation as well as naming the matters at hand, that is, the joys and the hopes, the pains and the agonies of women and men in Africa and an irrepressible desire to transform our lamentation and mourning to singing and rejoicing.

As an African woman theologian, I refuse to be silent until my voice and the voices of my sisters find their due and just places at the table of theological conversation and eucharistic encounter in Africa and elsewhere in the Church. To borrow the inspirational words of Ela,

> I dream of a[n African] "theology under the tree," which would be worked out as brothers and sisters side by side wherever Christians share the lot of peasant people who seek to take responsibility for their own future and for transforming their living conditions … perhaps this theology will not use the vocabulary of scholars and philosophers. But didn't God also speak the language of peasants and shepherds in order to be revealed to humanity? We must rediscover the oral dimensions of theology, which is no less important that the summae and the great treatises. Christian theology must be liberated from a cultural system that sometimes conveys the false impression that the word has been made text. Why can't the language of faith also be poetry, song, game, art, dance, and above all the gesture of humanity standing up and marching wherever the gospel elicits and nourishes a liberating effort?[31]

The resources for theology are abundant on the continent for African theologians; there is a variety of wisdom, narrative, story, myth, proverb, and music; the living, oral traditions of our people are primary resources for our theological imagination. The fruit of this imagination ought not to be a dry, abstract theology but a living, vibrant, and dynamic discourse incarnated in the joys and hopes, the pains and the anguish of the African people.

We can choose to start a new paradigm of African theology in the circle. The circle embraces all, feels all, and listens to all, as envisaged by Oduyoye and the Circle of Concerned African Women Theologians. I believe that in this circle theology, African women will be the strongest and most powerful part of Africa's liberation from poverty and disease. I invite you to join them in the circle of life and remember,

> From the day we arrive on the planet
> And blinking, step into the sun
> There's more to see than can ever be seen
> More to do than can ever be done
> There's far too much to take in here
> More to find than can ever be found
> But the sun rolling high
> Through the sapphire sky
> Keeps great and small on the endless round
> It's the Circle of Life.[32]

Endnotes

1   Jean-Marc Ela, *My Faith as an African* (Eugene, Ore.: Wipf and Stock, 2009), 180.

2   Mercy Amba Oduyoye, "The Church of the Future, its Mission and Theology: A View from Africa," in *Theology Today* 52, no. 4 (January 1, 1996): 494–505.

3   Julius Mutugi Gathogo, "A Survey on an African Theology of Reconstruction (ATOR)," in *Swedish Missiological Themes*, 95, 2 (2007).

4   Ela, *My Faith as an African*, 162.

5   Ibid., 164.

6   Ibid., 180.

7   Ibid., 181.

8   John Parratt, *Reinventing Christianity: African Theology Today* (Grand Rapids, Mich.: Eerdmans, 1995), 51.

9   Musimbi R. A. Kanyoro and Mercy Amba Oduyoye, "Introduction" in *The Will to Arise: Women, Tradition, and the Church in Africa*, ed. Mercy Amba Oduyoye and Musinbi R. A. Kanyoro (Eugene, Ore.: Wipf and Stock, 1992), 4.

10   Daisy N. Nwachukwu. "The Christian Widow in African Culture" in Oduyoye and Kanyoro, *The Will to Arise*, 54.

11   Kanyoro and Oduyoye, "Introduction," 1.

12   Mercy A. Oduyoye, "Reflections from a Third World woman's perspective: women's experience and liberation theologies," in *Irruption of the Third world: Challenge to theology: Papers from the fifth international conference of the Ecumenical Association of the Third World Theologians* (Maryknoll, N.Y.: 1983), 246.

13   Ela, *My faith as an African*, 171.

14　Pope Francis washes feet of young detainees in ritual; www.usatoday.com/story/news/world/2013/03/28/pope-frances-washes-feet/2028595/.

15　www.thecirclecawt.org/profile.html.

16　Ibid.

17　Mercy Amba Oduyoye, "Re-reading the Bible from where we have been placed: African Women's voices on some biblical texts," in *Journal of African Christian Thought* 10, no. 2 (December 2007): 6.

18　Agbonkhianmeghe E. Orobator, "Method and Context: How and Where Theology Works in Africa," in *Shaping a Global Theological Mind,* Darren C. Marks, ed. (Ashgate, 2008), 122.

19　Dambisa Moyo, http://bigthink.com/videos/dambisa-moyo-on-a-more-optimistic-outlook-for-africa.

20　Agbonkhianmeghe E. Orobator, *Theology Brewed in an African Pot* (Maryknoll, N.Y.: Orbis, 2008), 152.

21　Marc Lacey, "A Mother's Bitter Choice: Telling Kidnappers No" in *The New York Times,* January 25, 2003, www.nytimes.com/2003/01/25/world/the-saturday-profile-a-mother-s-bitter-choice-telling-kidnappers-no.html.

22　Ibid.

23　Emmanuel Katongole, *The Sacrifice of Africa: A Political Theology for Africa* (Grand Rapids, Mich.: Eerdmans, 2011), 154.

24　"Woman's mission for Burundi children was sparked by genocide," UNICEF, www.unicef.org/infobycountry/burundi_womans_mission.html.

25　Katongole, *The Sacrifice of Africa,* 161.

26　Ibid., 162.

27　Ibid., 172.

28　Ibid., 101.

29　Anne Arabome, "Gender and Ecclesiology Authorities, Structures, Ministries," *Concilium* 4 (2012): 115.

30　Ibid., 114.

31　Ela, *My faith as an African,* 181.

32　Elton John and Tim Rice, "The Circle of Life," from *The Lion King.*

Women and the Church in Africa: Allies or Strange Bedfellows?

Marguerite Akossi-Mvongo

Introduction

W
hat is the true role and the real place of women in the Church? Are they seen and do they live as created in the image of God and therefore benefit from all the prerogatives attached to their baptism? Are they priests, prophets, and kings, or are they only followers, second-class Catholic citizens who know how to remain in their places and be satisfied with pre-established limits? The first challenge of this debate is personal; we must ask ourselves such uncomfortable questions.

The Catholic Church is presented as an immense flock of followers, they are accompanied by various male and female religious, guided by the consecrated, and headed by a pope, cardinals, and bishops. Those who shepherd the flock are men, and those shepherded are for the most part women. From the point of view of gender analysis, women are confronted by forms of discrimination linked to their status as women. Whatever their qualities and competencies, they cannot have access to all positions in the Roman Catholic Church in Africa and elsewhere in the world. Feminist theologians are therefore right in claiming that women continue to struggle to find their true places in the Church today.

Notwithstanding formidable challenges in Church and society, since Vatican II, the role and place of the laity and especially of women has not stopped growing and has even revolutionised the Church's practices. The two African synods (1994 and 2009) have reaffirmed the principle that we should work to integrate women at different levels of the Church. In fact, we are witnessing a true dialogue of the deaf; some (the clergy) count the improvements, the positive changes that have taken place, while others (feminist theologians and many Catholics) pose a question of principle: can a human being created in the image of God – with faith in Jesus Christ and having been baptised – be prevented from serving everywhere if that person has the vocation and the skills, because that person does not have a penis? The answer to this question is as critical as the situation of women in the Church is complex.

The issue is much more complex for a committed lay Catholic woman like me whose research specialty relates to questions of gender and who is campaigning for social equality and particularly for the abolition of gender discrimination. How can I reconcile my scientific knowledge with my faith? Must I discontinue my research and questioning at the doors of the church and simply blend in and fade away with the crowd? How do I live with this absolute inconsistency? Am I supposed to separate myself from the Church, as many intellectuals have, or take refuge behind the distinction between what belongs to Caesar and what belongs to God (Luke 20:24–25)? I think it is possible to remain anchored in the Church of Jesus Christ and not be afraid to ask the disturbing questions to resolve the situation.

My aim in this chapter is to lay out my questions, analyses, and sentiments on the position taken by the Church and particularly the actual practices of the Church in Africa today with regard to women. Far from indulging in an exegesis of Scripture, I simply ask my questions and pronounce my frustrations as a Catholic woman who was baptised at a very young age, who was raised in the values of the Church, and who has tried in a variety of ways to contribute a little to the spread of the gospel: teaching catechism, choir, family commission, parish council, and the Legion of Mary. My objective is to propose a middle ground between church teaching and my interests.

My analysis is divided into three major parts: a diagnosis of the situation of women in the Church today, what is involved in being a woman intellectual, and some concluding questions.

1. Diagnostic: The Place of Women Today

As and when possible it is important to distinguish between what comes from the discourse of the Church and what is the result of cultural patterns and traditions. The Roman Catholic Church has evolved since the time when a woman who sought to be educated was viewed as a witch and suffered punishment for it. Despite this undeniable progress, the Church still seems today to reflect reactionary aspects and practices of societies in regard to women, both in the family and the matrimonial home in relation to the commitment of service in the Church.

1.1 The "Revolution": Vatican II and the African synods

Vatican II, already fifty years old, set for the Church the objective of finding ways and means to speak to the men and women of our times of the immutable and eternal message of the gospel. It was the culmination of reflections undertaken for a long time mainly in Europe and repeatedly interrupted by events and wars. The Church had the courage to pose questions to itself on its history and its practices, notably the slave trade and colonialism. It made this fundamental observation: if the message of the gospel is unchanging, it is nevertheless essential to find ways and means to communicate it to the men and women of today and to develop a cultural anchor of faith for each of the believers because at Pentecost, each heard distinctly the apostles in his or her own language. It was important that each appropriate the message individually and collectively. It was therefore necessary to speak to the people of the twentieth century in a way that would be accessible to them. Many changes are occurring for both laity as consecrated.

1.1.1 Women in Ordinary Life

Significant progress has been made in the context of worship and celebration; there are no more separated sitting places for men and women during Mass. The Bible has been translated into many languages, making it easier for women with lower levels of literacy to understand and appropriate the message. Moreover, the two African synods called for the integration of women at all levels of decision making in the Church. The significant place occupied by women in the practical organisation of the church is visible. In Côte d'Ivoire, for example, many parish councils are headed by women. Most of those who teach catechesis, who provide many different services, and who constitute committees for parish life are likely to be women. But it is necessary to take a closer look at this idyllic picture and examine thoroughly the message conveyed to women particularly in the preparation for marriage, when the church try to shape families, the domestic church, the basic unit of the universal church.

1.1.2 Women in Consecrated Life

The situation of women here seems quite complex. There are traditional religious congregations, new communities that emphasise evangelism and women who are trying to manage women in special platforms within the church. The congregations are particularly active in the charitable arena; they care for the poor and work to educate others; the religious congregations provide the humanitarian outreach of the Church and reflect in their everyday lives the gospel message for believers and nonbelievers. New communities focus on the transmission of faith and evangelisation. In this context, female Christians are well-known animators of evangelisation sessions and active members of the Catholic Evangelisation Service that preaches a bit like evangelical churches and is really successful among the faithful in Côte d'Ivoire. However, their relationships with parishes remain somewhat ambiguous.

Significant progress has been made, but there is still much to be done, not least on the issue of ministerial priesthood. An apparently nonnegotiable point exists in the code of canon law of 1983: "Only a baptised man validly receives sacred ordination." Why? Because, according to John Paul II, this is a state exclusively reserved to men since the origin of the Church.

1.2 Women and Church

The relationship of women with the Church must be considered not only in relation to official pronouncements and discourses but also by paying attention to concrete realities that shape the lives of women as constitutive members of the body of Christ and the people of God. In regard to the laity, I have observed that women take more active roles at the level of church organisation. To caricature this a bit, when it comes to ensuring material organisation, taking care of people, creating the basic community, and transmitting the faith to future generations, women have a dominant role recognised and valued by the church. But when it comes to the ministry of spirituality, gender discrimination appears. Recent news and media coverage of the election of Pope Francis has enabled every citizen of the world to realise he was elected solely by men. There is nothing new in this practice; it an age-old practice that the clerical class takes for granted and rarely if ever questions.

The situation of women in the Church makes me think of Luke 10:38–42, where Martha and her sister Mary received Jesus. Mary sat at the foot of the Jesus and listened to his words while Martha busied herself with multiple domestic chores. When Martha asked Jesus to tell Mary to help her, Jesus said, "Martha, Martha, you are worried and you have the concern for a lot of things, but only one is necessary. Mary has chosen what is really good and no one will take it from her." I find this text particularly edifying because this division of labour is well observed in the church. The women are the Marthas of the Church, preparing everything, organising everything, and taking care of everything; this is akin to what Pope Francis has described and denounced as "servitude". Yet, the best task, the one chosen by Mary, is denied them.

This text is also interesting because a feminine figure, Mary, is held up and valued by Jesus for avoiding tasks and the usual role assigned to people of her gender in order to devote herself to the Word of God.

Even after Vatican II, the Church calls for integration of women into all levels of the Church except where decisions are taken, where the Church of tomorrow thinks the roles of each is defined, where we discuss the doctrines and laws of the Church; it is therefore not surprising that in practice these same contradictions resurface.

1.3 Daily Practices

Among the laity, the first surprise comes at the time of preparation for marriage. The family commission is charged to help future spouses to prepare for their vocations of Christian husbands and wives. In "good faith" the instructors explain that God's plan calls the woman to be submissive, while they ignore the remarkable writing of Pope John Paul II in his rereading of Genesis and the letters of Saint Paul, which show that in marriage there is reciprocal submission. Strangely however, during marriage preparation, it is the traditional African conception of men as head of the family that is underscored. The women in the household are invited to take on all financial and material responsibilities but above all to remain silent and let the "head" of the family make the big decisions. This message of the Church will have difficulty being understood among the young generation of Africa who are more inclined to make decisions on the basis of competence; they have grown up in a society in which women (even if their numbers are still limited) find themselves in real decision-making roles not in line with the roles in the home or elsewhere in terms of gender. Many have seen their own mothers or neighbors actively fulfilling the needs of the household sometimes alone. Thus, in this context, faithfully preaching the tired message of gender submissiveness and subordination places the Church at the rear end of historical progress.

As I have argued above, the Church at the local level promotes the role of women in everything that involves practical organisation but tends to exclude them from the theological sphere, even when this has been authorised since Vatican II. For example, several parish councils in the archdiocese of Abidjan have women as heads. Women direct various movements and parish entities, and most catechists in urban parishes are women. Although this is not the case in rural parishes, the situation is a reflection of the fact that catechists need to know how to read and write, not a genuine resistance to the idea of women being catechists.

By entrusting all these "caretaking" tasks of organising, nourishing, maintaining, and enforcing guidelines to women, the African Church gives the impression that it is modern and has a place for women. However, once the slightest debate occurs, resistance surfaces. Recently a bishop in Abidjan decreed that young girls should no longer serve at Mass, as had been the practice in the past. Only boys could be Mass servers; girls could only be porters of collection bowls. Such a message leads young African girls to wonder about their value and place in the community of the faithful.

As an African intellectual, I was shocked to hear a stormy parish-council debate on the subject of women being extraordinary ministers of the Eucharist. The parish priest's explanations that there was no impediment in the canons of the Church regarding this were not sufficient to pave the way for the acceptance of women as extraordinary ministers of the Eucharist. These are just a few examples of actual resistance to women taking certain roles in the life of the Church.

The Church is in an ambiguous position in respect to the role and place of women in its midst. The Church affirms the message that there are limitations to the role of women in Church and that they do not have access to the fullness of the responsibilities of their baptism because of their biological nature. At the same time, it says and writes that all baptised have the same opportunities to realise their ministerial vocation of service in the church. In the face of this fundamental contradiction, Africans in the Church further limit the role of women not as a function of the Word of God but as a function of their experiences and cultural references. This is perhaps a perverse effect of the culturally anchored roots of Vatican II.

2. To Be an Intellectual Woman

My personal experience in this area invites me to live my relationship with God in a calm manner. My approach is to assume my own reading of texts and practices and to situate the church in its historical context because the arguments used to justify this fundamental contradiction rely on tradition, and traditions evolve.

2.1 Creation: The Original Ambiguity

"God created man in the image of himself. In the image of God he created him. Male and female he created them" (Genesis 1:27). The origin does not seem to mark differences or establish different specialisations for one or the other; man and woman received together the order to populate the world and exercise stewardship in relation to creation.

Original sin appears to have marked the end of equality. In the Genesis account God told the woman she would be dominated, and since the expulsion from the Garden of Eden masculine figures seem to have appropriated a position of superiority over and about feminine figures. From this follows multiple acts of gender-based injustice: man becomes suspicious of woman; she is branded the temptress and the origin of evil and the fall. Is this where the church derives justification for relegating women to a subordinate place?

Pope John Paul II, although opposed to the ordination of women, has refuted this opinion by his reading of Genesis and the letters of Paul, stating that the domination of man over woman is a sin, contrary to the divine plan of communion of persons; that the submission must be "reciprocal" between spouses. He has by this fact put an end to any question about the dignity and equality of women in the institution of marriage.

2.2 The Place of Women in the Church: Judaism and Christianity

In the Old Testament world the place of women in Judaism appears limited; they seem doomed and confined to domestic chores and material tasks while the men manage the sacred realm. In Israel, Levites, members of one of the twelve tribes, were responsible for official worship. Every male among the children of Aaron could eat this part of the dish of Yahweh (Leviticus 6:11); Leviticus specifies who may exercise the function of priest and clearly excludes women from it. There are therefore no woman priests in the Jewish tradition.

We all know that the message of the Bible supports life and is registered in history and human cultures. The Bible and sacred texts arising from it speak of God in the context of human realities. The Bible presents different points of view. Each epoch, each society, pretends to "forget" whatever does not form part of its own social practices. It is therefore not surprising that the message of the Bible has been interpreted in the light of the ancient patriarchal society in which it was difficult to imagine the "secondary" citizens (woman, slaves) officiating in the sacred space. But the coming of Christ changed this old order. Jesus offered a way of understanding the historical aberrations: this is part of the law of Moses that God allowed to be instituted at the beginning because of "the hardness of your hearts" (Matthew 19:8). Paul wrote, "Nobody will be just in the eyes of God in obeying the law" (Galatians 2:16). He also wrote,

> All of you have been baptised in Christ and you have become like him. There is therefore no longer any difference between Jews and non-Jews, between slaves and free persons, between men and women. In effect, you are all one in Christ Jesus. And if you belong to Christ, so you are the family of Abraham, you are heirs as God has promised (Galatians 3:27–29).

Vatican II was full of promise for all who felt the law and the tradition set the pace on the message of the love of Christ.

2.3 Vatican II and African Synods

Vatican II certainly led to many positive changes, but as I wrote earlier, fifty years ago, the traditional model of the patriarchal family was the most prevalent (father-provider and father-protector; and mother maintaining, tending the domestic). How many women participated at that council? The number of subjects to be dealt with and the real revolution in progress it had to digest did not make gender discrimination a subject of concern at that time. The African synods have tried cautiously to insist on the growing place of women in the Church.

2.4 Women and the Church

In this context, how can we consider the relationship between women and the Church? Women and the Church are certainly allies; women represent the vast majority of practitioners, and they account for the material and domestic aspects that include the charitable dimension. The Church needs women to transmit values and anchor families in Christendom. When women conform to prescribed models, as religious or wife, they are strong allies of the Church. (It is not surprising that many saints are virgins and were not aware of many aspects of life in the outside world).

They are allies also because in West Africa women in traditional religions are regarded as connected to the sacred, as Aihiokhai demonstrates in his essay. The transition to Christianity was made more easily by women than men, who often leaned toward polygamy.

But what strange bedfellows when we begin to raise questions! How can we reconcile women's faith and confidence in the message of the love of Christ and all the reassuring signs he directed to women (the first at the tomb, the sinner washing his feet, the adulterous woman) with the patriarchal organisation of the Church? How can we listen to the voice of women who study, reflect, and think about the world and the church when they are excluded from the centers of decision? Why have they nothing to say in the choice of the pope? How can they not feel a bit schizophrenic when they no longer know if protesting and rebelling against such discrimination is not a sin against God? We go to confession – again, exclusively to men!

The challenge is important; I believe that a good part of the defections of women to evangelical churches is linked to this historical gender-based discrimination.

3. My Questions

The Church in Africa and elsewhere would gain greatly if it made a real place for women in it by allowing them to play all the roles of the baptised. The presence of women, their increasing levels of education, and their availability to perform the work of the Church present real opportunities for the Catholic Church, especially in places in the world where it is slowing down and has big deficits of priests. Certainly, such changes require a reorganisation of the system, but perhaps we should clarify what actually contradicts the message of Christ and what is merely the result of human practices and traditions.

Raising debate that disturbs but contributes to the evolution of the Church in a positive way is important. For a number of years now, the Methodists have had women pastors! But the main obstacle often arises from the fact that all the faithful are not on the same wavelength. If each change brings about resistance and even schism (for instance, communities of the Society of St Pius X after Vatican II), we must above all give ourselves time for a debate of contradictions and not close the door to reflections by taking positions of rigid principle not drawn from Scripture.

It is becoming more and more difficult to justify the positions taken by some in the Church that do not directly have their origin in Scripture but that result from tradition. Tradition has evolved and continues to do so. Man/woman relations have changed enormously in society. How would the message of love of Christ be affected by the integration of women into ministerial roles? This question is similar to that of mandatory celibacy for priests. Material questions cannot block the spiritual evolution of the people of God. To continue to ensure the spread of the gospel, the good news of salvation to the men and women of our time, the church must speak to all in a language they understand and impose on them only the rules required by the love of God. Everything that falls under tradition and the law can ultimately evolve to make room in all hearts for the new order proclaimed and instituted by Christ.

The Place of Women in the Catholic Churches of Africa: Using Inculturation as a Model for Inclusion of Women in the Ministerial Life of the Church

Simon Mary A. Aihiokhai

Introduction

The Catholic Church, since the Second Vatican Council, has engaged in a critical reflection on its identity as a priestly people. Efforts have been made to stress the equality of all Christians by virtue of their baptismal identity as members of the priestly people of God.[1] In the dogmatic constitution of the Church, *Lumen Gentium*, the magisterium has stated categorically that the Catholic Church is constituted as the people of God who have been called to live fully the teaching and mission of Jesus Christ.[2] This community of the chosen people of God is also constituted hierarchically for the purpose of carrying out the mission of Christ and his church.[3] The ordained state is reserved solely for men. Women, though they constitute majority of the laity, have observable restrictions placed on them in regard to ministerial roles by the fact they are female. One may opine that these restrictions have cultural or sociopsychological roots. They also reinforce the perception that the church is an institution run exclusively by men.

It could be argued that some restrictions on the role of women in the church originate from a particular understanding of hierarchy and patriarchy. There is need to differentiate between gender and hierarchy. The latter has historically been understood to equate to maleness and thus limits or blocks any notion of viewing it as an office open to all Christians. To teach that the Catholic Church is constituted hierarchically need not be understood in such a way that aspects of such a hierarchical structure become limited to one gender. To do so could frustrate attempts at claiming a richer hermeneutics on what it means to be church and who can be part of it.

Women in the Church are endowed with charisms and gifts for the edification of the body of Christ. To deny or restrict these charisms and gifts amounts to imposing limits on the possibilities for receiving the liberating and refreshing role of the Spirit in the life of the Church. For now, the magisterium opines that the Spirit's role must be within the hermeneutic taught by it in relation to how it has understood the mission of Christ handed down through the apostles.

A one-sided reading of the historical development within the Church, however, fails to account for the complex, vibrant roles performed in the life of the early Church in which women held important positions of ecclesial and ministerial leadership. To prefer a simplistic historical narrative of the role of women in the Church is to espouse a cultural narrative on how women have been treated in the cultures that shaped the Church, especially those of the Greco-Roman communities.

It is important to acknowledge the fact that in the decades since Vatican II, women have been allowed to perform nonministerial functions in the life of the church to some degree.[4] However, there still exist elements of discrimination toward women that at times have been couched in arguments based on a tradition itself based on discrimination against females. For example, altar boys are preferred to altar girls because the service of altar server has been considered a way of encouraging vocations to the priesthood.[5]

Also, while men who are members of the choir can be within the sanctuary, when the choir includes women, the magisterium instructs that the choir ought to be outside the sanctuary.[6] Such policies pose a challenge to the theological understanding of baptismal identity shared by all equally in the Church.

To foster a different approach that allows women to be more integrally part of the ministerial life of the church, this chapter will use the church's understanding of inculturation as a justification for the need to transform those practices in the church that discriminate against women, who constitute a larger portion of its lay members than do men. Particular focus will be given to the African context because it has a rich heritage on the role of women in the ritual life of the people in African traditional religion.

Trends and Implications of the Meaning and Practice of Inculturation as Understood by the Magisterium

Inculturation can be said to be a continuous incarnation of Jesus Christ in the life of a faith community; inculturation makes present the incarnate Christ to a faith community in its cultural boundaries while also inviting the community to engage other faith communities. The incarnate Christ serves as the bond of communion among the believing communities.

However, though Christ serves as the bond of communion, the response of the different faith communities cannot and ought not be uniform without regard for the particular experiences of each community. This view is what today is lacking in attempts to inculturate the liturgy in the Roman Catholic Church. Any insistence that all attempts to inculturate the liturgy must take the Roman liturgical custom as the norm fails to take seriously the unique experiences of churches outside the historical influence of the Roman culture and tradition.[7] Sub-Saharan Africa has unique experiences and traditions that ought to be reflected in the subcontinent's attempt to engage the incarnate Christ. Rather than make the Roman liturgy the guide for inculturation, the incarnate Christ ought to be the norm. The creedal truths in Christ ought to be reflected in the liturgical life of each community; this should be the boundary of orthodoxy and nothing else.

One can opine that this was the case among the churches during the beginnings of the Christian faith. Faith in Jesus Christ was the boundary for orthodoxy for these churches, and they had unique liturgical expressions determined and shaped by their cultural realities.

Mere translation of the liturgical texts does not amount to inculturation. The Roman liturgical texts are themselves shaped by the cultural experiences of the Roman Church. Oftentimes these experiences conflict with the cultures in Africa and cannot be the markers for determining the validity of their desires to inculturate the faith in their contexts. This point has been stressed by the Asian bishops. They insist that "clinging too much to the 'substantial unity of the Roman Liturgy' may end up in rigidity that obstructs proper incarnation of Christian faith."[8] Their concern ought to be the concern of the African churches, since the religious and cultural experiences of the people differ significantly from those of Rome and Western European cultures. To trivialise the magnitude of this issue is to trivialise the importance of making Christ's Word truly and fully present to the African people.

At the heart of the Church's understanding of inculturation is the person of Jesus Christ. The incarnation event demonstrates the divine link in the process of inculturating the salvific message in any particular culture. Hence, inculturation, though it touches aspects of communal faith-based life, is essentially linked to the human person. The aim, process, and purpose of inculturation must not and cannot be removed from the human person living in a particular cultural milieu.

As observed by the International Theological Commission in its document "Faith and Inculturation," the incarnation is "a cultural incarnation."[9] Appropriating the conciliar view, this commission reminds us again that the salvific event of the incarnation played itself out in a particular culture – the Israelite culture – and in a particular time and place.[10] This insight has far-reaching implications, part of which I intend to demonstrate in this chapter. For now, certain questions ought to be asked: What limitations in the Israelite culture of Jesus' time shaped the kerygma that has been handed down from the apostles? What limitations in that culture are today reflected in the life of the church and how the church understands itself?

These questions will need another chapter to be fully addressed, but one can perceive cultural biases in the New Testament in attempts by the authors to present the kerygma to the new members of the ecclesial communities. For example, Paul's advice to the Church in Corinth on the role women should play in that Church demonstrates a cultural bias that helped form his view on how a Church should operate (1 Corinthians 11:3–16). Also, Paul's attempt to engage the issue of slavery is another cultural flaw that coexisted with the attempt by the ecclesial communities of his time to live truly the Christian message (Letter to Philemon).

The Catholic Church has and continues to teach that the message and person of Jesus have to be at the center of any inculturation attempt. In other words, cultural biases, even those that may have existed for centuries, ought to be absent in any attempt to inculturate the Christian message. This, as noted by the International Theological Commission, was the practice adopted by the early Church during the Jewish and Hellenistic conflicts in its circles.[11] Rather than follow the Jewish cultural practice on circumcision, the Hellenistic converts were excluded from such practices.

This is not the complete truth on the matter. At least, the solution proposed by James, the head of the Church in Jerusalem, did not completely do away with all Jewish cultural and religious practices that had nothing to do with the Christian message (Acts 15:19–20). The point here is that even though attempts continue to be made to inculturate only the Christian message in any particular culture, the cultural biases of missionary agents have not always been eradicated in the process.

It is now left for the Church to be truly aware of how such biases endure and sometimes hamper the growth of the Christian faith in the culture receiving it. Although the process of inculturation ought to be focused only on the kerygma, missionary agents are always limited by their own cultural biases. It will be impossible to completely eradicate the biases of culture; what is needed is a humble awareness of the enduring presence of traces of these biases.

Inculturation, when focused on the human person, attempts to transform a person's approach to the divine in a way that puts Christ at the heart of the process. In the African context, this understanding has grave implications, especially when many of the cultures on the continent have ritualistic roles for men and women. Inculturation in this context will have to engage the role of the genders as well as their understanding of the teaching and person of Jesus in the roles they perform in liturgical rituals.

The agents of authority in the Church with regard to their gender ought to be engaged through theological and cultural lenses alike. To teach, as did Pope John Paul II, that Jesus' life and ministry transcended his culture should not be understood as a denial of a very vital element of the consequences of his being human.[12] To be under the influence of the limitations of one's culture does not equate to culpability on the part of the one inhabiting the culture. Let me state it practically: though Jesus was against slavery, he probably ate food cultivated by slaves. By implication, one can begin to see how or to what extent gender roles in the culture of his time may have also shaped his life.

Relating this to contemporary society, one can be limited by the evils of a democratic society without necessarily being culpable for those ills. That Jesus did not denounce slavery during his ministry or make women part of the twelve does not mean he condoned slavery or wanted women to be excluded entirely and permanently from the ministerial life of the church. The wisdom of Jesus is alive in his Church through the voices that call on the Church to be an instrument of change in these areas. Thus, when members of the Church argue for an inclusive approach to ministry in the hierarchy, they continue the ministry of Jesus to the world and to the church. After all, the gift of the Spirit to the Church is a gift meant to continue the work of God through Christ by those who accept it.

The prophetic witness of Christ did not end with his death; it continues through the church not only to the world but to itself in its attempt to model itself along the teachings and practices of Christ. The fact that Christ challenged some negative gender restrictions on women ought to prompt the Church to be truly inclusive in all aspects of its life.

Since inculturation is ultimately person centered, it will be truly insightful for the Catholic Church in Africa to engage how it has dealt with the agents of worship in its rich heritage with particular focus on indigenous religions. This is particularly important because on the continent of Africa, many indigenous religions have women who serve as priestesses, healers, prophetesses, diviners, and exorcists. Christian missionaries simply ignored these women agents of worship in indigenous religions because the Christian Churches in Europe did not have such roles for women. This failure to include women as legitimate agents of worship has impoverished the Christian identity on the African continent.

In the next section, I will explore the role of women in African indigenous religions and show how such a rich heritage ought to be engaged by the Catholic magisterium in its attempt to inculturate the Christian faith in Africa.

The Role of Women in African Indigenous Religions

Women have played and continue to play very prominent roles in the ritual practices of African religion throughout Africa. In the Nigerian context, most fertility cults are headed by women. It is not surprising then to find women priestesses in the shrines of such deities as Osun among the Yoruba people of western Nigeria. Within the Yoruba pantheon of deities, Osun is the deity responsible for child bearing. She brings healing to the sick and wealth to the poor and marginalised. She is the goddess of comfort for those who suffer and who are at the margins of society due to misfortunes.[13]

Currently among the Yorubas, there is a false belief that priesthood in the Yoruba religion is predominantly a male affair. The historical facts dispute this belief; Yoruba priests (diviners) have never been solely men. Historical accounts show that prior to the coming of Christian missionaries to the Yoruba people, there were women *babalawo* (Ifa priests).[14] The term *babalawo* (father of mystery) is sexist because it glosses over the place and role of women priestesses in the priesthood of the Yoruba indigenous religion.[15]

Again, the role of women in Yoruba religion is so vast that it will be a betrayal and an aberration to simply deny that women have no place in the religious sphere. As noted by Dorcas Olubanke Akintunde, in the metaphysical realm, women play prominent roles in preserving harmony in the community. Hence, the Yoruba believe that "*aje funfun* (white witches) are benevolent female spirits who are consulted in times of national or tribal crisis."[16] These female witches protect the community or nation from being destroyed. It is their responsibility to guide the community out of the crisis by providing wise advice to the leaders through the priestesses who act as their medium of contact between them and the community in question.

Among the communities of southeastern Nigeria, the *Mami wata* cult is prominent. This cult is associated with the female goddess of the water responsible for the gifts of fertility, wealth, health, and happiness. She willingly bears the burden of her devotees so they can experience joy and happiness. In the *Mami wata* cult, women have prominent roles in the rituals associated with the deity; they are the healing agents of the deity and spokeswomen of it as well. The cult extols the beauty and virtues of womanhood.

On another note, among the Bini of midwestern Nigeria, there are many creation myths. One of these myths stands out because of the prominent role women play in it. The creation myth claims that *Osanobua* (the supreme God) had three children (all women) whose names were *Obiemwen, Olokun, and Ogiuwu*. When *Osanobua* wanted to create the world, he sent his three daughters as intermediaries. The eldest, *Obiemwen*, was given a snail shell by a bird, *Owonwon*. She turned the shell upside down, and a good amount of sand came out; it was enough to create land.

Later, *Osanobua* divided the earth among his three daughters. To the eldest, he gave control over childbirth and fertility. To *Olokun*, the second daughter, he gave control over riches and wealth. And to the third daughter, *Ogiuwu*, he gave control over death.[17] It is worth noting the significance of this myth. The entire gamut of human existence is tied to female deities. This Bini myth acknowledges the role women play in bringing life to the world, sustaining and nurturing it, and also journeying with the matured life through the death process. This female role is not simply existential but is tied to religious worship. Women thus cannot be denied a place of leadership in the ritual worship of the people because they are at the heart of collective human existence in Bini cultic rites.

Among the Tiv of northeastern Nigeria, a woman is regarded as both an emblem of communal continuity and a sacred representation of divinity. The Tiv believe that God has given them the knowledge of manipulating the *Akombo* (sacred object that links the community/family/individual with the divine) for personal protection as well as for the protection and survival of the community or nation.[18] Again, just as there are individual or familial *Akombo*, there is also great communal *Akombo* whose function it is to protect the entire community.

A breach of the regulations surrounding the use *Akombo* and relating with it demands a detailed ritual that at times involved human sacrifice during precolonial times. As noted by Bruce Lincoln, there is a close connection between the great *Akombo* and a woman. Just as the former protects the community from extinction, the latter through fertility guarantees the continuous existence of the community.[19] Women who have reached puberty are seen as the greatest *Akombo* among the Tiv people. This point is reflected in the tattoos drawn on the bodies of pregnant women. These tattoos are similar to the scarification on the great communal *Akombo* to protect the community when it is faced with grave danger that might lead to its extinction. The body of the woman becomes the symbol of purification and the continuity of the community. She bears on her body the past, present, and future of the community. In her body lies the meaning of existence of the Tiv people and becomes a testament for the community to be virtuous and holy.[20]

Practical Steps for Inculturating the Christian Faith in Africa

I have highlighted the role of women in the religious heritage of the African people in the context of African indigenous religions. To better understand how this can help shape the role of women in the life of the Church, we can explore the priestly identity attained through baptism. The foundation of the Christian life is rooted in baptism. The catechism of the Catholic Church refers to baptism

> as the basis of the whole Christian life, the gateway to life in the Spirit and the door which gives access to the other sacraments. Through Baptism we are freed from sin and reborn as [children] of God; we become members of Christ, are incorporated into the Church and made sharers in her mission.[21]

The membership in Christ and incorporation in the Church is a priestly one. As noted in the catechism, through baptism, one "shares in the priest-hood of Christ, in his prophetic and royal mission."[22] This point must not be lost to us as we engage the role of women in the Church. Canonical and liturgical norms that may be interpreted as distancing women from a variety of roles may signal forgetfulness concerning the rich identity we are called to embrace through the waters of baptism. If baptism makes us priestly people, prophets, and missionaries who are called and confirmed in the ministry of service through the sacraments of initiation, we, as Church, ought to ask ourselves how women perform these roles in the capacity as baptised members of the worshiping community.

It is not enough to claim theoretically that they participate in the royal priesthood of the people of God. The identity derived from baptism is not one without a mission; it is an identity that calls us to service in the Lord's vineyard. It is an identity tied to mission both *ad intra* and *ad extra;* to focus solely on the ad extra dimension is to risk advancing an imbalanced hermeneutics.

The gifts one receives through the sacraments of initiation are meant to edify the Church from within and without. The First Letter of Peter states this beautifully: "You are a chosen race, a royal priest-hood, a holy nation, a people of his own, so that you may announce the praises of him who called you out of darkness into his wonderful light" (1 Peter 2:9).

The gifts received through baptism are meant to be used in the mission Christ calls us to embrace through the Spirit of his Father. When women are not fully integrated into worship and ministry in our liturgies, the rich understanding of our royal priesthood is diminished.

With due attention to papal concerns about the issue of gender and ministry in the Church, it is my strong conviction that women can and ought to be allowed to perform other ministries in our Church that resonate also with the religious heritage of the African people.[23] The ministries of healing, prophesying, exorcising, and teaching are diaconal ministries that originate from the shared identity as members of the royal priesthood and not from the ministerial priesthood. There ought to be a revival of these ministries in the inculturated Churches in Africa and they should be open to women who through baptism are called to participant fully in the diaconal vocation of the Church. These ministries are found in the African religious heritage and can serve as a basis for inculturation. As noted above, the center of any inculturation is Jesus Christ, and any true inculturation must engage the role the people play in the life of the Church.

Since the sacrament of Holy Eucharist is the living fount from which we as Christians derive our strength and purpose as church, it has implications for the fundamental role of women in the Eucharistic celebration understood as a circle of life. One concrete way of achieving inclusiveness is through participation in diaconal ministries for women and men.

There is an account of a deaconess in the New Testament that justifies the argument that women deaconesses are part of the Church's tradition (Romans 16:1). Also, in the life of the Church, women performed many diaconal services and held ministerial positions for centuries.[24] Thus the tradition of the Church justifies a place for women in the Church's hierarchical structures.

Women in African Churches ought to be allowed into the order of deacons as well as the other diaconal ministries mentioned above. By doing this, the Church in Africa will truly be living out its African heritage. To merely inculturate the liturgy and not attend to the roles of the sexes in the liturgical and ministerial life of the Church is to lack the prophetic courage to speak truth to our tradition. Inculturation ought to be engaged in with courage and trust in the Spirit of Christ, who challenges us at every epoch to reflect deeply on the life in Christ we are all called to embrace as priestly people.

The priesthood of women as members of the royal priesthood is not different from that enjoyed by males in the Church. To stress the relevance of this point, the hierarchy in the African Churches ought to engage in proper catechesis with their flocks, ordained and lay, to dispel centuries of gender biases against women in African societies.

Gender discrimination is very prominent in African societies and within ecclesial communities. Hence, the hierarchy ought to journey with their people on the path to intellectual conversion and appreciation of the well of riches the Church can tap into by allowing the fruits of the Spirit to blossom without restrictions based on gender identity.

Conclusion

The Catholic Church in Africa is undoubtedly a very vibrant Church with numerous parishes in numerous dioceses and it comprises a large percentage of the global Catholic population. Nonetheless, no matter how vibrant this Church is, it still needs to develop a clear African identity. Pre-Vatican II canonical restrictions that bar Catholics from marrying non-Catholics are still being observed by some provincial sees ignoring ecumenical developments that have shaped the global Church since Vatican II.[25] Many pastors enact noncanonical rules that bar lay members of their parishes from receiving the sacraments because they fail to contribute to the endless "second collections" without consideration for the financial situations faced by these lay members.[26] In all these instances, no attempt has been made to engage these practices as well as update the Catholic identity in light of the ecumenical and interfaith gestures going on in the global Church.

If the Catholic Church in Africa is to be truly African, it ought to take seriously the urgent need to engage critically the Catholic heritage inherited from the European missionaries as well as the cultural realities present in the continent's dioceses. Since women play prominent roles in the religious heritage of the people of Africa, this must be brought to bear on any attempt to inculturate the Catholic identity holistically.

The hierarchy of the Church in Africa can begin to explore the need to receive women into diaconal ministries of exorcists, healers, teachers, and prophetesses. These ministries are part of the African heritage and can truly make the growth of the Church one of depth as well as number; the latter is simply not enough. To state that the Church is growing in number but ignore the quality of that growth will lead only to an identity that will always remain alien to the African people.

Endnotes

1 See "Dogmatic Constitution on the Church: *Lumen Gentium*" (November 21, 1964), no. 32, in www.vatican.va/archive/hist_councils/ii_vatican_council/ documents/vat-ii_const_19641121_lumen-gentium_en.html. See also Code of Canon Law, Latin-English Edition (Vatican City: Libreria Editrice Vaticana, 1983; Washington, D.C.: Canon Law Society of America, 1998), canon 208.

2 *Lumen Gentium* no. 9.

3 Ibid., no. 18.

4 See "The Church and the International Women's Year 1975" (Vatican City: Pontifical Council for the Laity), nos. 105–11.

5 See "Congregation for Divine Worship and the Discipline of the Sacraments, Vatican Communication on Female Altar Servers" (March 15, 1994) in www. ewtn.com/library/curia/cdwcomm.html.

6 Second Vatican Ecumenical Council, "Instruction on Music in the Liturgy: *Musicam Sacram*" (March 5, 1967), no. 23 C, in www.vatican.va/archive/ hist_councils/ii_vatican_council/documents/vat-ii_instr_19670305_musicam-sacram_en.html.

7 See "Constitution on the Sacred Liturgy: *Sacrosanctum Concilium*" (December 4, 1963), nos. 34, 38, 62b, in www.vatican.va/archive/hist_councils/ii_vatican_ council/documents/vat-ii_const_19631204_sacrosanctum-concilium_en.html.

8 See Jonathan Y. Tan, "The Responses of the Indonesian and Japanese Bishops to the Lineamenta," in *The Asian Synod: Texts and Commentaries,* Peter C. Phan, ed. (Maryknoll, N.Y.: Orbis, 2002), 61.

9 International Theological Commission, Faith and Inculturation (1988), Section II no. 12, in www.vatican.va/roman_curia/congregations/cfaith/cti_documents/ rc_cti_1988_fede-inculturazione_en.html.

10 See "Decree on the Mission Activity of the Church: *Ad Gentes*" (December 7, 1965), no. 10, in www.vatican.va/archive/hist_councils/ii_vatican_council/ documents/vat-ii_decree_19651207_ad-gentes_en.html.

11 International Theological Commission, "Faith and Inculturation," Section II, no. 24.

12 John Paul II, Apostolic Letter: *Mulieris Dignitatem* (August 15, 1988), no. 26, in www.vatican.va/holy_father/john_paul_ii/apost_letters/documents/ hf_jp-ii_apl_15081988_mulieris-dignitatem_en.html. See also Apostolic Letter: *Ordinatio Sacerdotalis* (May 22, 1994), no. 2, in www.vatican.va/holy_father/ john_paul_ii/apost_letters/documents/hf_jp-ii_apl_22051994_ordinatio-sacer-dotalis_en.html.

13 See Modupe Oduyoye, "The Medicine Man, the Magician and the Wise Man," in *Traditional Religion in West Africa*, E. Adeolu Adegbola, ed. (Ibadan, Nigeria: Sefer Books, 1998), 112–20.

14   See Peter McKenzie, *Hail Orisha! A Phenomenology of a West African Religion in the Mid-Nineteenth Century* (Leiden, New York: Brill Koln, 1997), 409. Also, see Elizabeth M. McClelland, *The Cult of Ifa among the Yoruba* (London: Ethnographica, 1982), 88.

15   Dorcas Olubanke Akintunde, "Women as Healers: The Nigerian (Yoruba) Example," in *African Women, Religion, and Health: Essays in Honor of Mercy Amba Ewudziwa Oduyoye*, Isabel Apawo Phiri and Sarojini Nadar, ed. (Maryknoll, N.Y.: Orbis, 2006), 164.

16   Ibid., 164–65. See also S. C. Onwuka, "I was a Juju Priest," in *Traditional Religion in West Africa*; T. Olunlade, "Ipa Ti awon Obinrin ko ninu eewo to jewo nipa Asayan Oriki at Orile Yoruba," in *Yoruba: A Journal of the Yoruba Studies Association of Nigeria* 1 (1999): 44–54.

17   The complete narrative on Bini creation myth is from Cynthia Admabua Iruobe, "The Olokun – The Sea Goddess," *The Guardian* (Saturday, August 24, 2002) in Edofolks.com, www.edofolks.com/html/pub106.html.

18   Bruce Lincoln, "The Religious Significance of Women's Scarification among the Tiv," in *Africa: Journal of the International African Institute* 45, no. 3 (1975): 316.

19   Ibid., 318.

20   Ibid., 325.

21   *Catechism of the Catholic Church. Second Edition* (Vatican City: Libreria Editrice Vaticana, 1994; Washington D.C.: United States Catholic Conference, 1994), 312.

22   Ibid., 323.

23   John Paul II, *Ordinatio Sacerdotalis*, no. 4.

24   See Kevin Madigan and Carolyn Osiek, eds. and trans., *Ordained Women in the Early Church: A Documentary History* (Baltimore and London: The John Hopkins University Press, 2005).

25   I was a witness to these practices in the archdiocese of Onitsha in 1995 and in the diocese of Awka in 1997, while I was a member of the Holy Ghost Congregation, Province of Nigeria.

26   I witnessed instances in Benin City Archdiocese of pastors locking the doors of their churches to prevent members of the parish who failed to pay the dues imposed on them by their pastors from participating in Sunday Eucharistic celebrations.

Leadership/Governance and Religion in Africa: Is Religion an Asset or an Obstacle?

Aloyse-Raymond Ndiaye

The second special assembly for Africa of the synod of bishops that gathered in Rome in 2009 made a link between governance and the difficulties that weaken Africa today. Pope Benedict XVI also referred to this issue in his postsynodal apostolic exhortation, *Africae Munus*, dedicating a paragraph to the "good governance of states."[1] Because religion has been in the past and even today an obstacle to the Light that liberates through its ambiguous positions and even indulgence to political authorities who held low regard for "good governance," it is legitimate to wonder whether religion can help Africa progress in the path of an "enlightened governance."[2] Can the Church influence states and by so doing contribute in a positive manner to good governance of states if it fails itself to live up to the values it recommends to states? The concern here relates to institutional and political governance which, to my mind, determine social and economic governance and equally determine the solutions to present-day African challenges. I intend to answer, in three stages: governance and religions in the African context, faith in the public sphere, and governance and Christian commitment to citizenship.

1. Governance and Religions: The African Context

Africa is a religious continent that still lives by its customs. There are in Africa a number of belief systems, monotheistic religions, and traditional religions that impact its development. The cohabitation between religions and beliefs is generally calm. That is why the ongoing interreligious conflicts in Africa, which almost appear to be religious wars, and of which there are Christian and Muslim victims alike, seem to me rather a caricature of religious conflict than in the real sense political machinery aimed at controlling power for economic and financial domination of wealth and natural resources. Muslim fundamentalists operating in Nigeria, Sudan, Somalia, and Kenya, for instance, claim responsibility for murderous attacks on and spearhead killings of Christians. Religious intolerance seems on the increase. Cistercian monks were slaughtered in Tibhirine, Algeria; to date, Christians still suffer persecution in their own countries, yet in some of these countries of the "Arab Spring," Christians were the first settlers. In Central African Republic, the religious persecution of Muslims and Christians is mutually devastating for adherents of both faiths.

These tensions do not derive from religious motives at all. Their *raison d'être* must be beyond the religions themselves. If one were to consider religions alone, like our languages, religions could naturally coexist in Africa and make the continent a land of tolerance in which everybody feels at home. Let us not forget that Alexandria and Hippo were in the past cultural melting pots like Toledo in Spain. There was a true interpenetration between the East and West.

Again, when Spain and Portugal became radicalised and evicted the Jews, the Islamic North Africa was among the regions that sheltered them and in which they enjoyed political freedom and self-governance. In his intervention during the synod of bishops, the patriarch of the Ethiopian Orthodox Church, Téwahédo, said that Africa is not only the cradle of humanity but also the source of civilisation and land of reception: it is in Egypt and in Ethiopia that Jews and the prophet Jeremiah found refuge. It is again in Egypt where the holy family took refuge to avoid the threat of Herod. All these are signs that the call of Africa is "to look after humanity." Ethiopia, which is the seat of the African Union, would represent this tradition of hospitality and tolerance threatened today in Africa by the rise of extremists and fundamentalists.

Jean-Marc Éla therefore had every reason to say that in the religious world of the African, there is always a place for God, for the human being, and for the ancestor. He makes the distinction, however, between the ancestor, that is, the grandparent, and the spirits, that is, the object of superstitious beliefs.[3] The ancestor has the right to a cult. It is the religion of custom that understands itself in its relation to the family, the basis of culture. This anthropological view is opposed to that of modern society. Two completely different anthropological views are at play here.

That of Western, modern society dominated by science and technology, emphasises the individual cut off from the group and rests on the logic of individualism. The other, that of African societies that keep their traditions, emphasises solidarity among its members and refers to a communitarian logic founded on custom and usage.

What is important to underline is the double origin of the society in Africa: simultaneously ancestral or customary and divine or supernatural; in other words, the ancestors and the gods. Otherwise stated, custom, the religion of the ancestors, is the source of law in African society as it determines the rules of social behavior, the status of persons, the rules and the criteria of the good, moral, and upright life. The religion of the ancestors is also the foundation of the religious community. At this level, religion is seen as the link between the living and the dead; it ensures the continuity of life.

The norms of social life and religion are not separated. Our values of solidarity, brotherhood, freedom, dignity, pride, and true nobility have their origin in custom and mix with the religious values. It is what makes us say that Africa is a religious continent. How then can one imagine that on this continent, where the reference to religion is present in the daily life of the people, religion as such cannot have something to say about governance?

In *Africae Munus*, Pope Benedict XVI did not exclude the traditional leaders in the process of setting up good governance. "The traditional leaders," he wrote, "can contribute in a very positive way to good governance."[4] Why? It is obvious that the one who holds power in the pure African tradition exercises it as a moral authority, necessarily respectable, with the mission to look after social cohesion through a strict adherence to custom. This allows us to think that custom can be a very positive contribution in governance. Tradition can contribute to the proper management of our states, and, in fact, religion can contribute to it positively. It is necessary, however, to also take into consideration the context of globalisation with respect to some of its mainsprings, science and technology, which have conferred on humanity unlimited power characterised by remarkable successes and progress.

Good governance must be illuminated by two sources: reason and faith. If Africa wants to develop, it must embrace modern science and technology. If it wants to stay true to itself, it must reappropriate the wisdom of the ancestors, the source of law, moral values, and religion. We, however, need to be cautious, for not everything in our traditions is worth keeping. There is a need for a critical mind. That said, the wisdom of the ancestors spiced with the salt of charity becomes an opening to the universal with respect of the equality of all people, of their spiritual nature, and of their "kinship with God."[5]

A New Way for African Theology?

Contemporary history shows us that when we are faithful to our cultures, to what in them elevates us to the spiritual values they contain, we manage to safeguard peace and live together in harmony. The current situation in Mali illustrates this well. The recent invasion of Mali by Islamists who virtually divided the country into two pieces, with the north under their control, led to a movement of the population to nonoccupied zones. The refugees, among them Christians and Muslims, were hostile to the *sharia* law; they could not understand the practices that were being imposed on them; they were different from their customs and cultures. They showed strong belief in their cultures without having to abandon their faith. By doing that, the Muslims remained faithful to their religion.

At the start, there was a Muslim community in Mali that considered the Islamists and their vision of a violent religion as incompatible with the culture of the population. By so doing, they reinforced the authority of the state in its determination to assert its commitment to the principles of secularism, democracy, respect for the rights of persons, and the defense of the integrity of their territory.

Religion, in this case Islam and custom, played a positive role in consolidating national cohesion, thereby contributing to the implementation of the conditions for good crisis management with the help of the international community, African states, and France. It is a good example in which faith guided political action for the interest of all and the wellbeing of all, but it was also a case in which the religion of the book, Islam, and custom could meet to contribute to peace. They are not necessarily in a conflictual relationship. Edmond Ortigues pointed out the fact that religions of the book are still nourished by the sap of traditional religions they have tendency to forget.[6]

What is happening in the Arab world today in Tunisia, Morocco, Egypt, and Yemen is a sign of tension within Islam towards a form of living together compatible with good, enlightened governance, which implies democracy and a culture concerned with the primacy of the law and a respect for differences. From this situation, one may ask, on what condition is religion an asset to the promotion of good governance? It is only when it gives its own spiritual values as assets that it can help political power.

The recent crisis in the Ivory Coast is a clear example. The exploitation of religion for political motives in this crisis led to the adoption of a critical stance by some religious leaders; all religions taken into account did not serve in the effective management of the crisis. It will be necessary to go further than proclaiming only spiritual values and to accompany with good works the efforts of the state to promote a culture that takes into consideration the primacy of the law.

By stressing the religious dimension in the African context, I wanted to stress the fact that Africa religion cannot be indifferent to the management of politics. The values of the republic are always balanced by those of religion. In this way, tensions with religious undertones that we observe do not have to make us think they are aspects of religions. We may lament that religions are easily exploited. The most dramatic example is the conflict in the Central African Republic. Here a country in which Christians and Muslims had always lived in mutual respect of their religious beliefs and always lived together in harmony was brusquely led into an interreligious conflict for the first time. It was exploited by the struggle of politicians to have control over power. Is Christianity in Africa an asset? It is this question I need to answer.

2. Faith in the Public Sphere

Let us return to the Post-synodal Apostolic Exhortation of Benedict XVI; it stresses the importance of politics as a "major instrument in the service of reconciliation, justice and peace." Its essential duty "is to set up and manage a fair order." This latter in turn is "in the service of a vocation of communion of the people."[7] At this level, Benedict XVI remained faithful to the spirit of Vatican II, which had made politics one of its major priorities. The social doctrine of the Church makes it clear that "the common good is the *raison d'être* of political authority."⁸ There is a strong link between politics and the common good, and one can only judge political action in relation to the common good, that is, politics at the service of people and society. To engage in politics is to wish to serve others and not the self.

To accomplish such an ideal, "the Church in Africa must contribute to enlighten the society in collaboration with governmental authorities and private and public institutions involved in the promotion of the common good." More precisely, it "commits to promote within itself and within the society a culture concerned about the primacy of the law."⁹ As an example, Benedict XVI chooses elections as a

> place of expression of the political choice of a people and sign of legitimacy for the exercise of power.... The non-respect for national constitution, for law or for verdict of ballot, where elections were free, equitable and transparent, would demonstrate a serious failure in governance and mean a lack of competence in the management of the *res publica.*¹⁰

The future of the continent and its culture lies on this primordial concern. It is therefore in politics, especially in promoting respect for the primacy of the law, that the Church in Africa must emphasise its assets and collaborate with states.

The context of this collaboration is neither stimulating nor rewarding; it is a discouraging and distressing environment marked by conflicts for many different reasons. Among the factors of conflicts, there is a presence of authoritarian and tyrannical regimes that emerged in Africa since the collapse of the Soviet bloc at the end of the Cold War. Under the pretense of the principle of national sovereignty and nonintervention, African states have operated politics of suppression, exclusion, and marginalisation against their own populations and have done all this with total impunity.

Everybody considered the time of *coups d'état* in Africa a bygone era, but suddenly Mali reminds us that the risk is always real and present. Leopold Sédar Senghor thought it was because of lack of culture that his peers were involved in *coups d'état*, tyrannical and bloody regimes, misappropriation of public funds, violations of human rights, and intolerance. If conflicts in Africa have lasted for such a long time, it is probably because they were managed by incompetent and heartless politicians who were concerned only with their personal interests to the detriment of the promotion of peace and the common good. The observation of the poet-president and Christian humanist is still pertinent.

Something new that we have been observing is the risk of conflicts whenever there are elections. Generally, elections contest give rise to outbreaks of violence that manifest the will of the leaders to maintain power by all means in spite of democratic reasons to transmit the mantle of leadership to others; they engineer chaos to disrupt a peaceful process for the succession of power. From this resistance of politicians follows the resistance of the people. Having been subjected by antidemocratic regimes and intense suppression for a long time, the people have learned not to lower their heads and be subjugated but to claim their right of resistance, their right to freedom, to democracy, and to development. The right to resist is acknowledged by the social doctrine of the Church.

> It is legitimate to resist authority in case it violates gravely and in a repeated manner the principle of natural right (law). The resistance to authority aims at reasserting the validity of a different vision of things, as well when one tries to acquire a partial change, by changing certain laws for instance, that when one fights for a radical change of situation.[11]

These situations of resistance are not rare. In spite of this, in the *Instrumentum laboris* of the synod of bishops in 2009, it was admitted that in Africa there were signs "of a new epoch and the beginning, although timid, of a democratic culture."[12] Nevertheless, in spite of this awareness, huge challenges still need to be addressed, especially in certain countries of the continent in which violence and instability result from disputed electoral processes. The major challenge is especially about the need to improve the integrity of electoral processes. It is therefore on this particular point that the church in Africa is called to. What assets does the church dispose to help political power recover its first motivation? I shall offer an answer by referring to the Church's mission of announcing and awakening, of reconciliation and forgiveness, each of which contributes to creating favorable conditions for good governance.

3. Governance and Christian Commitment to Citizenship

Announcing and Awakening

To illustrate the mission of announcing and awakening of the Church, I have chosen the example of Senegal, one among many on the continent. But let us first specify the contents of this mission by referring to the social doctrine of the church. It says that "the Church does not tire in proclaiming the Gospel that brings salvation and genuine freedom to temporal realities."[13] The Church takes on entirely this function of announcement, which also entails a function of denunciation.

The Church, aware that its essentially religious mission includes the defense and promotion of human rights, "holds in high esteem the dynamic approach of today which is everywhere fostering these rights." The Church profoundly experiences the need to respect justice and human rights in its own ranks. This pastoral commitment develops in a twofold direction: in the proclamation of the Christian foundations of human rights, and in the denunciation of the violations of these rights. In any event, "proclamation is always more important than denunciation."[14]

This was the attitude of bishops, priests, and laypeople in Senegal on the eve of the presidential elections in 2012. This double function was at the heart of the open letter to the president: "The Christian community owes nobody any debt of recognition, except God!" It was sent by a parish priest and widely broadcast by mass media during the strained preelectoral period. In order to explain his approach, the author evoked the figure of Saint John the Baptist.

So the political situation of Senegal during the presidential election of 2012 gave the Church an opportunity to get involved in the political arena. Considered as a model of democracy in Africa, Senegal had the reputation of being a stable country that has never known a *coup d'état.* Its constitution asserts its commitment to the republic, to democracy, and to the secular state. From its independence, Senegal instituted a mode of governance that progressively led to concentrating all power in the hands of one man, its president. This reinforcement of the executive power, its presidential pole, was expressed by its progressive rise over the legislative and judicial powers. This situation was, however, worsened by the combination of the function of the president of the republic and the leadership of his party. Consequently, these apparent dysfunctions and drifts impelled the new regime of 2001 to question the management of public affairs.

Successive reviews of the constitution resulted in acts of violence on the eve of the presidential elections; this period of turmoil prompted a resolute commitment to public action by Church authorities. The open letter to the president of the republic pointed out the determination of the bishops of firmly reminding him of the need to respect the law. "The Message of Bishops of Senegal on the occasion of the presidential election of February 2012" was broadly broadcast and relayed by the Commission for Justice and Peace, whose mission it was to assist in the preparation of the elections and to oversee the commitment of the parties involved to electoral procedures, communication, training, and prevention of conflicts in conjunction with other organisations. The commission reechoed the contents of the message of the bishops, whose intervention was decisive in calming the political arena and restoring trust among political actors.

Reconciliation and Forgiveness

Senegal managed to have transparent elections in a calm atmosphere, but this is not always the case in other countries. In these critical situations, difficulties begin after the cessation of conflict, when one did not know how to prevent them. How could we reconstitute the unity of a nation whose members and groups were divided and opposed by war? What strategy of conflict resolution could we put in place to ensure a lasting peace, democracy, and development so all could enjoy the leadership of a state at the service of the common good and revitalise links of solidarity in families and society in its various components? The solution found falls in line with religion; whence truth and reconciliation commissions. While the justice and truth commissions intervene before elections to inform citizens about the risks of conflicts, the vocation of truth and reconciliation commissions is to intervene after the cessation of conflicts.

The Republic of South Africa first experienced this original conflict-resolution track by combining truth, justice, and reconciliation, and it is now followed almost naturally everywhere in Africa where solidarities are threatened. The truth and reconciliation commission was entrusted to the archbishop of Cape Town, Archbishop Desmond Tutu, by the president, Nelson Mandela. Mandela, president of the ANC, had to act with firmness and determination to impose on and convince his own people, who were then skeptical, that it was necessary to make a *tabula rasa* of all the atrocities committed during the apartheid era for the benefit of peace. It was also necessary to admit the fact that if the South African people wanted to survive as a nation, it was necessary for them to forgive and reconcile. The religious connotation of forgiveness here appears inseparable from reconciliation. The religious dimension of forgiveness, introduced by the archbishop of Cape Town, appeared to be essential for genuine reconciliation.

The South African model has been followed, with a few variations, in several countries of Africa where antidemocratic processes and violence have led to serious trauma, for example, in Sierra Leone, Liberia, Togo, in Guinea-Conakry, and Cote d'Ivoire. In the case of Rwanda, it is the international criminal tribunal in Arusha that has been responsible for judging the key masterminds of the genocide. It is interesting to note that the Rwandan government has, however, considered it useful to install parallel to the international criminal tribunal for Rwanda a structure drawn from deep-seated cultural judicial practices among the people of Rwanda, the *gacaca* courts. These provide a remedy through dialogue, the meeting between executioners and victims, and allow reconciliation for the future.

African traditions seem to warn that reconciliation cannot see the light of day unless it is associated with forgiveness, for it is not only a question of judging but also and especially forgiving and reconciling. It is possible to forgive, to render fair justice, only when the truth of the facts is established and acknowledged. That is what the archbishop of Cape Town understood. He was, however, reproached for having introduced a spiritual and Christian dimension to the concept of reconciliation. Yet, if one remains faithful to African traditions, the spiritual or religious dimension is always part of reconciliation. The spiritual dimension partakes of custom. It is present in the Rwandan tradition of *gacaca*. It is therefore the ancestral models such as *gacaca* that restore implicitly the truth and reconciliation commissions. It is because they make allusion to the African culture or better because they are co-natural to it that they are adopted almost naturally, without too many reservations by the African countries where they were established, while the efforts at mediation by international or regional organisations are not always well received or accepted. There therefore seems to be a continuation between these experiences, which reveal a cultural unit of populations not only in the Great Lakes region and South Africa but also in all African countries as well.

After the crisis in Cote d'Ivoire, the authorities set up the "Dialogue, Truth and Reconciliation Commission." Unlike the South African commission, the Ivorian commission is chaired by a committed layperson of the church. Would this choice of a layperson be explained by the partisan behavior of the country's religious leaders during the crisis? That would have raised questions of credibility with regard to their impartial commitment to the search for truth, justice, and reconciliation. In the majority of the structures of dialogue for reconciliation, politicians have called on prelates, high religious personalities of the Church, including Msgr Isidore De Souza in Benin, Msgr Ernest Kombo in Congo Brazzaville, and Msgr Laurent Monsengwo in D. R. Congo. It was again prelates who were solicited to mediate during periods of political crisis or rebellions: Msgr José Camnate of Bissau, Msgr Robert Sarah of Conakry, and Cardinal Theodore Adrien Sarr of Dakar.

Among all these prelates, one can remember, for instance, the figure of Msgr Isidore De Souza, Archbishop of Cotonou, who chaired the first structure of dialogue of this kind, set up in Africa in 1990, called the "Conférence Nationale des Forces Vives." It was during a period of great instability, and he devoted himself to define a new order.

It is however necessary to acknowledge that in most cases, the prelates achieved their mission successfully and showed the expertise of the church, its usefulness, and the effectiveness of its help to the states in terms of crisis management. But this does not prevent us from questioning the motives for choosing religious people for peace mediation while sidelining the laity. Would it not be more appropriate, and more in accordance with their vocation, to call on the laity rather than prelates, whose mission and roles are different?

The choice of the prelates is easily understood: their competence is not in doubt, nor is the knowledge they have of problems of their society. From their functions they lack neither experience nor authority. Generally well informed, they enjoy a broad consensus among the citizens and political actors who appreciate their impartiality. And especially, they are credible because they do not have political ambitions. Religious enjoy favorable repute, which is not the case for laypeople who are easily suspected of partiality, corruption, or political ambitions even when they are not connected with the ruling regime.

We face an internal concern in the Church. It is not a question of doubting the participation of religious in the temporal domain, which has been successful so far, but rather wondering if it really is their role to be involved in the political arena instead of the laity. By not promoting with their multiform support the commitment of Christians in society, do religious not contribute to weakening the laity and delaying their exercise of responsibilities in public life? There is a conflict of powers or competences, a mixture of detrimental consequences to the ecclesial community. We know,

> the social doctrine belongs to the Church because the Church is the subject that formulates it, disseminates it and teaches it. It is not a prerogative of a certain component of the ecclesial body but of the entire community; it is the expression of the way that the Church understands society and her position regarding social structures and changes. The whole of the Church community – priests, religious and laity – participates in the formulation of this social doctrine, each according to the different tasks, charisms and ministries found within her.[15]

There is a sharing of competences to be respected. The prominent role of prelates should neither replace nor undermine the critical role of laity.

> This social doctrine implies as well responsibilities regarding the building, organisation and functioning of society, that is to say, political, economic and administrative obligations – obligations of a secular nature – which belong to the lay faithful, not to priests or religious. These responsibilities belong to the laity in a distinctive manner, by reason of the secular condition of their state of life, and of the secular nature of their vocation. By fulfilling these responsibilities, the lay faithful put the Church's social teaching into action and thus fulfill the Church's secular mission.[16]

The laity has been deprived for a long time of any significant responsibility in the Church. It has been moved aside from making major decisions of the Church and reserved for some tasks such as being providers of funds and being assistants always at the service of religious. Even today, a part of the hierarchy is not ready to surrender part of the power it retains and share responsibilities with the laity unless it is for the clergy's advantage. Even in such cases, it is done under strong supervision.

Times have changed. The feeling of dignity and respectability present in people's minds today, inseparable from the quest for universal human rights in the Church as well as in society, is at the root of the laity's resistance or indifference to bishops. Their resistance is legitimate because some of them are more competent than are the religious. They have more experience of public life. It is a problem of democracy in the Church that we are facing today, democracy which must be participative and inclusive and that requires reforms. The mutual recognition of rights and duties, competences, and leadership is essential to establish relations of trust and solidarity between the laity and the bishops.

In *Africae Munus*, according to Pope Benedict XVI, lay people are "'ambassadors of Christ' (2 Cor 5:20) in the public sphere, in the heart of the world." It is highly recommended for them "to be equipped with a solid knowledge of the Church's social doctrine, which can provide them with principles for acting in conformity with the Gospel."[17]

They also have to know that "their Christian witness will be credible only if they are competent and honest professional people."[18] This recommendation is without ambiguity. As ambassadors of Christ, they are called to be in communion with the ambassadors who are nuncios and other pontifical prelates trained in diplomacy to represent the pope. However, the same professionalism demanded of the laity will also apply to religious.

The recent example of an African prelate who was going to chair the electoral commission of his country and whose impartiality was publicly questioned illustrates the risk of lack of preparation and a choice not properly discerned. One can lament the fact that in many of our countries, we have scandals due to the incompetence, lack of training, and inexperience of a large number of religious and lay people in the management of institutions or structures. This phenomenon is recurrent and can be explained by the culture of silence in the Church that hinders good governance. It is preferable to say the truth than always keep things secret.

Conclusion

It is possible for a religion to be an asset for the state by collaborating in the promotion of a culture in which the law has primacy. The Church in Africa participates especially in the efforts of the state in the framework of a multifaceted collaboration. By its works, it contributes to the fight against the wrongs that affect society and is at the root of conflicts and crises exploited by extremisms and fundamentalisms of all kinds. By favoring institutional governance, my interest was to emphasise the obvious role of the laity in the present situation of Africa. The Christian faithful are

full-time messengers of the Gospel; because it is through them that the Church assures its real presence within secular institutions. In other words, the lights of the world according to the spirit of the Gospel are those who commit themselves with abnegation and courage, a spirit of service and concern for the common good, in respect for human rights and who struggle against dictatorship, corruption, for honest and healthy management of natural and human resources, sacrificing themselves in order to built and consolidate democracy in order that law rules within the State.[19]

There is no doubt that these committed Christians exist. They need only to be trained, and this is the role of Catholic universities and cultural centers. The organisation of forums in which lay people in leadership positions and bishops meet and dialogue is essential for fostering better mutual knowledge and more-efficient collaboration. It is necessary to create spaces for reflection, cooperation, and dialogue at regional and continental levels to assure a more efficient presence of the Church by its laity who are engaged in the institutions run by the state.

Our reflection on the role of the Church in the resolution of conflicts has revealed the place of dialogue in governance. Any enlightened governance leads to development, but there is no development without democracy; neither is there democracy without dialogue. That is what truth and reconciliation commissions reveal to us.

Whatever form it takes, dialogue is very essential and is closely linked to an ancestral practice of African culture known as the palaver. It is about a talk that creates culture, establishes a link, a communication among people. This chapter is all about what people communicate; it is all about the truth that circulates in the community. That truth unites people, and intelligence and heart participate in it. True communication takes place between reconciled and sincere people who engage themselves wholeheartedly. By calling on the Church, politicians acknowledge that it is better prepared than any other institution. The mission of the church is to proclaim the Word. People long for dialogue. They expect to be taught how to dialogue by the church. But can a church far from the world dialogue with that world? It is necessary for the Church to consider and take care of culture and traditions. Of course it will not be an easy task, but perhaps this is another way of conceiving the proclamation of the Word in Africa.

Translated from the French by
Abdon Rwandekwe, SJ, and
Kpanie Addy, SJ.

Endnotes

1   Benedict XVI, Post-synodal Apostolic Exhortation *Africae Munus* (Vatican City, 2011), no. 81, 67.

2   Albert Tevoedjre, *Symposium International des Indépendances Africaines* "L'audace unique défi pour une Afrique nouvelle." *Le Manifeste du cinquantenaire* (Porto-Novo. Office du Médiateur de la République. 2010), 15.

3   Jean-Marc Éla, *Ma foi d'Africain.* Préface d'Achille Bembé. Postface de Vincent Cosmao (Paris, Karthala, 2009), 35–56; *Repenser la théologie africaine* (Paris, Karthala, 2003).

4   *Africae Munus,* no. 81, 68.

5   Benedict XVI, Encyclical Letter *Caritas in veritate* (Vatican City, June 29, 2009), no. 30, 52.

6   Edmund Ortigues, *Religions du livre, religions de la Coutume* (Paris, 1981).

7   *Africae Munus.*

8   *Compendium de La doctrine sociale de l'Eglise* (Paris, Cerf, 2008), no. 168, 94.

9   *Africae Munus,* no. 81, 68.

10 Ibid.

11 *Compendium de La doctrine sociale de l'Eglise,* no. 400, 225.

12 Synod of Bishops Second Special Assembly for Africa *Instrumentum laboris* (Vatican City. 2009), no. 7, 3.

13 *Compendium de La doctrine sociale de l'Eglise,* no. 2, 1.

14 Ibid., no. 159, 89.

15 Ibid., no. 79, 43.

16 Ibid., no. 83, 46.

17 *Africae Munus,* no. 128.

18 *Africae Munus,* no. 128, 103.

19 *Instrumentum laboris,* no. 138, 49–50. Original in the French: "Les messagers à part entière de l'Evangile, car c'est par eux que l'Eglise assure sa présence effective au cœur des institutions séculières. En d'autres termes, les lumières du monde selon l'esprit de l'Evangile sont ceux et celles qui se sont engagés avec abnégation et courage, esprit de service et souci du bien commun, dans le respect des droits humains et qui luttent contre la dictature, la corruption, pour une gestion saine et honnête de toutes les ressources naturelles et humaines, se sacrifiant pour construire et consolider la démocratie afin que le droit règne dans l'Etat."

Leadership and Governance in Africa: Is Religion a Help or a Hindrance?

Elias Omondi Opongo

Introduction

An analysis of leadership and governance in Africa draws attention to the current status of the social, economic, and political situation in Africa today. This chapter examines the diverse perspectives on African leadership and governance and the role religion has played and can play on the continent today. The primary question is, to what extent has religion been a help or hindrance to leadership and governance in Africa?

To unpack this question, I will discuss four main perspectives on African leadership and governance and demonstrate how religion has played a role in them. First is to understand how the African conflicts demonstrate a serious lacuna in leadership and governance and how religion has played both positive and negative roles in this.

My second task will be to examine the democratic processes in Africa, the positive experiences of change, and the challenges of the democratisation processes as well as the role of religion.

The third aspect entails an analysis of leadership and governance in economic reforms and development.

Fourth, I will consider the concerns over the management of natural resources and the implications on leadership and governance and the role of religion.

Religion plays a vital role in influencing the leadership in the society. Scott Appleby reiterates that religion cannot be immune to the temporal changes in history. The Catholic Church, he affirms, which has approximately one billion adherents, has "pre-positioned itself *vis-à-vis* the state and civil society, retreating from entangling alliance with the former to assume a constructive and sometimes prophetic role within the latter."[1] Thus, since Pope Leo XIII's encyclical in defense of labourers, *Rerum*

Novarum (the Condition of Workers) in 1890, the Catholic Church has been instrumental globally in rallying for the defense of the common good of all people. In Africa, religious leaders have played this role in diverse ways.

The discussions in this chapter will identify some of the positive initiatives by religious institutions in influencing change in African society and how these institutions have equally contributed to the task of transforming African leadership and governance. This chapter will not pretend to represent the full reality of the continent as far as leadership and governance is concerned; however, anecdotal examples will highlight some of the major concerns the continent needs to deal with.

Conflicts in Africa and the Challenge to Leadership and Governance

One of the major concerns in Africa today is the conflicts that do not seem to cease from being associated with the continent despite the fact that most countries have had fifty years of independence. Seventeen countries and also regions on the continent are either in conflict or recovering from conflict, including Democratic Republic of Congo (DRC), Darfur in Sudan, northern Uganda (which has had a ceasefire since 2006), Mali, northern Kenya, Ivory Coast, Zimbabwe, Egypt, Libya, Somalia, Ethiopia-Eritrea border tensions, Guinea Bissau, and Nigeria, to name but a few. These conflicts have impacted the host and neighbouring countries and have led to internal displacements and large influxes of refugees. Communities that have experienced conflict are often left divided along ethnic and political lines. Conflicts also increase poverty on the continent, which continues to struggle with unemployment and food sustainability.

These conflicts demonstrate the lack of good leadership and governance on the continent. Diverse factors lead to these conflicts, but most of these conflicts have their roots in poor governance. First is the lack of political inclusion in the decision-making processes. When part of a population is left out of the national governance structure and distribution of natural resources, there is high likelihood of violence and conflict.[2] Hence, inclusive governance is vital for political stability. Lack of political inclusion in governance structures has led to conflicts in Rwanda, DRC, Chad, Sierra Leone, Ethiopia, Libya, and Egypt, among others.

In most cases, religion has played a marginal role in these conflicts, but most Arab states in the northern part of Africa have synchronised Islamic laws into the political structures and constitution. This has helped create harmony between religion and political leadership. However, it has also created tensions when the population has pushed for democratic change. For example, the recent popular uprising against the Muslim Brotherhood government in Egypt, leading to subsequent *coup d'état,* was largely due to the imposition of Islamic laws, poor political leadership, and lack of adequate economic reforms.

In a number of countries in Africa, the Church has played a positive role in postconflict reconstruction. Historical evidence in Sierra Leone, DRC, Rwanda, Uganda, Ivory Coast, Nigeria, Kenya, Zimbabwe, and many other countries shows that violence can still erupt when deep-rooted economic and political issues are not properly addressed. Postconflict reconstruction is a proactive response that aims to bring an end to conflict by addressing both the root causes and the sustaining factors of conflict. It is important to identify these issues, analyse them in relation to the whole conflict, and work out immediate, short-, and long-term responses.

In South Africa and Mozambique, the Church was instrumental in peace building. The Church in South Africa joined hands with other religions in the fight against apartheid. With the end of apartheid in 1994 and 1995, the Church was asked to play another important role of reconciling the whole nation. Thus, a seventeen-member Truth and Reconciliation Commission (TRC) was formed and was headed by Nobel laureate for peace Bishop Desmond Tutu. The committee was given two years to "hold hearings on allegations of human rights abuses committed from March 1 1960, through December 6, 1993."[3] The healing process still goes on.

The bishops have commonly used pastoral letters to speak against violations of human rights, political freedom, and citizen participation in democratic processes as well as to speak on economic and social rights. The bishops of the Great Lakes region, for example, in speaking against genocide, wrote, "The protection of people from genocide ensures that the human person is not subjected to the immense suffering and trauma that accompany an experience of genocide."[4] The Great Lakes region has been faced with fratricidal conflicts that have left millions dead. In an effort to address these conflicts, the region's bishops have made attempts to form a regional consultation body of bishops from northern Uganda and eastern DRC. These efforts have, however, been faced with the challenge of the complexities of the conflict and difficult political terrain in the region. Besides, the Church has no sufficient financial resources to fully realise this initiative. The persistent wars have also created a situation of apathy against social action in general society.

In a recent pastoral letter by the African bishops under the umbrella of the Symposium of Episcopal Conferences of Africa and Madagascar (SECAM), entitled "Governance, Common Good and Democratic Transitions in Africa," the African bishops stated,

> The Church ... has been at the heart of all efforts towards better governance. In many countries, during the delicate democratic transitional period of the 1990s, the Church played a clearly visible role of support. Five out of the eight National Transitional Conferences that were organised during this epoch were chaired by Catholic Bishops. This intervention by the Church helped, in many cases, to ensure peaceful democratic transitional processes with a lot of success, through inclusive consultations and dialogue. Many Christians in some volatile situations helped in bringing about peace and reconciliation. The Church has to take her responsibilities in the socio-political domain. She has to be fully involved in the in-depth transformation of our society.[5]

The above description of the prophetic role of the church has been evident in interventions in political crises in the DRC, Congo-Brazzaville, and Guinea-Conakry, among others. These interventions have sometimes led to the death of Church leaders, including Bishop Muhinzihirwa in Eastern Congo, who spoke strongly against the Rwandan invasion of DRC, and Archbishop Okulu in Uganda, who spoke against human-rights abuses by the government and was later murdered by the then-president, Idi Amin.

Democratic Processes in Africa and the Role of Religion

Many African countries have experienced democratic transitions since the 1990s. These transitions have been difficult and have sometimes been marred by violence. Democratic processes demand political, social, and economic reforms but, more important, genuine reforms in leadership and governance structures. The failure of African leadership to enforce genuine democratic reforms has been attributed to a number of factors, chiefly, the lack of a consistent political ideology in post-independent Africa. African leadership has often oscillated between dictatorship and semi-democratic approaches to state governance. In most cases, the expansion of the democratic space became possible because of the pressure exerted by the World Bank and International Monetary Fund (IMF), which linked access to foreign aid with democratic reforms. A number of states were thus pushed to the democratisation process without much conviction; this led to a multiplication of political parties and national elections without genuine institutional reforms at the executive, legislative, and judiciary levels.

Religious leaders have been at the forefront in advocating for effective political leadership in Africa. In Malawi, the 1992 bishops' pastoral letter against the dictatorship of the then-first president, Kamuzu Banda, led to a sudden turn of events, and the government succumbed to pressure and allowed multipartism. The letter led to mass arrests, threats to the lives of the bishops, and international solidarity, particularly after twenty-three international episcopal conferences asked the European Union to intervene. President Banda was eventually defeated in multiparty elections in 1994.

In Kenya, the interreligious initiative in the late 1990s known as the *Ufungamano Initiative* developed an alternative process of constitutional review that put pressure on the government to create a more inclusive approach to the review process. The government succumbed to the pressure mounted by this initiative and approved a more inclusive approach. However, it was not until 2010 that the country realised its new constitution.

Ellen Johnson-Sirleaf, the current president of Liberia, asserts that we should be open to accepting that the doctrine that purports free and fair elections are

> preconditions for democratic leadership. Because genuine democratically elected presidential leadership entails a building of a nation based on equitable dispensation for justice, equality, freedom, equal opportunity and the full participation of women and all, in the nations' affairs.[6]

The elections have emerged as one of the most important aspect of national stability in Africa. The competitive nature of the elections and the fact that politics has been ethnicised and ethnicity politicised has meant that the Church faces the task of responding to the challenge of uniting the countries while calling for the civic right to vote. The bishops in Kenya stated:

> The right to vote bears positive fruits for the country when the people choose good leaders for presidency and for membership of the parliament ... We strongly advocate sending representatives to our new parliament who are ... people of genuine integrity, moral courage in the cause of truth and justice, and who are competent for the posts entrusted to them.[7]

However, the experience of elections in Kenya, Zimbabwe, and Ivory Coast has been violent and has led to ethnic and religious divisions. Polarised politics have filtered into the church leadership, leading to open and hidden divisions that have damaged the integrity of the Church.

The Second African Synod of bishops considered elections to have an important impetus on the political stability of a country. The synod fathers acknowledged that elections have been a difficult challenge for many countries.

> Elections represent a platform for the expression of a people's political decisions, and they are a sign of legitimacy for the exercise of power. They provide a privileged opportunity for healthy and serene public political debate, marked by respect for different opinions and different political groupings. If conducted well, elections call forth and encourage real and active participation by citizens in political and social life. Failure to respect the national constitution, the law or the outcome of the vote, when elections have been free, fair and transparent, would signal a grave failure in governance and a lack of competence in the administration of public affairs (no. 131).

Popular participation of citizens in the electioneering process calls on elected leaders and government officials equally to respect the rights of the people and to establish systems of governance that are accountable to the people they govern. It is therefore important that citizens, NGOs, religious institutions, and civil society be knowledgeable about constitutional, legislative, executive, and judicial structures that govern the country.

Lack of governmental transparency in constitutional reforms in Zimbabwe has denied the people the full participation of their democratic right to determine how the country should be governed. Constitutional and political transitions in Zambia, Zimbabwe, Malawi, Ethiopia, Equatorial Guinea, Tanzania, etc., will continue to be litmus tests in Africa. The religious leaders in South Africa, Zimbabwe, Ivory Coast, Kenya, Uganda, and South Sudan, to mention but a few, have been at the forefront of reconciliation efforts in their countries. In most post conflicts situations, the religious leaders are wounded healers who journey with the people at times of joy and distress while maintaining prophetic commitments to social transformation.

There have, however, been situations as in Rwanda, where the Church leadership has struggled to regain its credibility in playing its role of leadership in the sphere of forgiveness and reconciliation. This has largely been attributed to the accusations against some of the Church members who were perceived to have participated in the genocide. Although few in number, those accused have tainted the image of the Church and compromised its leadership role.

In Kenya, Madagascar, and DRC, religious leaders have been perceived as divided and not speaking with one voice at the height of political tensions and social divisions.

The challenge for the religious leaders in most of the conflict situations is to develop a reconciliation process that integrates both political and spiritual perspectives. In most cases, reconciliation exercises have been confined to political processes or truth and reconciliation commissions without a spiritual healing process. A big gap between political reconciliation and spiritual healing processes exists; religious leaders need to engage with political leaders in a dialogue that can effect social and political change. Hence, religious leaders ought to claim a place in the political processes of reconciliation to effectively apply the psychospiritual dimensions of reconciliation.

Furthermore, religious leaders need to invent creative ways of helping people to reconcile with the dead. How, for example, would an aggressor reconcile with a dead victim? How can religious leaders initiate rituals that are culturally grounded in healing the population of past atrocities and establishing mechanisms of reconciliation founded on religious faith and cultural values? One way would be to engage in dialogue with cultural leaders and members of civil society. Such a dialogue would produce creative ways of healing people through a genuine process of reconciliation.

Engaging with structures of governance is equally critical. A number of episcopal conferences have tried to engage with parliamentarians and other governance structures. This has been important particularly in contributing to policy formulation on important national issues of debate. In South Africa, for example, the Southern Africa Bishops Conference runs a Catholic Parliamentary Liaison Office (CPLO) that conducts research and makes policy recommendations to parliament. Through briefing papers, submissions to parliament, and roundtable discussions, CPLO has been able to engage with structures of governance in very effective ways. The briefing papers, for example, intend "to provide a short and accessible overview of a piece of legislation or a current issue of policy or politics ... written, first and foremost with the leadership of the South African Catholic Church in mind."[8]

Fr Peter-John Pearson, director of the Catholic Parliament Liaison Office, asserts that the CPLO office

> is focused on: enhancing peace through encouraging public debate around key policy issues based on values geared toward transforming the injustices and indignities of the past which if not reversed carry the potential for a severe undermining of the new democracy, of the bid to promote good governance and the strengthening in both civil society and state institutions so that they, in turn, contribute to democracy and peace.[9]

In Zimbabwe, Zambia, and Kenya, among others, there are attempts to develop the parliamentary liaison offices to the level of the CPLO in South Africa.

Leadership and Governance in Economic Reforms and Development

Leadership in economic policies and sustainability is critical for peace in Africa today. Religious leaders in Africa have not played very active roles in monitoring development policies in Africa. However, a few religious institutions and universities have been involved in the monitoring of development policies or speaking against policies that marginalise the poor. African leaders have in most cases adopted economic policies they could not adhere to. External financial aid has sometimes ended up in ghost projects or blatant misappropriations of funds. These situations have increased Africa's external debts and reduced its financial capabilities. Religious institutions, while providing 30 to 40 percent of basic social services, such as health and education, have sometimes been accused of misappropriating funds. It is critical that religious leaders demonstrate leadership in the management of the common good and particularly financial resources.

In his post-synodal exhortation, Pope Benedict XVI addressed the African Catholic bishops in the following terms: "Make your message credible, see to it that your dioceses become models in the conduct of personnel, in transparency and good financial management."[10] The emphasis on financial transparency and accountability by the pope demonstrates that there have been serious concerns about the Church's manner of managing its financial resources, and this situation has weakened the Church's capability of acting as a prophetic witness against corruption and financial misappropriation by government and public officials.

Religious and political leadership in economic spheres is critical for countering potential conflicts on the continent. In recent years, scholars have attributed most civil conflicts to economic conditions in any one country. Paul Collier and a team of scholars assert that the "key root cause of conflict is the failure of economic development."[11] Countries that depend greatly on primary commodities for their exports and provide few economic opportunities for its citizens are at a high risk of civil wars. The basic maxim therefore, according to Collier et al., is, "War retards development, but conversely, development retards war."[12]

Economic disparities evidenced by inequality of household incomes and ownership of land[13] as well as poor economic performance of a country also can lead to conflict. These conditions breed general discontent against the government and encourage the formation of armed guerrilla groups while luring unemployed youth to the power of the gun, hence creating an alternative source of income through extortion and other criminal activities.

Religious leaders need to emphasise that development is key to liberating human beings from the oppression of poverty and suffering. This concept has constantly been used to refer to the material consumption and progression in society; material consumption becomes the measuring index for progress. But the debate has recently shifted to focus more on the human person as the object of development. Thus, development ought to be reflected in the people's conditions of life and accessibility to the basic commodities.

Management of Natural Resources

One of the major factors that provoke and sustain wars based on economic conditions is the management and control of natural resources such as oil and minerals. Communities that live in the "lucky" localities of such resources often demand control of the benefits of the resources,[14] particularly if these communities had been marginalised. Inequitable sharing of revenues from natural resources by corrupt or oppressive governments can lead to rebellion. Conflicts that develop over control of natural resources are often fueled by emphasis on the people's local identity and differentiation from the rest of the country, and this can lead to demands for secession.

Several African countries, including South Sudan, Tanzania, Sierra Leone, Ghana, Angola, DRC, and Zambia, among others, face the challenge of properly managing natural resources. These countries' governments have signed mining contracts with multinational companies that reap maximum profits while leaving the countries very poor. The working conditions in these mines are degrading, and the mining and drilling practices have serious negative impacts on the environment.

Linked to the management of natural resources is the challenge of making economic policies accountable. Many African countries adopt economic systems that are geared towards marketisation of the economies and utilisation of the population as mere tools of labour without adhering to fair-wage policies, promoting dignified conditions of labour, or fairly distributing economic resources. Lack of transparency on the part of governments and multinational companies has led to poor economic policies that often victimise the poor. According to the World Bank report "Rising Global Interest in Farmland,"[15] Western countries as well as China have been at the forefront of large-scale acquisitions of farmland in Africa, Latin America, Central Asia, and Southeast Asia. The report states that between 2007 and 2009, close to 45 million hectares (111 million acres) of farmland were leased out compared to 4 million hectares leased in 2008. More than 70 percent of the deals took place in Africa, mainly in Sudan, Mozambique, Liberia, Ethiopia, Nigeria, and Madagascar. According to World Bank's managing director, Ngozi Okonjo-Iweala, "These large land acquisitions can come at a high cost. The veil of secrecy that often surrounds these land deals must be lifted so poor people do not ultimately pay the heavy price of losing their land."[16]

These aggressive land leases have been pushed by the high demand for food in China and Western countries, the rising cost of food experienced in 2007–2008, and the limited availability of water and arable land, among other factors.[17] These land leases have further complicated the perennial problem of food insecurity in Africa that has led to perennial hunger in some parts of the continent. According to the "Africa Human Development Report 2012," in most cases,

> misguided policies, weak institutions and failing markets are the roots of sub-Saharan Africa's food insecurity … Sub-Saharan Africa needs a new agenda for social justice that empowers the rural poor and especially women, who hold the key to greater food security and human development.[18]

To address the problem of management of natural resources, religious leaders must collaborate with institutions of higher learning in researching governments' policies on management of natural resources, existing contracts, working conditions at the sites of exploitation of natural resources, and the management of revenues from these resources. Natural resources are a common good that ought to benefit all; the exploitation of natural resources ought to promote human dignity and the integrity of creation.

Conclusion

The question about whether religious leaders are a hindrance or a help in leadership and governance in Africa can be answered fairly only with the recognition that the religious leaders have critical roles to play as the conscience of society. In this sense, they need to show moral leadership and work closely with the political and social structures of governance. In most cases, religious leaders in Africa have not found effective means of engaging with political leaders in structured ways apart from anecdotal and time-bound interventions such as participation in truth and reconciliation commission or conferences for national reconciliation.

The credibility of religious leaders lies in their capacity to stand against ethnic and political divisions and embrace a path that heals nations emerging from war. They must call for a commitment to healing a society in conflict to embrace love and forgiveness again. It is critical that the religious leaders devise means of dialogue with the decision makers. This can be done through quiet or corridor diplomacy as well as research and advocacy. Religious leaders and representatives of religion have a lot to learn in regard to engaging and promoting effective and accountable leadership and governance in Africa.

Endnotes

1   Scott S. Appleby, *The Ambivalence of the Sacred: Religion, Violence, and Reconciliation*. (Lanham, Md.: Rowman and Littlefield, 2000), 41.

2   Frances Stewart, *Horizontal Inequalities and Conflict: Understanding Group Violence in Multiethnic Societies* (Basingstoke: Palgrave Macmillan, 2008).

Mike Pothier, *The State of the Nation Address, Response,* (Cape Town: Southern African Catholic Bishops' Conference Parliamentary Liaison Office, 2011).

3   Lynn S. Graybill, "South Africa's Truth and Reconciliation Commission: Ethical and Theological Perspectives" in *Ethics and International Affairs,* ed. J. H. Rosenthal (Washington, D.C.: Georgetown University Press, 1999), 372.

4   AMECEA Documentation Service, "Message of the Bishops of the Great Lakes Region of Africa" no. 465 (February 15, 1997), no. 3.

5   SECAM, *Governance, Common Good and Democratic Transitions in Africa* (Accra: SECAM, 2013).

6   Amos M. Sirleaf, *Visionary Liberia leader: Ellen Johnson-Sirleaf* (Bloomington, Ind.: Author House, 2009), 30.

7   Kenya Episcopal Conference, "Pastoral Letter on the Occasion of the 1988 Elections" nos. 4–5 (1988).

8   Mike Pothier, *The State of the Nation Address, Response* (Cape Town: Southern African Catholic Bishops' Conference Parliamentary Liaison Office, 2011).

9   Peter John Pearson, "God Hears the Cry of the Oppressed: Parliament as a Place of Conversation: The Church's Ongoing Role in Parliamentary Debate" in *Peace Weavers: Methodologies of Peacebuilding in Africa,* ed. Elias O. Opongo (Nairobi: Paulines Publications–Africa), 71.

10 Pope Benedict XVI, *Africae Munus:* Post-Synodal Exhortation (2009), no. 104; www.vatican.va/holy.../documents/...africae-munus_en.html.

11 Paul Collier et al., *Breaking the Conflict Trap: Civil War and Development Policy* (Washington D.C.: World Bank and Oxford University Press, 2003), 53.

12 Ibid., 1.

13 Ibid., 66.

14 Ibid., 60.

15 World Bank, *Rising Global Interest in Farmland,* World Bank, 2010; siteresources.worldbank.org/INTARD/Resources/ESW_Sept7_final_final.pdf.

16 World Bank, *World Bank Report Sees Growing Global Demand for Farmland,* World Bank, 2010; web.worldbank.org/WBSITE/EXTERNAL/NEWS/0, contentMDK:22694767~pagePK:64257043~piPK:437376~theSitePK:4607,00.html.

17 L. Cotula et al., "Land grab or development opportunity? Agricultural investment and international land deals in Africa," World Bank, 2010; www.ifad.org/pub/land/land_grab.pdf.

18 UNDP, *Africa Human Development Report,* 2010; www.undp.org/.../hdr/africa-human-development-report-2012.

Conclusion:
Bread for an Unfolding Journey

Agbonkhianmeghe E. Orobator

At the risk of inadvertently attenuating the intensity of theological perspectives and positions in this volume's essays, these concluding remarks aim to distill lessons we can derive from the ongoing theological research project inaugurated by TCCRSA. This book is the first of an anticipated three volumes detailing the findings of this project. We are still at the beginning phases of an unfolding journey.

A palpable energy and excitement emanated from the theological approaches of these African authors during the colloquium's sessions. Each author is eager to break new grounds and do theology differently by experimenting with new ideas and methods. Although the overall aim relates to theology in Africa, and I have tried in my introduction to identify the points of intersection of their conversations, these authors do not offer identical accounts of what African theology entails. They dispel the myth of a homogenous and static African theology and aptly recall and appropriate the title of a pioneer text in African theology, *a theology en route*.[1] What goes for African theology also holds true for the continent; it is a flexible and unfolding rather than a rigid narrative. Africa is the subject of ongoing adaptation, change, and transformation, and theology must strive to keep up with this process.

In these essays are several recurring themes, including the role of culture, an especially important consideration in Africa. How do we assess culture's role? Is it all good or all bad or six of one and half a dozen of the other? The reader will find hints of all three lines of approach in this volume's essays because the authors do not agree with each other though all refer to and acknowledge the significance of culture.

The methodology of inculturation has varying degrees of appeal to the authors perhaps as an outcome of this lack of consensus. It is the way forward for some, but others relegate it to the past. Although this debate is not settled in this volume, the authors underscore its urgency and pertinence.

Vatican II is a recurring point of reference evoked to validate a particular position or critique it. The prominent role Vatican II plays in African theology confirms the thesis I advanced in a different context that although Africa was not adequately represented at the council, the Church in Africa and African theologians have had to look back to receive and implement the teachings and theological principles, norms, and guidelines of Vatican II.[2]

Another point of agreement relates to the praxis of Christianity and Church in Africa. All the authors would agree with Pope Francis that the Church needs to be on the streets with the people, battered and wounded, for its message to respond effectively and credibly to what ails Africa. In Francis' words, "I prefer a Church which is bruised, hurting and dirty because it has been out on the streets, rather than a Church which is unhealthy from being confined and from clinging to its own security."[3] Likewise, theologians must follow suit and be highly creative and imaginative in their research – not as guardians of arcane museum artifacts but "midwives" of a new heaven and earth.

The profile of African theology that emerges in this volume shows gaps and promises. One such gap is the dearth of expertise in the study of Scripture capable of combining exegesis and theology. Notwithstanding, the profile is rich in culture, experience, and religious tradition; it casts critical attention on the local and demonstrates constructive passion for the global.

Based on the analyses in this volume, theologians in Africa or elsewhere ought to pack their toolkits with basic methodological tools and attitudinal dispositions including abilities to listen, discern, dialogue, include, converse, collaborate, and immerse.

Notably, the overall aim of the TCCRSA project, demonstrated in this volume, is to make theology an intensely collaborative effort or teamwork of laypeople, clergy, nuns, and bishops. There may be leaders and facilitators, but all are valued and respected participants, not spectators or bystanders. As a fundamental rule, in this communal enterprise, monopoly is a pathology of manipulation and monologue a symptom of deafness. Both contravene the ethics of palaver and Ubuntu.

What unique attributes does Christianity in Africa possess? What does it contribute to the practice of Christianity in the global Christian community? A short answer is all that can be proposed at this point evidenced by the contributions our authors have made to this volume. The practice of Christianity in Africa prioritises community and interrelationship. In various and diverse ways, several authors affirm this truism, but we cannot claim this as something new. Christianity began as a community of disciples. The opening chapters of Acts and several Pauline letters paint a picture of a family Church in which communal relationship mattered more than doctrine and dogma. The gradual historical codification of Christian creed and the ensuing elaboration – mired in controversy – of complex and convoluted doctrines and dogma would have as a side effect if not as a direct effect the sundering of Christian unity. Set against this backdrop, there is nothing new in the emphasis on community and relationality in African Christianity except that African Christianity retrieves and places at the service of the world Church an ancient truth, namely, that Church is *the* family of God, *the* community of the risen Christ, and all are welcome members. This truth offers us sustenance for a yet-unfolding journey.

Endnotes

1   Kofi Appiah-Kubi and Sergio Torres, eds., *African Theology en Route* (Maryknoll, N.Y.: Orbis Books, 1979).

2   Agbonkhianmeghe E. Orobator, "'After All, Africa Is Largely A Non-Literate Continent': The Reception of Vatican II In Africa," *Theological Studies*, Vol. 74 (June 2013): 284–301; "Look Back to the Future: Transformative Impulses of Vatican II for African Catholicism," *Concilium International Journal of Theology* (2012/3): 97–102.

3   Pope Francis, *Evangelii Gaudium*, no. 49.

Contributors

(In Order of Contribution)

Laurenti Magesa from Tanzania is a Priest of Musoma Diocese, where he did pastoral ministry for several years. Since 2008, he has taught theology at Hekima College, Tangaza College and Maryknoll Institute of African Studies, in Nairobi, Kenya. In 2011/2012, Prof. Magesa was an international visiting fellow at Woodstock Theological Centre, Georgetown University, Washington, D.C., USA. He has recently published *What is Not Sacred? African Spirituality* (Orbis, 2013).

Teresa Okure from Nigeria is a Sister of the Society of the Holy Child Jesus (SHCJ). Professor of New Testament and Gender Hermeneutics at the Catholic Institute of West Africa, Port Harcourt, Nigeria, she has authored many books, chapters in books, and articles in scholarly journals; she continues to lecture globally, conduct research on biblical, African, church and gender issues, work with women and religious groups and do mentoring worldwide. Currently she is the Foundational President of the Catholic Biblical Association of Nigeria (CABAN) and a member of the Anglican Roman Catholic International Commission (ARCIC) representing Catholic Africa.

Eloi Messi Metogo from Cameroon has been a Dominican priest since 1980 and a Professor at the UCAC since 1995. Prof. Messi Metogo was a visiting professor at *Lumen Vitae* (Belgium) in 1991 and an associate teacher at the Catholic Institute of Paris in 1998 and 1999. He is also a member of the Board of Editors of *Concilium*. Prof. Messi Metogo has participated in several seminars.

Paul Béré from Burkina Faso holds a doctoral degree in Sacred Scripture from the Pontifical Biblical Institute (Rome). Since 2008, he has been involved in the Synod of Bishops. In 2009, Pope Benedict XVI appointed him as Consultor to the Secretariat of the Synod of Bishops (Vatican). He teaches the Old Testament and biblical languages at the Institut de Théologie de la Compagnie de Jésus (ITCJ) in Abidjan, Côte d'Ivoire, and in other institutions. His current research focuses on the Old Testament exegesis and Aural Criticism (the aural reception of the written text). His publications cover the areas of exegesis, theology and ecclesiological issues.

Nsongisa Kimesa Chantal from Congo is member of the Congregation of the Daughters of Our Lady of the Sacred Heart. In May 2009, she graduated as Doctor in Biblical Theology at the Gregorian University where she specialised in the letters of Saint Paul. Since 2010, Dr Nsongisa teaches at Saint Eugene of Mazenod Institute in Kinshasa. In 2010-2012, she was appointed lecturer at the Catholic University of Congo in Kinshasa. Dr Nsongisa teaches Biblical Hebrew as well as Greek, the "Pauline Corpus", and sometimes directs seminars. In 2011, she was admitted as post doctoral researcher at Catholic University of Tilburg, Netherlands.

Eunice Karanja Kamaara from Kenya is a Professor of Religion at Moi University, Kenya, and International Affiliate Professor of Indiana University Purdue University, Indianapolis (US). She has a doctorate in African Christian Ethics and her research interest is inter-disciplinary: theological, ethical, medical, socio-anthropological, and gender approaches to church and development in contemporary Africa. Individually and with others, she has carried out major research projects, presented hundreds of papers in local and international forums and has over fifty publications. She is trainer of trainers in Gender and Development, Sexual Health issues including HIV/AIDS, and in Higher Education Management. She has also consulted for national and international organisations.

Daniel Assefa Kassaye from Addis Ababa, Ethiopia, took his final vows with the Capuchin Order in 1992 and was ordained to priesthood in 1993. He holds an MA from the Pontifical Biblical Institute in Rome. Br. Assefa was the rector of the Capuchin Franciscan Institute of Philosophy and Theology (1998-2001), Ethiopia. He also holds a PhD from the Catholic Institute of Paris, in Biblical Theology (2002-2006). From 2007 to July 2012, Br. Assefa was rector at the same institute. He is currently the director of Research and Retreat centre. He is a Member of "Enoch Seminar" and Society of Biblical Literature. His main area of research includes: Apocalyptic literature, Second Temple Judaism, Origins of Christianity, Ethiopic literature (especially in the First Book of Enoch). His pastoral commitment is biblical courses for the laity.

Stan Chu Ilo is a professor of religion and education and the Director of Field Education in the Faculty of Theology, University of St Michael's College, in the University of Toronto, where he teaches the following courses: Embracing World Christianity in Theological Education; Theological Reflection Seminar; Teaching and Learning in the Spirit of Augustine; Theories of Leadership and Christian Praxis; Faith Development Across the Life Span, and History of Religious Education. He is the series Editor of the African Christian Studies Series for Pickwick Publications, publisher of the online Journal of African Theology (www.theologyinafrica.com) and co-founder and director of the Canadian Samaritans for Africa.

Josée Ngalula from the Democratic Republic of Congo is a nun with the Order of Religieuses de Saint André. She has a PhD in Theology from the Catholic University of Lyons (France). Dr Ngalula teaches systematic theology in theological institutions in Kinshasa and is a member of several theological associations. She is also a researcher in African theology, New Religious Movements in Africa, Ecumenism on the African continent, African theological feminism, and Christian lexicology for the African languages. Dr Ngalula is co-founder of the Association of African Theologians (ATA) and is the initiator of the collection "Bible et femmes en Afrique."

Bishop Kevin Dowling from South Africa is a member of the Congregation of the Most Holy Redeemer, more commonly known as the Redemptorists. He serves as the Bishop of Rustenburg and is Co-President of the Pax Christi International Board. He has been Chairman of the International Sudan Ecumenical Forum through which he engaged in the Sudan Peace Process. As a trustee of the Ecumenical Solidarity Peace Trust, he is involved in research of human rights abuses in Zimbabwe.

Bishop Rodrigo Mejía Saldarriaga from Colombia joined the Society of Jesus in 1956. He first came to Africa in 1964, to the DRC. He attained a Licentiate Degree in Philosophy and Classical Letters at the Xaveriana University in Bogotá in 1963. In 1979, he attained a Doctorate in Theology at the Gregorian University in Rome. Bishop Rodrigo has worked as Parish priest, Professor of Philosophy and Rector in Canisius Institute of Philosophy (Kimwenza – Kinshasa) from 1979 to 1984. In 1985-1995, he was Professor of Pastoral Theology in Hekima College and CUEA in Nairobi, Kenya, and Provincial of the Eastern Africa Province from 1995 to 1998. Bishop Rodrigo was Secretary of the Archdiocese of

Addis Ababa from 1998 to 2001, and then went on to become Director of Galilee Spirituality Centre in Debre Zeit (Ethiopia) from 2001 to 2006. He is now Emeritus Bishop of the Apostolic Vicariate of Soddo.

Bienvenu Mayemba from Kinshasa, DRC, is a Jesuit Priest. He holds a PhD in Systematic Theology from Boston College, USA, MPhil from the Institut Saint Pierre Canisius, in DRC, and STL in Theological Anthropology from Weston Jesuit School of Theology, USA. Dr Mayemba is Professor of Systematic Theology, African Christian Theology and Postcolonial Theory at Institut de Théologie de la Compagnie de Jésus, Abidjan, Côte d'Ivoire. He is Visiting Professor of Environmental Ethics at Loyola University Chicago, USA, and Visiting Professor of African Philosophy and Critical Theories at Arrupe College, Zimbabwe. In 2010, he received The Donald J. White Teaching Excellence Awards at Boston College and was named Boston College 'The Heights' 2010 Person of the Year.

Marinus Iwuchukwu is an Assistant Professor in Theology Department at Duquesne University, Pittsburgh, Pennsylvania, USA. He specialises in Interreligious Dialogue, Religious Pluralism, and Media and Religion. He has authored a book and co-edited another. He has several journal articles published in different peer review journals and some book chapters. He is currently working on the manuscript of another monograph and is the current chair of Duquesne University Christian-Muslim Dialogue Committee and the International Outreach Editor for the Journal of Interreligious Dialogue.

Lilian Dube from the USA teaches theology at the University of San Francisco. Her research focus is on the intersection of religion, gender, and sexuality in HIV/AIDS Contexts. She developed an international service-learning program focused on community response to AIDS and has led USF students through the month-long program in Zambia since 2010.

Emmanuel Katongole from Uganda is associate professor of theology and peace studies at the Kroc Institute for International Peace Studies at the University of Notre Dame. His research interests focus on politics and violence in Africa, reconciliation, and Catholicism in the global South. He earned his Ph.D. in philosophy from the Catholic University of Louvain (Belgium) and a diploma in theology and religious studies from Makerere University in Kampala, Uganda. Prof. Katongole, a catholic priest of Kampala Archdiocese, has served as associate professor of theology and world Christianity at Duke University, where he was the founding co-director of the Duke Divinity School's Centre for Reconciliation. As a major part of his research at the Kroc Institute, Katongole will contribute to Contending Modernities, a cross-cultural research and education initiative examining catholic, Muslim, and secular forces in the modern world.

Eugene Elochukwu Uzukwu from Nigeria is a priest of the Congregation of the Holy Spirit (C.S.Sp) since 1972. He is the first holder of the Rev. Pierre Schouver, C.S.Sp., Endowed Chair in Mission, in Duquesne University. He was Rector of Spiritan International School of Theology, Attakwu, Enugu, Nigeria (1987-91; 94-97). He is experienced in formation work in Nigeria and Congo and has lectured in broad areas of theology in Nigeria, Congo, France, Ireland, and USA. His areas of interest include: Liturgy-Sacraments, Mission, Ecclesiology, contextual theology (Africa). He is the Editor of *Bulletin of Ecumenical Theology*.

Anne Arabome is a member of the religious community of the Sisters of Social Service in Los Angeles, California. She holds a Doctor of Ministry degree in spirituality from Catholic Theological Union in Chicago. She is presently working on a second doctorate degree in Systematic Theology at Duquesne University in Pittsburgh, Pennsylvania, USA.

Marguerite Akossi-Mvongo from Abidjan, Côte d'Ivoire, is a Multilingual Psychologist working as University Researcher. She has a solid field experience in human resources management and vocational counseling, including measuring human behaviour and how the differences in personality impact various behaviours in everyday life. Akossi's major fields of interest are gender issues (including violence and marital relationship), health, and learning abilities. She is the past-governor of Zonta International (a charity organisation advancing the status of women worldwide). Akossi is a married catholic woman, involved in different positions in the Church. She was the Coordinator of French Catholic community in Nairobi, 2004-2009, and currently is a member of the Parish council in Abidjan Bon Pasteur, secretary of Family Commission, and member of *Legio Mariae*.

Simon-Mary Aihiokhai from USA is a lay Catholic theologian. He is currently a lecturer on comparative theology at Loyola Marymount University in Los Angeles, California. He has written extensively on issues related to interreligious dialogue and presented papers nationally and internationally on such topics as religion and political empowerment in Africa, religious identities and multiple religious belonging in contemporary societies, globalisation and the challenges of religious pluralism. Dr Aihiokhai has worked in areas of first evangelisation in Nigeria. He is currently interested in critiquing the missionary strategies employed by past and current missionaries in the African continent.

Aloyse-Raymond Ndiaye, from Senegal, is a Doctor of Philosophy, Doctor of Philology, Professor of Philosophy at the University of Dakar. He was Dean of the Faculty of Humanities of the University of Dakar (1985-1992). Prof. Ndiaye is currently Director of the Higher Institute of Arts and cultures (ISAC) of the University of Dakar (2007-2013). He is President of the Senegalese Association of the Sovereign Military Order of Malta, Director of the Cultural Centre of the Catholic Archdiocese Daniel Brottier Dakar (2010-2013). Aside from this, Prof. Ndiaye was Auditor at the Second African Synod (2009).

Elias Omondi Opongo from Kenya is a Jesuit Priest and the director of Hekima Institute of Peace Studies and International Relations (HIPSIR). Dr Opongo holds a PhD in Peace and Conflict Studies from University of Bradford, UK, and MA in International Peace Studies from University of Notre Dame, USA. He has published books and articles on conflict resolution, transitional justice, peace-building, and Catholic Social Teaching. He is a peace practitioner and conflict analyst.